A Passion for our Grandchildren:

Our Families Need Us Now

by Janet Mort
Illustrations by James Dodd

Contact J. Mort by fax at (250) 652-7889
or jmort@direct.ca

Canadian Cataloguing in Publication Data

Mort, Janet.
  A passion for our grandchildren

  Includes bibliographical references and index.
  ISBN 1-55212-281-6

  1. Grandparent and child. 2. Grandparenting. I. Title.
HQ759.9.M67 1999   306.874'5   C99-911138-8

TRAFFORD

This book was published *on-demand* in cooperation with Trafford Publishing.
On-demand publishing is a unique process and service of making a book available for retail sale to the public taking advantage of on-demand manufacturing and Internet marketing.
On-demand publishing includes promotions, retail sales, manufacturing, order fulfilment, accounting and collecting royalties on behalf of the author.

Suite 2, 3050 Nanaimo St., Victoria, B.C. V8T 4Z1, CANADA

Phone	250-383-6864	Toll-free	1-888-232-4444 (Canada & US)
Fax	250-383-6804	E-mail	sales@trafford.com
Web site	www.trafford.com	TRAFFORD PUBLISHING IS A DIVISION OF TRAFFORD HOLDINGS LTD.	
Trafford Catalogue #99-0032		www.trafford.com/robots/99-0032.html	

10   9   8   7   6   5   4   3   2

Dedication

It gives me great pleasure to dedicate this book, so appropriately, to my family:

- my Mom and late Dad, who created our original family with their commitment, hard work and never-ending love for their four kids, then delighted in and celebrated their grandchildren (all seven of them!)

- my loving sister Nancy, brothers Bob and David, and their families

- my husband Michael, the ultimate best friend and skilled counsellor who has such incredible insight into people, children in particular. He has made a great contribution to this book, debating and probing my assumptions, and even writing part of Lesson 23. He is a master of unconditional love and deep insight about all things family.

- our oh-so unique and special sons, Brad and Justin, who have brought us great joy…in many ways, including our new daughter Yvonne and, of course, grandchildren Natasha, Rory and Trevor, the inspiration for this book.

**Our families,
the richest possible legacy,
I love each and every one
of you
and always will.**

Thanks to...	**for...**
Mavis Andrews..............................	*initial layout concept, scribe*
Bob Ashford..................................	*fine editing*
Rob Destrubé.................................	*superb family photo shoot*
James Dodd...................................	*insightful artistry and friendship*
Wendy Graham.............................	*Granny consultant, Sunday Snowflakes*
Denise Nicholls.............................	*production of cover*
Gay Pringle..................................	*abiding love*
Bob Swain....................................	*beyond moral support*
Lynn Traunweiser...........................	*"Granny-in-a-Bag" dolls*
Judy Turner..................................	*patience, talent, and final layout*
Dee van Straaten............................	*cover design, concept consultant*
Trevor's mom, Sylvia.......................	*for sharing Trevor*
Judith Sales and Wendy Holob (teachers) and their Grade 6 & 7 classes (1998-99) at Lake Hill Elementary School and Strawberry Vale Elementary School respectively....................................	*for their touching stories*

...and all my special friends who listened, supported and advised throughout the year and a half of the book's development

PS: Al Traunweiser

A Passion For Our Grandchildren:
Our Families Need Us Now

Introduction: The Evolution of My Passion

The writing of this book has been an evolutionary process for me. There are three reasons why it has been particularly important to me and my family.

...Three Reasons Why...

1) I discovered my passion in my new role of grandmother.

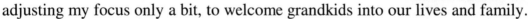

Becoming a grandmother was an exciting event. Rory was our first as he and his mom married into our family. Becoming a grandma overnight was a unique experience. Starting from scratch with a four-year-old grandson has its own challenges and rewards. One of my greatest satisfactions in our relationship comes from the fact that we were able to, step by step, construct a trusting connection by earning it each step of the way and now, eight years later, our bond is strong.

Becoming a "birth" grandmother was another and different thrill. I anticipated the event with confidence. My career in education was a choice to dedicate the majority of my adult life to the service of children with a specialty in educational innovation – making a difference for kids and their well-being. It seemed like a natural transition, adjusting my focus only a bit, to welcome grandkids into our lives and family.

I was unprepared for the passion I felt as I held newborn Natasha and, with only God as my witness, I promised to protect her forever, to teach her everything I knew about life, to make the way easier for her. That moment has defined and guided our relationship and that of our other two grandchildren, Rory and Trevor.

Early in my grandparenting, I found myself searching for the answers to a number of questions:

- Is grandparenting the same in 1991 as it was in 1961?
- What is our purpose?
- What is the difference between the parent's role, the teacher's role, the grandparent's role, and that of the great-grandparent?

- What difference could the new technologies make in long-distance relationships?
- How could the skills and knowledge I'd gained in my educational career be applied to my role as grandparent?
- How would I be different with my grandkids than I was with their parents?

As I struggled with the answers to these questions, and acknowledged that indeed I *was* struggling, I recognized that others would be too, since my age puts me on the leading edge of many of the baby boomers. We are becoming grandparents in our fifties, retiring with time to spare and a passion for our grandchildren. This book began to evolve from my own experiences with our three terrific grandkids.

…Three Reasons Why…

2) I needed to find my own new reality.

The second stage of the book's evolution was a frustrating one for me – after thirty years of a dynamic career in educational administration, I was diagnosed with scleroderma, a degenerative and sometimes life-threatening disease. This led me to my greatest struggle of all – new questions:

- Who am I and what is my purpose now?
- How long will I have, will I see my grandkids marry?
- What is there left for me to do and how can I still contribute to the world of children?
- How will I balance my need to find new meaning in my life but no longer able to do what had become a pivotal part of my adult life, education?

The answer began to grow around the words "children," "teacher," "grandmom," "love," "depth," "purpose," "writing," "rest," "independence," "health," and "contribution" – and then it started to take shape – a book for, and about, grandkids and grandparents.

In a practical way, it fit within my health issue; it was still about the work I love with the focus on children; the rest I need to keep my life and health manageable; and the sense of purpose which has always pro-actively challenged me to make a difference for kids.
In May 1998, I decided to write this book.

...Three Reasons Why...

3) The passion became a mission...

Only the first chapter was completed when the horror of the Columbine shootings and subsequent nightmare unfolded. A horror-stricken world asked why? What's gone wrong? What is our youth missing? How can we make a difference now? Almost all media coverage focused on parenting and the family and what parents could do differently. A few samples of quotes from international newspapers:

- "...if they had grown up with love and respect..."
- "...if there had been adults, even just one who reached out and held on through the turmoil of adolescence..."
- "...so hug your kid...and look to your own life for solutions..."
- "...there is something wrong when parents are so out of touch they don't know bombs are being built in their own houses..."
- "...there are four gifts a village gives its children: kinship, mentorship, friendship and worship..."
- "...we can respond by 1) giving our children a more intimate form of kinship...; 2) redesigning time so our children do not raise themselves; and 3) recapture the art of loving companionship – to walk and talk with them, sit around the campfire sharing our stories. Let them hear stories of family heroes..."
- "...youth needs the wisdom and compassion of elders to mentor them and listen..."

I agonized, as did the world. I thought of Rory and Natasha and Trevor. It reminded me of the promise I had made – to protect them, to guide them, to always be there for them – and my resolve was strengthened.

Then came the frustration again, because if I were still a school principal or Superintendent or teacher, I knew what we would do to support not only my kids but all those in my care.

And then it came to me...even if I couldn't contribute in person, I could in spirit –and it was then that this book entered its third stage of evolution. Based on my educational training, experiences in leadership positions, my connections to classrooms and kids, I could promote the discussion about, and possibility of grandparents as key players in the solution.

Experts have proposed the notion of attachment theory, that every child needs a connected bonded adult. We elaborate on this notion throughout the book. Some experts go so far as to say that in order to feel secure, safe and connected, each child needs tight bonds with between four and six significant adults.

In our research, we discovered that some kids today have as many as seven living grandparents and most have four or five, due to the frequency of blended families in today's culture.

This book proposes that if all grandparents would make a commitment to develop tight bonds with their grandchildren, whether near or far, we would be one giant step closer to saving our kids – and that's what this book is about – building that bond and being there for our families – with a clear vision and a passion, in new and old ways, in innovative and tried and true ways...

We invite you to join us with…

A Passion For Our Grandchildren
Our Families Need Us Now!

Sincerely,

Janet N. Mort

The Book's Framework

Lessons: The book has fifty numbered lessons which are either generated by a story or interview or by my family's experiences. These are not intended to be imposed on the reader rather thoughts to reflect and/or act on. We won't be offended if you disagree with some of them. They are intended to generate discussion.

Stories and interviews: Every lesson connects to or emerges from the story or interview. Approximately fifty adults were interviewed as a part of the research for the book. Most of the stories and interviews appearing in the book are excerpts of longer pieces. Most of the adults interviewed were grandparents already. If they were not, they were asked to reflect on their experience with their own grandparents.

The students were in either grade six or seven at Lake Hill and Strawberry Vale elementary schools in the Greater Victoria School District. Their contributions were a result of class discussions with the author, their own interviews with their parents about their grandparents or their personal writing. We felt it was important to respect the style of the storyteller so minimal edits were made. Special thanks to all contributors and regrets to those whose stories were not used only because of space limitations.

Janet's Postscript: The author's postscript is a reflection on the story or interview based on the author's knowledge of the person, subject or her own personal experience. It provides a link between the story or interview and the suggested "Try This" activities.

Try This activities: Every lesson has between three and five "Try This" activities which are tried and true experiences for grandparents and grandchildren. These activities were chosen for the purpose of generating the experience described in the story or interview, so that the experiences can be recreated and personalized by the reader. They are only 'starter' suggestions. We anticipate that through these initial experiences, the reader will discover spin-offs that take them down their own experiential paths. There are over 200 suggestions for:

- being and doing together (Chapter One);
- exploring and creating treasures and traditions (Chapter Two);
- nurturing self-esteem (Chapter Three);
- loving unconditionally (Chapter Four); and
- teaching and monitoring the development of new skills (Chapter Five).

These five chapters overlap in nature. It is intended that after a scan of the lessons and related parts, the reader will pick and choose a focus for the development of their own special bond and connection with their grandchild. One chapter may provide a focus for a few months, or a variety of random experiences throughout the book may prove to help you find the focus that will be unique to your interests, time and needs as well as those of your grandchild.

Conclusion: Each conclusion provides an overview of the intent of the chapter often including previously unused and pertinent quotes from the stories and interviews contained in it.

We expect that some readers will be very experienced with child development and would use the book as a source of useful ideas not yet explored while readers with limited experience will use it as a guide until their own path starts to take shape.

Finally, although this book is written for grandparents, its content is based on the best research on child development. It is written by an experienced educator, and as such is suitable for any child and adult relationship, including parents. It could have been called: A Passion for Our **Children**: Our Families Need Us NOW!

We are already beginning Volume II and are inviting readers to make contributions. Further details can be found at the end of this book.

I wish for you rich and rewarding relationships with all the children in your lives. I hope this book will make a positive contribution to those relationships.

Table of Contents

Chapter 1:
Let's Make Memories: Being and Doing Together

	Let's Make Memories: Being and Doing Together	1
Introduction:	The Gift of Time	2
Lesson 1:	**We only need to go as far as our own backyard to create a magic time for our grandchildren.**	3
Try This #1	Scavenger Hunt	4
Try This #2	Rock and Wood Art	5
Try This #3	Yikes! Ant Lions	5
Try This #4	Borrowing an Ant Hill	6
Lesson 2:	**When we awaken new interest and new talents as we sit side by side with our grandchildren, we are sharing at a deep and satisfying level.**	7
Try This #5	A Grandchild's Stained Glass	8
Try This #6	Vegetable Prints	9
Try This #7	Marbled Art	9
Try This #8	Wax Resist Art	10
Try This #9	Rock Art	10
Lesson 3:	**There are countless things you can do together, but the richness will come from the conversations you have while you are doing them.**	11
Try This #10	Role Models All Around Us	13
Try This #11	Actively Influence Their Choices	13
Try This #12	Encouraging Good Language	14
Try This #13	Make an Activities Calendar	15
Lesson 4:	**The Rules CAN be Different At Grandma's House.**	16
Try This #14	Family Play Day	18
Try This #15	Camp Out in the Living Room	19
Try This #16	Family Dance Party	20
Try This #17	New and Old Group Games	20
Lesson 5:	**The quality time and the lessons therein will be what our grandchildren remember about us, forty years later.**	21
Try This #18	Hopscotch	23
Try This #19	Snap	25
Try This #20	Slapjack	25
Try This #21	Who Has the Coin?	26

Lesson 6:	**An investment in our grandchild's education will be our living legacy for their lifetime.**	27
Try This #22	Support for Success	28
Try This #23	Accepting and Praising Their Efforts	30
Try This #24	Going for a Walk with a Prereader	31
Try This #25	Encourage Your Child's Learning	32
Lesson 7:	**Children learn through action, experience and reflection: these words should drive the activities we plan for our grandkids**	34
Try This #26	Interview Your Grandchild – Then Have Them Interview You	35
Try This #27	Our Similarities and Differences	36
Try This #28	Who Can I Count On?	37
Try This #29	Using Television Appropriately	37
Lesson 8:	**We must remember to honour and reinforce our grandchildrens' relationship with their parents as well.**	40
Try This #30	Egg Candles	40
Try This #31	A – Clay-Pot Candles	42
Try This #31	B – Other Ideas For Clay-Pot Candles	43
Try This #32	Playdough Decorations	44
Try This #33	Uncooked Salt Dough	45
Lesson 9:	**When grandchildren come to visit, tell them the things you have to do, and ask them how they'd like to be involved.**	46
Try This #34	Oranges en Surprise	48
Try This #35	Playdough You Can Eat	48
Try This #36	Cornflake Crunchies	49
Try This #37	Popcorn Pops	49
Lesson 10:	**Grandparents can be the matchmaker between a grandchild's interests and talents, and arrange lessons to invest in long term success.**	50
Try This #38	Make Library and Bookstore Tours	51
Try This #39	Health and Learning Walks	51
Try This #40	A Community Commitment to Kids	52
Try This #41	Phone Book Fun	54
Conclusion:	The Voices of the Grandchildren	55

Chapter 2
Treasures and Traditions: The Connection to Family Values 59

Introduction:	Our Grandchildren, Our Treasures	60
Lesson 11:	**Powerful family values wait patiently to be explored.**	62
Try This #42	Begin Your Autobiographies With A Timeline	64
Try This #43	Start Your Autobiography	65
Try This #44	Timelines Through Pictures	65
Try This #45	Simple Journals	66
Lesson 12:	**Treasures and traditions are simply eloquent memories of the feelings we felt in the best times.**	67
Try This #46	Photo Essays And Captions: A Great Way To Tell The Story	70
Try This #47	Recycling Old Photos With History As A Focus	70
Try This #48	Sharing Photo Stories	70
Try This #49	Check Your Timelines To Guarantee Order	71
Lesson 13:	**We can discover powerful family values as we reflect upon "beginnings" and "endings".**	72
Try This #50	Touring The Treasures: Looking For Qualities	74
Try This #51	Every Family Has Heroes	74
Try This #52	Baby Treasures	75
Try This #53	Connecting To Your Far-Flung Family	75
Lesson 14:	**Handwritten messages from the past can speak volumes to future generations.**	76
Try This #54	Tried And True Traditional Postcards With A New Twist	77
Try This #55	Creative Postcards From The Kids	78
Try This #56	Picture Treasure Chests	78
Try This #57	Thank You Notes	79
Lesson 15:	**What we learned from our parents needs to be put into words.**	80
Try This #58	Teaching The Interview Process	81
Try This #59	Prepare For The Interview	82
Try This #60	During The Interview	82
Try This #61	After The Interview	83
Lesson 16:	**The best relationship with our grandchildren will be built on history, strength, love, kindness, time, teaching, storytelling and safety.**	84
Try This #62	Writing Poems Together	86
Try This #63	Webbing	87
Try This #64	A Scrapbook Of Values	88
Try This #65	Collecting Family Recipes	89

Lesson 17:	**We need to create opportunities to discuss our values, family values and the emerging values of our grandchildren.**	90
Try This #66	Searching For Character	93
Try This #67	Keeping Peers In Perspective	94
Try This #68	It All Boils Down To Respect	95
Try This #69	Getting To The Root Of Their Problems: The Fishbone	96
Try This #70	Making the Action Plan: The Fishbone	99
Lesson 18:	**Whether we've met them or not, our ancestors can teach us important values through stories of their past.**	100
Try This #71	More Sophisticated Diaries	101
Try This #72	More Challenging Timelines	102
Try This #73	Hints For Encouraging Young Writers	103
Try This #74	Grandparents: Building On Early Writing	104
Lesson 19:	**Let them know they have a special place in your home, as well as in your heart.**	105
Try This #75	Make a Place In Your Home…	106
Try This #76	How To Respond To A Child's Work	106
Try This #77	Your Child's Craft Corner For Creating Treasures	107
Try This #78	Tips For Saving Your Grandchild's Art Treasures	108
Lesson 20:	**When generation after generation repeat celebration in ritual ways, the family ingredients must be worth studying.**	109
Try This #79	A Scrapbook Of Family Traditions	111
Try This #80	Create A New Family Tradition	111
Try This #81	Start A Lifelong Treasure Chest	112
Try This #82	What Is Family Fun?	112
Conclusion:	So Many Different Choices	112

Chapter 3
"I Am Lovable": Nurturing Their Self-Esteem

		115
Introduction:	Unconditional Love	116
Lesson 21:	**Being cherished as a person nurtures the feeling of being loved.**	118
Try This #83	Celebrate The Arrival	121
Try This #84	A "Cherished" Photo Shoot	121
Try This #85	Celebrate The Arrival – Video Version	122
Try This #86	Celebrate the arrival – how to cherish	122
Lesson 22:	**Our young ones will feel cherished when we take the time to "find each other."**	123
Try This #87	Being Observers Together #1	124

Try This #88	Being Observers Together #2	125
Try This #89	Celebrate Being Together #3	125
Try This #90	Spying Underwater	126
Lesson 23:	**The cornerstone of the love that nurtures is psychological safety.**	**127**
Try This #91	About Encouragement Instead Of Praise	129
Try This #92	Setting Limits	130
Try This #93	Choices And Consequences (Not Punishment)	131
Try This #94	Bullying: A Culture Of Violence	131
Lesson 24:	**Children survive on acceptance but they blossom on love.**	**132**
Try This #95	Create Matching Gardens	134
Try This #96	Store The Memories Of Your Gardens	134
Try This #97	Winter Flower Candles	135
Try This #98	Decorate Your Garden	135
Lesson 25:	**A hundred years from now, all that may matter is that the world will be a better place because we were important in the life of a child.**	**136**
Try This #99	Personalized Pillow Cases	137
Try This #100	Granny-In-A-Bag	138
Try This #101	Savings Piggy Banks	139
Try This #102	Make A Christmas Tree Skirt	140
Lesson 26:	**We can learn to appraise our potential, then set goals to achieve it.**	**141**
Try This #103	Past Success With Goal Setting	143
Try This #104	Possible Success With Goal Setting	144
Try This #105	Planning Success By Goal Setting	144
Try This #106	Goal Setting In Relation To Problem Solving	145
Lesson 27:	**We must dream our dreams with them, then pave the way for the dreams to come true.**	**147**
Try This #107	Their Dreams, Our Dreams	148
Try This #108	Opening Doors	149
Try This #109	Supporting Teens	149
Try This #110	Staying Connected	150
Lesson 28:	**Self-esteem blossoms when we are clear on our belief system, learn new skills and are supported by those around us.**	**151**
Try This #111	Getting To Know You Better	153
Try This #112	You're A Great Family	153
Try This #113	Develop A Family Slogan	154
Try This #114	Develop A Family Coat Of Arms	155
Try This #115	A Family Chain Letter	155

Lesson 29:	**Excerpts from a grandmother's letter to her grown children.**	156
Try This #116	Family Roots	159
Try This #117	Their Support Networks	160
Try This #118	Success Is…	160
Try This #119	I Trust You, You Trust Me	161
Lesson 30:	**Over the years, our strong and deeply felt love and encouragement can help them find hope and purpose forever.**	162
Try This #120	"I Like Me Because…"	166
Try This #121	"We Know Each Other, Don't We?"	166
Try This #122	"I'm Really Okay"	167
Try This #123	Helping Them Make Positive Changes	167
Conclusion:	"I am Lovable" : Nurturing Their Self-Esteem	168

Chapter 4:
Unconditional Love

		170
Introduction:	A Joy That Brings Peace To The Soul	171
Lesson 31:	**Unconditional loving is the best feeling in the world, the deepest form of joy.**	173
Try This #124	Face Painting Preparation	175
Try This #125	Book Search	175
Try This #126	Face Painting Clown Fun	176
Try This #127	Body Painting Brain Storm	177
Lesson 32:	**When someone over time shows they care about us, we feel a strong and lasting connection to them.**	178
Try This #128	Koosh football	180
Try This #129	Playful Koosh Games	180
Try This #130	Relay Hysteria	181
Try This #131	Playful Tag And Hiding Games	182
Lesson 33:	**The greatest love of all lies inside of me.**	183
Try This #132	A More Orderly Display	185
Try This #133	So Many Ways To Say They're Special	186
Try This #134	Your Local Photo Place	187
Try This #135	Fridge Fun	187
Lesson 34:	**We need to listen as they "ramble on and search for answers".**	188
Try This #136	Love Nicknames	190
Try This #137	Building A Spiritual Connection	191
Try This #138	Make A Date With Their Spirit	192
Try This #139	All Feelings Are Okay	193

Lesson 35:	**A recipe for loving can be found in the joy of cooking together (caramel apples).**	194
Try This #140	Double Trouble Peanut Butter Cookies	196
Try This #141	Grandma's Rice Krispies Square With A New Twist	196
Try This #142	Great Grandma's Incredible Coffee Ring	197
Try This #143	Grandma Joan Hall's Easy, Quick And Delicious Banana Cake	198
Lesson 36:	**Our aboriginal cultures have a lot to teach us about unconditional love. Theirs is passionate, wise and deep.**	199
Try This #144	A Grandbaby Shower	201
Try This #145	Hand And Foot Records	202
Try This #146	Garden Stepping Stones	202
Try This #147	A Handful Of Love	203
Lesson 37:	**The connection is not dependent on the amount of time spent together, it is the quality of the small and sometimes long-distance connections.**	204
Try This #148	Be Brave: Take On Technology!	206
Try This #149	Sending "Do-It" Stuff	207
Try This #150	Focus Your Letters	208
Try This #151	Photo Diary	208
Lesson 38:	**With the unconditional love of an extended family, we can discover and create multiple connections and life-long relationships.**	209
Try This #152	Multiple Possibilities	211
Try This #153	Tried And True Outdoor Games	211
Try This #154	More Family Fun	212
Try This #155	T-shirt Memories	213
Lesson 39	**There's a grandparent nearby for each of us...blood is not always thicker than water.**	214
Try This #156	A Grandparents Wanted society	215
Try This #157	Powerful Bonds Between Young And Old	216
Try This #158	Neighbourhood Kids Helping Seniors	217
Try This #159	A Senior Services Study Group	218
Lesson 40:	**Unconditional love is like being best friends. It's the difference between flat and flying, between the mundane and the magical.**	219
Try This #160	Develop A Family Mission Statement	222
Try This #161	Narrowing The Focus	223
Try This #162	Mission Checkpoint	223
Try This #163	A Family Focus On Its Mission	224
Conclusion:	Near or Far, It's Unconditional	225

Chapter 5:
Grandparents: Teaching With the Winning Touch
227

Introduction:	Education Is A Critical Key To Their Future	228
Lesson 41:	**The key to unlocking the door to an unlimited future is reading and getting the best education.**	230
Try This #164	Make Reading A Necessity	230
Try This #165	Read To Them Daily	230
Try This #166	Encourage Independent Reading	230
	Reading: A Standards Guide K–3	232
	Reading: A Standards Guide 4–7	234
	10 Reasons to Read to Your Child	235
Lesson 42:	**If our children can read these words "by sight", they'll be 245 steps ahead in the reading "game".**	236
	Basic Sight Words	237
	Basic Sight Word Phrases	239
Lesson 43:	**When we insist on accuracy in a young child's writing, we run the risk of inhibiting their inspiration to write.**	241
	Writing: A Standards Guide K–3	242
	Writing: A Standards Guide K–3	243
Lesson 44:	**Awareness of how to deal with and express emotions in a socially acceptable manner leads children to function independently and in cooperation with others.**	244
Try This #167	Emotional and Social Development	244
Try This #168	Accepting and Expressing Emotion in Socially Acceptable Ways	244
	Social and Emotional Development of Our Grandchildren, Birth–7	245
	Social and Emotional Development of Our Grandchildren, 7–13 years	247
Lesson 45:	**"Living in harmony with other human beings may be one of the outstanding challenges for the whole human race."**	249
	Social Responsibility of our Grandchildren, Birth–7	250
	Social Responsibility of our Grandchildren, 7–13	252
Lesson 46	**By giving our kids a solid foundation of family values, we will provide them with the capacity to withstand the inevitable growing pains and stress of life.**	254
Try This #169	Encouraging Family Values	255
Lesson 47	**"Enjoy the one you have, not the one you think you should make him into."**	256
Try This #170	Golden Rule 1: Always Love the One You're With	256
Try This #171	Golden Rule 2: Nurture Her Strengths and Lessen Her Weaknesses	256

Try This #172	Golden Rule 3: Accept and Appreciate Your Toddler for Who She Is	257
Try This #173	Golden Rule 4: Cherish Your Child's Individuality	258
Lesson 48:	**"If I could tell you what I mean, there would be no point in dancing."**	259
Try This #174	Aesthetic and Artistic Development	259
Try This #175	Physical Development	260
Lesson 49:	**Play is important...and it keeps us young at heart!**	261
Lesson 50:	**50 Ways to Show You Care**	262
Try This #176 to #225	50 Ways to Show You Care	
	Conclusion: When They Are Grown	264

Conclusion:
A Passion For Our Grandchildren

266

Chapter 1

Let's Make Memories:
Being and Doing Together

Let's Make Memories:
Being and Doing Together

Introduction: THE GIFT OF TIME

Gordon Neufeld, a professor at the University of British Columbia, is provocative in his portrayal of how young children go wrong as they reach their pre-adolescent years, and he thinks we can do something about it. In essence, he says that as kids age, an orientation to peers strengthens, mob rule or "Lord of the Flies" syndrome sets in, and all too often parents and teachers are left in the dust.

Providing kids with busyness in the form of sports lessons is not the solution, he says. Although well-intentioned, such activities often lack the closeness of an adult with whom children can bond, and they turn their attention to peers who cannot provide the stability, empathy, understanding and security they need.

He points out that things began to change with the baby boomers, the first mass youth culture in North America. Today's youth are the children and grandchildren of the first deeply peer-oriented group, and the phenomenon has compounded. With parents increasingly absent, impersonal day cares and social centres taking on more parental functions, and television having increasing influence on children, the essential primary bonding mechanism of childhood is being destroyed, and therein lies the problem.

…here's where we grandparents can be pivotal; we can be a significant part of the solution. We can be a lifeline, an anchor point, a psychological womb.

Neufeld says children need to be proactively wooed. We need to harness their attachment instinct, provide closeness spontaneously and generously through touch, attention, love, affection, closeness, connectedness, delight, enjoyment, interest and significance.

"Time," he says, "one-on-one time!" Over and over in our interviews with kids they identified time as the thing they valued most. During that time they valued doing things together: walking, painting, just being together and talking together. So . . . that's what this chapter is all about!

A Lesson We've Learned

1

We only need to go as far as our own backyard to create a magic time for our grandchildren.

SEIZING THE MOMENT

I lived with Nana at Honeymoon Bay for a while when my sister was in the hospital and my parents were still working. I was maybe three. We were walking from Nana's house to Mrs. Westwick's house, and as you went along there were icicles that had formed and were hanging down from a cliff face on the other side of the road. I wanted to go over and play with the icicles. They were huge – they must have been thirty feet long. So Nana took me across the street and she picked up a stick and started to hit the icicles, and they made different sounds. We stood there on the road playing icicle music until we were so cold we had to keep going or Mrs. Westwick would wonder where we were. And I'll never forget that, because it was so unusual for Nana, and they were just there, and they sounded incredible, and it was something I never would have done if I hadn't been with her. The only reason she did it is because she had done it as a child in Denmark. When the icicles would hang down from the houses they would hit them and they would make different sounds. So that's like one really special thing from Nana.

Wendy Holob, a memory from the '50s

"The family is one of nature's masterpieces"
George Santayana

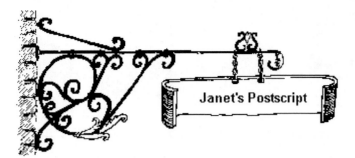

Janet's Postscript

I used to spend considerable time and money planning special outings for the grandkids. It should be no surprise that some of our most memorable events have been those connected with nature.

♥ take a can of nails and a hammer to a beach to build a raft;

♥ hike the woods and pastures for wildflowers, take them home and press them for a memory book. Check out your local library or bookstore for outdoor activity books…there are endless ideas;

♥ pick wild berries for a great ice cream sauce;

♥ take a glue gun to the seashore, an old plate or paper plates and collect sea shells, rocks, dry seaweed, feathers and other collectibles for a magnificent wall sculpture

In fact, in our survey of students, taking walks with grandparents was one of the most highly rated activities.

TRY THIS #1

SCAVENGER HUNT

When I was a child it was common practice to plan scavenger hunts through our neighbourhoods, knocking on doors and asking strangers to join in the fun. No longer with the child safety issues we are forced to pay attention to. We can still have the same thrills by paying attention to safety.

These rules will help:

• choose enclosed space where all children will be in sight, or

• organize children into small teams with an adult leader who can maintain sight contact

• pre-visit the site so you have knowledge of items to be found

• make a list of 30 or so items. Make them obscure by using rhyming words or other clues. Example on a beach hunt: "Find something that rhymes with feed." Answer: "seaweed"

• give points for the fastest team, the most creative finds, the most finds, etc.

Suggested sites: beach, playground, park, garden, campground.

TRY THIS #2

ROCK AND WOOD ART

Since the beginning of time man has left a legacy of art
using natural things. Gather an interesting collection of rocks or pieces of beach
wood. Arrange them in shapes like animals or buildings or simply build an
interesting sculpture by placing articles that balance well. Blend rocks and wood
if you like. Leave your sculpture for the world to enjoy.

Recently an anonymous person(s) gathered dozens of wooden logs on a Victoria
beach and created the most amazing large scale art even seen on local beaches.
When the sun came up, there it was. Hundreds went to visit after a picture in the
local paper highlighted it. The mystery of the creation was the best part of all.

TRY THIS #3

YIKES! ANT-LIONS!

Ant-Lions are one of the world's best kept secrets. If you find an anthill in a
sandy area there are probably ant-lions nearby. These are little creatures with
big pinchers who wait to trap and eat ants. Look for little funnels in the sand. At
the bottom of the funnel is the ant-lion. He waits for an ant to come by, the ant
slides down the side of the funnel, the pinchers reach up and grab the ant and
pull it under the sand. If you wait a few minutes, the ant-lion spits the dead ant
out of the funnel after sucking the juice out, then waits for another. To catch the
ant-lion you have to quickly scoop the funnel and the sand under it as they are
very fast to burrow out of harm's way.

If you want to keep them as pets for a while just put the ants in the jar with
them, as that the ant lion's daily food. Poor ants!

 *"Children are poor men's riches."*
English Proverb

TRY THIS #4

BORROWING AN ANTHILL

This is only permitted if you take good care of it and put it back in a few days. Search for an anthill in a sandy area. Using a garden trowel, scoop part of the anthill up being careful to leave behind a livable home for those you don't take. Look for different kids of ants, some large, some small, some carrying food or eggs and especially look for the Queen ant. If you find her, your nest will last longer and the ants will work harder to create her new home.

Put the ants and dirt from the hill into a glass container that is fairly narrow so that as they build their tunnels you will be able to see them. Tips for a successful in-your-home anthill:

- put damp pieces of sponge in so they have water
- feed them cereal, small seeds, sugar, crumbs left over from picnics
- cover the jar with fabric so they can breathe but put a tight elastic around it so they can't get out
- put the jar in the dark between observations
- check each day to see that they have food and water
- be sure to dig out books or check the Internet so you can learn everything you need to know about your new friends

Everyday you'll see changes. Put them back at the same anthill within a week so they can rejoin their friends and families.

A Lesson We've Learned

2

**When we awaken new interests and new talents
as we sit side by side with our grandchildren,
we are sharing at a deep and satisfying level.**

TWO BUDDING PICASSOS

I often find that things happen in a happenstance kind of way with my grandchildren. I had decided to teach myself the art of painting with acrylic paints and had purchased a beginning set (which you can purchase for about $30-35) and a set of brushes. My first portrait was a portrait of our black Persian cat, Garbo. It came out looking like a cartoon Garbo with big yellow dazzling eyes, and black hair sticking

out all over. Natasha was quite entranced when she saw that I had painted a real-life creature from our life, and she asked if she could try to do the same with paints. I was skeptical that a six-year-old could manage acrylic paints; however, they are washable, and we decided to give it a try. There was a big bouquet of flowers on the kitchen table. The two of us sat around the flowers and we decided that we would each paint the bouquet. For any of you who have engaged in painting, you will recognize the euphoria and the peace that comes with the quiet concentration and emerging creativity.

Janet Mort

"There is no vocabulary for the love within a family, love that's lived in but not looked at, love within the light of which all else is seen, the love within which all other love finds speech.

This love is silent."

T.S. Eliot

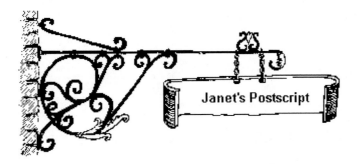

Janet's Postscript

What a wonderful experience it was for the two of us to find that zone together. The silence was punctuated by Natasha glancing over at my painting and saying, "Oh, Grandma, that's very, very good. That's so creative!", or me glancing over at hers to say, "I love the two colours you put together there." It was a wonderful way for her to learn how to appreciate another person's production, the quiet communing throughout our painting, and the excitement of being able to hang on our wall a Tasha composition and a Grandma composition side by side. It wasn't surprising to find that her creation was even more creative than mine. This was a joyous experience, and I recommend it to anyone.

TRY THIS #5

A GRANDCHILD'S STAINED GLASS!

Sometimes we as grandparents have to take a deep breath and let go! Find a window or a mirror in your house that you are willing to share. Using thick poster paint or acrylic paints, then paint designs on the window with your grandchildren. This activity has a particular attraction for young children who often are chastised for putting sticky fingers, noses and tongues on our finely polished glass. Just wash it off once they've left!

–Pick a Theme–
Jack-o'-lanterns for Halloween –Santa and his reindeer for Christmas –Hearts for Valentine's Day–or how about a mural of all the members of your family! We suggest that the adult participating in the activity outline the figures that the children draw to put a finishing touch on the portrait. Grandkids get a particular kick out of this kind of activity, because it's almost guaranteed at some point in their life someone has said NO. The forbidden is always attractive.

TRY THIS #6

VEGETABLE PRINTS

Choose a variety of vegetables to make your prints. Cut the vegetables at odd angles and experiment with the kind of print that can be produced by the vegetable using sheets of newspaper. Practicing for 10 or 15 minutes will make your grandchild confident about their ability to make interesting patterns.

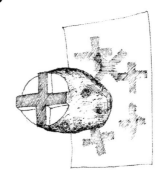

Some of the best vegetables to use are hollow vegetables such as squash, peppers, celery, large mushrooms. Once you are confident about your printing ability, try patterns on white poster board, which then can be used to cover shoeboxes or tin cans to make colourful holders as gifts to take back home to Mom and Dad. This is also a way of honouring the parents and will give you an opportunity to talk positively about special qualities of other members of the family. Engaging in art activities together is a great way to open the door for conversations about many important topics.

TRY THIS #7

MARBLED ART

In throwaway containers, mix a small amount of the paint with a small amount of turpentine and mix it well. Very carefully pour the oil paints into the water in different areas of the dishpan. Using a stir stick, stir the paints, making an effort to create interesting patterns. It is important that the paints are well mixed. Be careful not to stir too actively. Use a piece of paper which is smaller than the size of the dish pan and place it carefully on the surface of the water. Pick up the paper by one corner and pull it carefully away from the water. Set aside to dry. This makes wonderful wrapping paper, as well as covers for boxes or cans.

You Will Need:
- a dishpan half filled with water
- several colours of oil paints
- turpentine

TRY THIS #8

WAX RESIST ART

Decide on a theme for you and your grandchild. It could be a seasonal theme or a scenery theme or an outdoor theme. Draw your pictures with the wax crayon, pressing heavily to ensure that the wax is thick on the paper. The brighter the colours are, the better it will look on paper. Paint over the wax drawing and let it dry. For young children, seeing the wax appear through the paint will seem like magic.

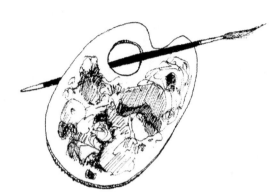

You Will Need:
- wax crayons and a dark colour of poster paint, or watercolours
- paintbrushes
- poster board or construction paper (a heavier weight than newsprint as it will absorb some of the paint)

TRY THIS #9

ROCK ART

On one of your outings, look for smooth, round rocks of any shape or size. Acrylic paints are best used on rocks or pieces of wood, and these make wonderful gifts and paper weights on desks at the office or gifts to members of the family or, if they're large enough, door stops.

One of our sons (presently 33) found a large oval rock which had broken in half. He stood each of the rocks on the broken end and painted bright sailboats against a blue background and gave them to his father for Christmas. 22 years later in our empty-nest home, his door stops are used every day to prop doors open. Several rocks can be put together to create a caterpillar. On a flat broad rock an animal can be painted curled up asleep. Pick out some animal and insect books at your local library and look for matches between the shape of your rocks and the creatures' photos in the book. Flat pieces of driftwood collected at the beach make a wonderful palette for pictures of birds.

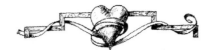

A Lesson We've Learned

3

There are countless things you can do together, but the richness will come from the conversations you have while you're doing them.

WE LISTEN TO EACH OTHER

The most significant time is on the weekend. I usually take grandma out to eat. She always smiles and she always invites us in for a little snack. I go with her on Saturday.

My grandparents are special because they love us and care. You don't have much time with them, so make the best of it. My grandparents always come to the recitals with us and go back to our house. We usually listen to each other do things. For example, I will play the piano, she will listen. She will usually teach me how to do chores and I listen. So that is like a bond.

My grandparents do a lot of things that are special to me that I just can't say in a whole page. One of them is she lets us work in her garden and she usually lets us have a great time there.

A lesson that I learned from my grandparents is that make the best of your life and another is how to do things such as chores. One more thing is how to write a bit of Chinese.

Michael Quan
Lake Hill
Elementary School

Snapshots

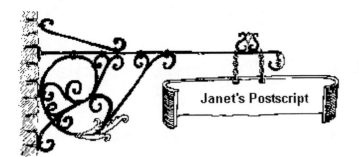

Janet's Postscript

When we were interviewing the Grade 6–7 students in elementary schools, we held a brainstorming session about what they *do* with grandparents that is special.

Following is what stood out as most important to them:

- shopping
- walks
- going to movies together
- sleepovers
- dressing up to go somewhere
- games, including video games, dominoes, crokinole, checkers, Chinese checkers, rummoli and hopscotch
- making bread, then eating it
- helping with the baking and cooking
- helping with the garden

In all of the conversations we had with the Grade 6–7 students about their experience with their grandparents, the following point was made:

"It's about quality time with them that you can't spend with anybody else."

When you are looking for things to do with your grandchildren, plan for activities which provide maximum time for interaction, both verbally and physically. Going to a movie is a passive activity, if that's all there is. However, holding hands in the movie, putting an arm along the back of their seat, touching their shoulder, brushing the hair out of their eyes and little squeeze in exciting or scary moments, all are ways of increasing connection. Having a conversation about the movie and predicting outcomes, speculating about the characters or the events in the movie, talking about what you hope to get out of the movie experience, and then discussing the movie after is an important way to make a further connection.

*"If one extends knowledge to the utmost, one will have wisdom.
Having wisdom, one can then make choices."*

Cheng Yi

TRY THIS #10

ROLE MODELS ALL AROUND US

Regardless of where your activity takes you, point out the role models that abound around us. If it's a movie, ask your grandchild to identify the positive characteristics that they see in role models in the movie. The child might respond with words like 'strength' or 'honesty' or 'braveness'. Discuss each of the characteristics that are raised. Counter-question by asking whether the quality could ever be a negative characteristic. Extend the conversation by identifying together role models in your town or role models in your family. For each member of your family ask the child to identify one characteristic that they admire most in each member of the family. This will provide you with a great opportunity to understand the developing values in your grandchild and the opportunity to positively influence and broaden their thinking.

Brave Honest strong

TRY THIS #11

ACTIVELY INFLUENCE THEIR CHOICES

We are well aware of the negative impact many television shows, video games and the internet have on our children and grandchildren. Suggestion: in advance of your grandchild's visit, ask them to identify their favourite TV shows, web sites, video games, etc. During the visit, arrange to visit the sites. You might record the television show prior to their visit, or play their video games with them. Prior to their visit, choose some you think they might really like but haven't experienced. Once you have finished your sharing, pose probing questions such as:

- What makes that show particularly interesting to you?
- Do you see any negative learning?
- Is there anything about this game/site/TV show that you wouldn't want your daughter or son to watch or experience?
- How does that game represent positive choices that you are making?

As your grandchild answers each of the questions, feel free to express your viewpoint, too, but be careful that your comments are only about the experience and do not directly make a value judgment about the child's choices. Listen and show you're listening by responding appropriately.

TRY THIS #12

ENCOURAGING GOOD LANGUAGE

- They encourage, through modelling and practice, the rich, colourful and precise use of words.
- They neither push nor patronize the child.
- They encourage many forms of expression through the use of body language, facial expression, and noise as well as words.
- They offer the child a varied and legitimate audience for his or her attempts to communicate.
- They recognize that it is harder to generate language than receive it. In this connection, you could do the following:

1. Get a double set of magnetic letters and create personal messages on your fridge door.
2. Make a game of memorizing children's poems or nursery rhymes together.
3. Work together to make bright, colourful labels for objects in the kitchen.
4. Offer to label any drawing your child makes.
5. Provide your child with an audience for his or her work.

6. Expose your child to many different types of music.
7. Provide opportunities to play word games and practice spelling.
8. Use magazine pictures to create cut-out stories.

9. Answer questions about word meanings with trips to the dictionary, help your child look up definitions.

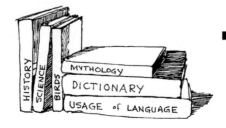

TRY THIS #13

MAKE AN ACTIVITIES CALENDAR

This is a wonderful activity for collaborative planning.

Pin up a large piece of paper on a wall or tape it to a window, and divide it into three columns. At the top of the first column put "What I like to do". At the top of the second column put "What is important to me?" and at the top of the third column put "What I am good at". Explain to your grandchild that in order to plan your activities for the year you need to know as much as you can about them.

Put up a second sheet, draw the same three columns, and complete the same chart for yourself. Together, have a discussion about which items are a match between your grandchild's sheet of paper and yours. Identify where the most significant differences are between your grandchild's chart and yours.

On a third chart, make a list of the places there are in your area where you might go to experience some of the things you're good at and would like to share, as well as some of the things which are important to you and some of the things you like to do. If you are short on ideas, get out your phone book and turn to the yellow pages – 'let your fingers do the walking!' You might find art galleries you didn't know about. You may discover a heritage organization you didn't know about. You might find clubs you want to join or courses you could take together.

On a fourth chart, list the months of the year and, depending on how frequently you are able to be together, identify target activities that give you a variety of rich experiences.

PLACES TO GO	
• museum	• fishing
• art gallery	• Witty's Lagoon
• bird watching	• mountain climbing

A Lesson We've Learned

4

The rules *can* be different at Grandma's house!

GRANDMA: JUST LETTING ME BE ME

Grandma had the big feather duvets, quilts, before feather quilts existed. Nobody had them except my Grandma, it seemed. And when we stayed overnight she would make up the bed in the living room. She'd fluff up the big feather bed. We would start at the back corner of the bathroom and we would run full tilt, right through the house, through the bathroom, through the kitchen, through the dining room, through the entry hall, through the living room and leap into this feather bed, and sink into the feathers. When we got out, Grandma would fluff up the feather bed again and we'd go back to the end of the bathroom and we would run… we would do this for hours. When you fell into the feather bed you'd start up really high and then you'd just sink and it would be like the feathers would come up over top of you and it

would be like this cocoon building around you. Grandma would laugh, always. The blanket would just cover over our faces. It was this feeling of being enclosed and warm and family and being wrapped in something. It's just something I always, always remember.

"It's not the years in your life but the life in your years that counts!"

Adlai Stevenson

It was so special because it was the only place we could do it. All my friends' grandmothers didn't have feather beds. They didn't have any idea what it meant to fall into a feather bed. It also brought back a sense of history, because it was from Poland, where my grandparents were from. It just felt like it was complete. Grandma let us run through the house. Nobody else ever let us run through the house.

Wendy Holob
A memory from the '50s

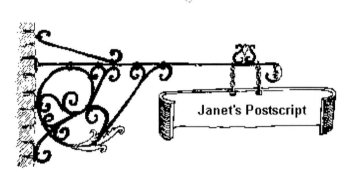

Janet's Postscript

When I first became a grandparent I thought it was important that parents and grandparents agreed on and expected the same kind of rules about deportment in our two homes. I've changed my mind about that. The rules in my house are very different from the rules in the children's parents homes. I asked Wendy, after she told me this story, if she would have been allowed to jump on the bed in her parents' home. Her answer was immediately, "Of course not!" But the question would be, "Was Wendy aware that the rules were different, and was she able to behave one way in one home and a different way in the other?" The answer is "Yes". Perhaps the rationale was that the bed at Grandma's house was stronger or tougher, or perhaps because the structure of a feather bed is different there was less possibility of damage to it. But on the other hand, perhaps it was simply that Wendy's grandma so enjoyed the excitement and laughter of the children that it was worth it to her in the short time Wendy visited to share that experience with the grandchildren.

I had an interesting experience shortly after Wendy told me this story. Natasha, aged 6, and Trevor, aged 3, from different families, were visiting at the same time. I was sitting across the room from the bedroom working at my computer when I suddenly saw and heard the two kids jumping on our bed. My instant response was a voice of reprimand which said, "Natasha, don't be teaching him that!" Her face fell and they both stopped jumping and got off the bed with both of them looking very contrite. Suddenly Wendy's story flashed through my mind and I realized that I didn't know why I had told them to stop jumping on the bed. There was no particular reason. The bed is very sturdy and in no way could those two small bodies damage it. So I asked myself, why would I tell them to stop?

"There would be fewer spoiled children if we could spank grandma"

(unknown)

That was a real lesson for me, and as I reflected on why that was my spontaneous response, I remembered that when I was a young child I was jumping on bunk beds at our summer cottage when the spring broke free from the wall (it was built-in bunk bed) and crashed to the floor. I remember being terrified at what my father would say because he had told us not to jump on the beds. Fortunately my big brother saved me by repairing it before Dad came home. So I reflect on the fact that so often our responses are triggered by what we experienced when we were children, yet to some degree that's the point of what this book is about. To plan for our experiences with our grandchildren, to be clear on our rules.

And that's probably the most important point of all. I don't think there's anything wrong with the rules being different at Grandma's house. However, here are the conditions I would put on that circumstance:

- that parents and grandparents are very clear on what the rules are in each house, even though they may be different;
- that behaviours which are permitted in Grandma's house reflect the values that both sets of parents hold true;
- when the children visit and their parents are present, the grandparents take responsibility for enforcing the rules of the grandparent home.

We recommend that parents and grandparents have a conversation about the rules in each other's homes, agree which ones are important to the parents to be enforced in both homes, and yet grandparents be clear on the rules that they would like to be different in their home. It is this kind of open conversation and collaborative planning that will make the situation much easier for everybody.

TRY THIS #14

FAMILY PLAY DAY

This is a cooperative event which is fun for all ages, no losers, just winners. This needs a fair amount of space as you will want to have five or six activities, depending on the number of people present. Choose different creative events for relays at each station, such as:

- carrying an egg on a spoon
- dart and balloon busting
- carrying water on your head in a flat dish
- raw egg catching
- apple dunking

The point is that each team starts at the first event and plays the relay, then an announcer/timer tells them to go to the next event after 5 minutes, until all groups have been around the circle. At the end share funny stories about incidents along the way.

TRY THIS #15

CAMP OUT IN THE LIVING ROOM

It may not be practical for grandparents to take grandchildren camping for a number of reasons. A recent Oprah show highlighted family campouts in the living room.
Try:

- a real pup tent, OR tents made out of blankets (Hint: use clothespins to make bigger tents)
- a campfire in the fireplace OR a light with sticks cleverly stacked around it
- try roasting marshmallows or hot dogs in the fireplace OR pack a picnic basket the night before
- OR order takeout food from Grandma's kitchen
- prepare some campfire songs and really good scary stories!
- arrange for tapes or CD's of favourite sing-along tunes.

Get the kids in on the planning. That will guarantee creativity. If you feel brave – invite them to ask a friend to the sleepover.

TRY THIS #16

FAMILY DANCE PARTY

Have every family member bring their favourite dance music and teach each other all your favourite dances.

Laughs are guaranteed on this one!

Variation: Dress up in costumes.

Try one of the videos on a new dance for all of you – for example, line dancing with everyone dressed up in Country & Western costume.

Family fun for this section is from Oprah, July 21, 1998.

TRY THIS #17

NEW AND OLD GROUP GAMES

Ask around, someone will remember the rules. And if not, make up your own!

- Bocce ball
- Tug-Of-War
- Frisbee
- Hide-And-Seek
- Horseshoes
- Bull's Eye
- Watermelon seed spitting

- Treasure hunts
- All kinds of tag
- Kick-The-Can
- Badminton
- Charades
- All varieties of races

One of my all time favourites is tying a balloon to every person's ankle on a foot long string. The object of the exercise is to see who can be the last person keep their balloon unbroken, once you yell "Go!" Imagine Granny climbing up onto the picnic table to get hers out of the stomper's way!

A Lesson We've Learned

5

The quality time and the lessons therein will be what our grandchildren remember about us forty years later.

REMEMBER THE QUALITY TIME

Before my Grandpa was dead we used to do everything together. I was two years old and my sister was just born. Me and my sister would go over to my grandparents' house early in the morning because my Mom worked full time. I would wake my Grandpa up and we would share a cinnamon bun together (but I would pick out the raisins). Then he would take me to skating. He would stay and watch the whole thing, then it was off to swimming. I was a pretty good swimmer so I already knew how to swim.

After swimming we would always go to the library. I would pick out lots of books for him to read to me later that day. Then we would go to the Buns Master Bakery. I would get an old fashioned doughnut. Then we would go home and play a game we made up ourselves. It was called Goldilocks and the Three Bears. My Grandpa is dead and my life is sure different. I miss him a lot and I feel that his death has taken a piece out of me.

Kristie Blain
Strawberry Vale Elementary School

"Memory is the treasury and guardian of all things."

Cicero

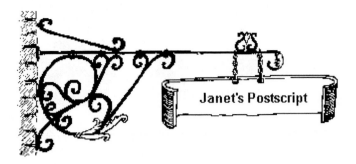

Janet's Postscript

Kristie's story is very revealing. She starts and ends the story talking about her grandfather's death, and in between she remembers what came first to her mind when she was invited to write the story.
She highlights the following activities:

- eating a cinnamon bun together, while picking out the raisins
- taking her to skating
- taking her to swimming
- going to the library to pick out books for him to read later that day
- going to the bakery to get an old fashioned doughnut, which must have been a special one for her
- going home to play a game

The story Kristie tells consistently identifies the gift of time that her grandfather gave her. Notice how she comments that he would stay and watch the whole thing when he took her skating. This confirms my own experience.

Natasha only enjoyed her gymnastics on the days that one of her grandparents, and it didn't matter which one, was there to watch her and her learning. Notice, too, that she comments that he would always take her to the library – but notice that she is picking out books for him to read to her later in the day. No doubt there were cuddles during the reading.

Then she comments that they play a game. Games by their very nature are interactive. In one day, it is remarkable the amount of quality time this young Kristie had with her grandfather.

The strategies which follow are simple and easy games that many of us played in our childhood.

The recipe for relationships in games includes:

**Fun ~ Challenge
Laughter ~ Joy ~ Excitement
Fairness ~ Companionship ~ Playfulness**

TRY THIS #18

HOPSCOTCH

*Play all the variations of this ancient sidewalk
game, then make up your own!*

Number of players: Two to four
Object of game: To hop through the diagram and pick up your marker
without making a mistake.

1. Draw one of these diagrams on a sidewalk with a piece of chalk or
   scratch it into the dirt with a stick. Each square should be about eighteen
   inches on a side. Add a line several feet below the bottom of the
   diagram.

2. Each player will need a marker. You can use anything small and easy to
   throw. Coins, stones, keys or bottle caps all work well.

3. The first player stands behind the line and throws the marker on square
   one.

4. Beginning at the Home square, the player must hop on one foot through
   the squares in the diagram, skipping the first square. When two squares are
   side by side, the player should land with one foot in each square.

5. Once she hops to the square marked *Goal*, the player must turn around in
   one jump and then hop back through the diagram. When she reaches
   square two, she must lean down and pick up her marker, then hop into
   Home.

6. The first player continues her turn, throwing her marker into square two.
   She then hops through the diagram, this time skipping over square two (or
   any other square with a marker in it), both coming and going. She will
   have to stop on square three on her return trip to retrieve her marker from
   square two.

7. A player's turn continues upward through the squares unless she makes
   any of the following mistakes: stepping on a line, missing the target
   square with her marker or having her marker touch a line of the square,
   stepping on a square with anyone's marker in it, or putting two feet down
   in a single box.

HOPSCOTCH continued

8. When she makes a mistake, the player leaves her marker in the last square it occupied before her turn ended, and waits for her turn to come around again. Then she must repeat the last round before she can throw her marker again.

9. If markers are blocking so many boxes that it becomes impossible to hop past them, temporary "boxes" can be drawn next to the occupied ones.

10. The first player to move her marker to the Goal and then hop back to Home is the winner.

IDEAS FOR VARIATIONS

Instead of throwing her marker and then picking it up again, a player must kick her marker to the next square on her return trip. If she loses her balance or misses the target square, her turn is over.

- OR -

When a player has gone through the entire diagram, she must hop to the Goal and back again, but this time she must balance the marker on one foot (or her head, finger, arm, knee or forearm) while she is hopping.

TRY THIS #19

SNAP

Watch for cards that match, then be the first to say, "Snap!"
Number of players: Good for two
Object of game: To get all the cards

1. Shuffle and deal out all the cards - including the Jokers.
2. Each player holds his pack face down.
3. Together the players say, "One, two, three." On the word *three*, the players quickly lay their top cards face up in the middle of the table.
4. If the cards do *not* match, the players repeat, "One, two, three" and lay down the next card.
5. If the cards match - two Kings, two 10's, two Aces - the first player to call out "Snap!" takes the cards.
6. If both players call "Snap" at the same time, neither player takes the cards.
7. If you say "Snap" by mistake, you have to give one card to every player.
8. If one of the Jokers turns up, it's as good as a match. Again, the first player to call out "Snap!" takes the cards.
9. The player who gets all the cards is the winner.

TRY THIS #20

SLAPJACK

You have to be fast to play this game.
When you see a Jack – slap it!
Number of players: Two to six
Object of game: To get all the cards

1. Shuffle and deal out all the cards.
2. Each player puts his pack face down on table in front of him.
3. The first player quickly puts his top card face up in the centre of the table. When putting down cards, turn them fast and do not peek!
4. The next player puts his card face up on top of the first card, and so on.
5. When a Jack is turned over, all the players try to slap their hand on it. The first player to slap the Jack wins the pile.
6. The next player then puts a new card out, and the game goes on as before.
7. If a player runs out of cards, he sits without playing until a Jack comes up. Then he tries to slap the Jack and get back in the game.
8. The winner is the one who ends up with all the cards.

TRY THIS #21

WHO HAS THE COIN?

This is an –under-the-table game that brings screams of laughter from adults and kids alike. It can be played by anywhere from 2 to 10 people but is best with about 6. It relies on all kinds of tricks and acting to keep the pace up.

Players team up evenly and sit on two sides of the table (although on ferry rides we've used a briefcase as the table and a newspaper too.) Toss the coin to see who starts. Each team designates a leader who has the final say in passing the coin and directing hands of his/her team. The starting team leader says, "Under the table!" and all hands of the team disappear. The leader has the coin and secretly places it in one person's hand. Team members use facial expressions etc., to try to hide what is going on under the table. When the placement is completed, the leader says, "Hands Up!" and all closed hands are placed on the table. The opposite team then tries to determine where the coin is.

Rules:
- They cannot touch. They have to ask their leader's permission to take a hand off if they believe it is not in a particular hand.
- The object of the game is to get enough hands off so that the pressure builds up until they order, "Coin!" and point at the guilty hand. If the coin is there, they win a point. If it is not there, the other team gets a point and the game starts over.
- Remember to always ask the leader before giving an instruction, or the order is lost.
- It is permitted to ask that hands be turned over or moved around so that tension of hands can be gauged. Some people swear by the heat test (hands held over the closed hands to test energy level). Others stare into eyes while asking, "Do you have it?" to test truth telling.

You get the point? It's a crazy game of psyche-out and everyone gets in the fun!

A Lesson We've Learned

6

An investment in our grandchild's education will be our living legacy for their lifetime.

WITHOUT MY GRANDMA IT COULDN'T HAVE HAPPENED

When I was twenty I decided that I was going to go back to school, to university. I had decided that if I was going to make anything of my life at all I had to do it, so I wrote exams as a private study student and got accepted by UVic. About two weeks before I was due to go, my Dad's mom was over for dinner. Usually Nana would winter in Florida or California, or she would go some place warm. Right in the middle of dinner, just before dessert, she said, "I think I'm going to go to university with Daphne." I thought, "Oh, please, Nana, no. I don't want this." She said, "Yes, I've got it all figured out. We'll rent a place together and I'll be able to visit my friends. I'll be in Victoria where it's nice and warm and for Christmas, too, and Daphne will be able to go to school. I'll cook dinner for her and everything will be wonderful. And there, it's settled." I didn't have a thing to say about it.

When I look back on it now, I realize that if it wasn't for Nana I really wouldn't have been able to do it. In my first year I had saved only $756. Most of that and more went for tuition on the very first day of registration. Nana paid the rent, I bought the groceries for that entire year, and she cooked the meals. There was over 50 years difference in our ages and I would get home from class or from work and Nana would be waiting for me. She had made dinner and kept it warm, and she would say, "Now, tell me about your day."

And I look at that as the greatest gift that anybody could have given me. We laughed a lot. She added her perspective to my view on the day, things that were important. I can remember at one point thinking that I was going to go and join a demonstration and she said to me, are you prepared to lose this whole year? Are you prepared to go to jail? Do you realize that these kinds of things could happen? You've made a big investment here – do you know what each lecture costs you? All of those kinds of things were her way of helping to ease me into and at the same time get very serious about doing the work at university and getting out and doing what it was I wanted to do.

And without her it couldn't have happened.

Daphne Macnaughton

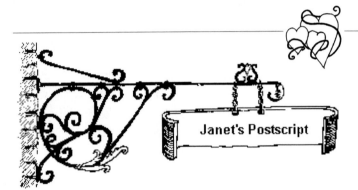

Janet's Postscript

Later in the interview, Daphne told me that her Nana knew some of the pitfalls she would run into moving from upcountry to the city, and felt that she could help to shape Daphne's view and purpose, hence her decision.

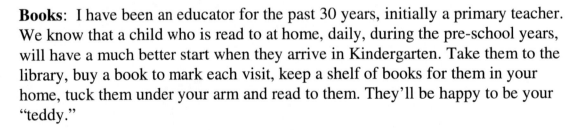

TRY THIS #22

SUPPORT FOR SUCCESS

There are many ways we can support our grandchild's education, from big (as in Daphne's story) to small:

Books: I have been an educator for the past 30 years, initially a primary teacher. We know that a child who is read to at home, daily, during the pre-school years, will have a much better start when they arrive in Kindergarten. Take them to the library, buy a book to mark each visit, keep a shelf of books for them in your home, tuck them under your arm and read to them. They'll be happy to be your "teddy."

Day Care: Most young parents work these days. Michael and I paid for Natasha's day care for half a day from age 3 to age 5 because her parents were struggling to juggle their work shifts to care for her. We chose a Montessori day care centre because of their excellent reputation in our city. The right educational centre will stimulate and motivate, help your young child learn to socialize and introduce readiness activities for reading.

Education Plans: There are many tax-deductible investment plans available. We put $75.00 per month into a plan for our three grandchildren. We don't really notice it and already the money has tripled itself. We just paid $10,000.00 for tuition for our 25-year-old for only one year. Most of our grandchildren will need help and need a post-secondary education. (Statistics indicate 95% of all jobs will require post-secondary education in the Year 2000.)

Toys: Look for educational toys. There are many choices available these days: puzzles that teach, audio tapes to sing along with, talking toys. Check out your area for a teacher's store where there will be a wealth of resources used in schools. Keep a closet full.

Technology: We bought a marvelous computer keyboard which plugged into my computer, and taught Natasha her ABC's through comic characters and games. Buy a used computer for your grandchild to take home. These days every child needs to be computer literate, but many of our kids can't afford the technology.

Daphne finished her story by saying, "And I had many, many chances over the years to thank her for that, and to laugh about that year." Daphne is now a very successful school principal, and we can bet Nana is proud.

TRY THIS #23

ACCEPTING AND PRAISING EFFORTS

- providing opportunities for them to draw, paint, cut and glue
- helping them learn letters, words and numbers in the world around them
- encouraging them to accept responsibility
- reading to them and encouraging them to discuss stories, poems and nursery rhymes
- giving them a background of experiences to talk about: visits to the park, the beach, the airport, the library, trips by car, boat, train, plane. By noticing together, you encourage them to be observant and give them opportunities to tell about the experiences you have shared.
- encouraging them to share with others
- providing them with opportunities to play with others and even to spend time away from home with friends in order to develop independence
- developing in them the knowledge that both of you are working together for their welfare
- talking positively about school experiences

Create a writing centre and stock it with these suggested types of writing materials:

- pencils
- crayons
- felt markers, broad and fine
- an old typewriter
- magnetic letters and numbers
- hard paper for covers
- a small chalkboard
- letter and number lists for copying
- labels for computer and printer
- envelopes, large and small
- a beginner's Dictionary
- stapler and hole puncher
- paper of all sizes, shapes and colours
- pocket charts (plastic shoe holders to tuck things away)
- wallpaper books rings for holding things together
- …and so on

A walk through a stationery supply store will bring you lots of ideas!

TRY THIS #24

GOING FOR A WALK WITH A PREREADER

Have you and your prereader looked at every storybook in the house so often that the pages fall apart at a touch? Are both of you looking for new ways to practise reading skills?

Almost everything a prereader does during the day can become a preparation for reading. Many familiar pastimes involve understanding symbols, following paths, and identifying objects, shapes or colours. Here are a few simple ways to offer practice in prereading skills, as you and your grandchild take a walk around the neighbourhood:

Read shapes. Many geometric shapes, already well known to a prereader, take on new meaning when they are spotted in objects on a neighbourhood walk. For example, on closer examination, a car is actually a conglomeration of circles, rectangles, squares and trapezoids.

Read logos. Are there restaurants or stores near where you live that feature prominent trademarks or logos? Point out any such logos to your child when you take your walk. Later, at home, you can draw the different logos on a piece of paper and ask your child to identify them.

Read a tree. Bark patterns in trees can look like pictures. Are there faces or other recognizable patterns in any old gnarled trees in your neighbourhood? The cracks and ruts in the bark's surface can also be used as maze paths to trace with a finger.

Read colours. As you walk along together, you can play the guessing game "I see something . . . ," using colours as clues. You can also turn the game around by asking your child to pick out something that's red, yellow, blue, green, gray, orange or brown.

Read letters and numbers. You walk could turn into a hunting game, as together you try to spot the numerals 1 to 10 on buildings, street signs or license plates. Children may enjoy hunting down the letters of the alphabet this way, too.

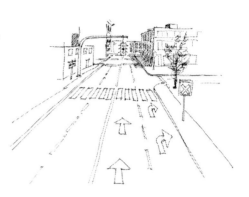

Read the sky. Cloud pictures are easy to spot on a clear day when the sky is filled with puffy cumulus forms. Scanning the sky for clouds that look like familiar objects is a game that changes every time the wind blows.

Read traffic signs and symbols. Once you have pointed out traffic signals and have explained the significance of the red, yellow and green lights, you can watch a signal direct traffic for a while.

Observing the lights at work will be a lesson in communicating with symbols.

You can also find arrows on traffic signs and those painted on the street and explain their functions. Observe them at work, as well.

If, after all of this outdoor prereading practice, you're still not ready to return to old, familiar books, why not put together your own neighbourhood book? Your child can dictate sentences to you about the things both of you have seen. For illustrations, you can include pictures drawn by your child, napkins (with familiar logos), photos of neighbourhood friends and places, and any other found or created objects.

(Source unknown)

Snapshots

Devin
1999

TRY THIS #25

ENCOURAGE YOUR CHILD'S LEARNING:
Create A Reading and Writing Centre

- read and re-read favourite stories
- share observations and predictions
- discuss and answer questions, especially "why?" questions
- read into a tape recorder for them to have at home
- role-play characters and different endings to stories
- use puppets to dramatize

Suggested types of reading materials:
- big books; ask at your bookstore – these are very big and great for new readers
- books with read-along tapes
- tried and true childrens' literature
- prize winning books such as Caldecott winners
- child-authored books
- research and theme books based on some of the activities you are having or corresponding about, and holiday or seasonal books for crafts, traditions, stories or field trip ideas
- poetry
- song books
- large chart paper to draw and write their stories on (just like at school)
- picture books, excellent for discussions
- their own tape recorder

A number of people proposed we provide a list of recommended books and computer software. Any such list would be outdated almost immediately. Just ask any reputable bookstore personnel and they'll be able to help you. If you are just starting a collection, the choices will be different than supplementing one with the latest.

"We make a living by what we get,
but we make a life by what we give."

Norman MacEwan

A Lesson We've Learned

7

Children learn through action, experience and reflection: these words should drive the activities we plan for our grandkids.

Researchers world-wide have come to significant conclusions about how children learn, a few of which would be relevant to how we spend time our children.

- **The prime need of all learners is to make meaning of their experiences.** (Caine and Caine, 1991)

- **Educators have now moved beyond thinking that learning is rote memorization.** (Cambourne, 1988)

- **Children learn through the process of play. Play is a natural universal learning activity of children and adults.** (Katz and Chard)

- **Children are naturally curious. From the time they are born, children want to know, and to act or interact.** (Clay, 1991)

- **Children learn through collaboration with others. Social, emotional and intellectual development is fostered through interaction with others** (Vigotsky, 1978 and Wells, 1986)

- **Children learn best in an environment that encourages risk-taking, and from their mistakes.** (Goodman, 1986 and Smith, 1974)

- **Children acquire, develop and express their understandings through the use of language – written and oral language develop concurrently.** (Bliss, 1980 and Lemke, 1989)

- **Children gain knowledge by creating relationships.** (Caine and Caine)

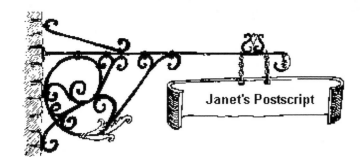

Janet's Postscript

The last statement stays with me. If this is true, that children gain knowledge by creating relationships, then far better it be caring grandparents than peers, baby-sitters or the person next door.

Even if we can't be with them, we can give them the gift of time. This book is based on the research in this lesson.

TRY THIS #26

INTERVIEW YOUR GRANDCHILD – THEN HAVE THEM INTERVIEW YOU

Use these questions, or make up your own:

1. Who are your role models? Why?
2. What is the job you like least? or most?
3. What has been your biggest challenge?
4. What has been your biggest success?
5. Who has helped you overcome challenges?
6. Which of your accomplishments are you most proud of?
7. How could I help/support you more?

Once the interviews are over, ask:

What surprised you the most?
What do you have in common?

TRY THIS #27

OUR SIMILARITIES AND DIFFERENCES:
DRAW A VENN DIAGRAM

You write the ideas, feelings, etc., that you both share in the overlapping section, and show your different viewpoints in the other two sections.

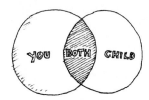

Interview your grandchild or have them interview you with questions that bring out feelings, viewpoints, ideas that you may or may not share. Try the following questions or make up your own, based on "want to know" or "need to know" topics:

1. What do we most like to do outdoors?
2. What TV shows do we think are best for kids?
3. What kind of pets would we choose if we could have anything?
4. If we could go on a fantasy trip?
5. What are our favourite foods?
6. What feelings do we feel most often?
7. What would we want in the ideal world?
8. What are the worst characteristics kids might show (adults might show)?
9. What are our most important values?
10. What would be the characteristics of our heroes?

This is only the beginning. Once you have your Venn Diagram done, pursue:
- why you put your priorities where you did
- what questions you have about the other person's choices
- how you could make a plan to do things together based on this information

Try Venn Diagrams to start other conversations!

TRY THIS #28

WHO CAN I COUNT ON?

Draw two sets of concentric circles on a large piece of paper. The purpose of this conversation is to identify, in both of your lives, who you can count on most in your life and to demonstrate that there are different layers of people, or different reasons why you count on them.

Write in the names of people for each of you

The important part of the exercise will be discussing after:

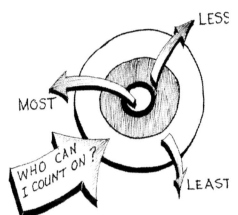

- why you put each person in which circle
- what you would count on them for
- what thoughts came to mind as you completed it
- if there are any gaps in any circle and how you might fill them

This opens up the opportunity to explore your grandchild's circle of friends and the degree of closeness or safety he/she feels with friends and family members. You might even learn something about yourself!

TRY THIS #29

USING TELEVISION APPROPRIATELY

Choose 2 or 3 television shows to watch together.

Provide each of you with a paper and pencil.
The task is for each of you to identify five appropriate and inappropriate social behaviours of characters in popular TV shows.

The last task for each of you to identify an area of social behaviour that you want to improve and set a goal for yourself as well as a timeline for reaching the goal.

A Lesson We've Learned

8

We must remember to honour and reinforce our grandchildrens' relationship with their parents as well.

PAINTING POTS FOR MOM

A wonderful thing to do with grandchildren is to impress upon them the importance of them honouring their fathers and their mothers by taking the time to do something special for them. Many children will take a piece of paper and fold it over and make a card, but this is a wonderful opportunity to engage in some of the recommended crafts, and work on them together as gifts.

For Mother's Day, I purchased two small clay pots. I already had my acrylic paints. I also purchased a latex paint in dark green, and prior to Natasha's arrival, I painted both pots green on the outside and the inside.

When Natasha arrived we got out the acrylic paints. We talked a bit about the kind of design we wanted to put on our pots. Natasha painted stick flowers on hers. I had a few real flowers on hand so that she could copy what the centre of the flowers looked like with stamens, therefore helping her get a bit of reality into her creativity. I also had moist sponges available so that when she was unhappy with the way the flower looked we could wipe it off quickly and she could try again, although I always left it up to her to decide if she needed help.

We painted bright-coloured borders around the tops of the pot. Mine was a series of zig-zag lines and dots. I keep a collection of clay pots on hand in Natasha's cupboard, so that any time she wants to paint a gift, the materials are there for her.

We also painted under dishes to sit underneath the pot. Her mother was thrilled with the gift, and it maintains a bright and happy spot in their house filled with flowers.

**CAUTION: If the owner of the pot intends to put earth directly into the pot, then the inside of the pot has to be painted either with a varnish or a paint in order to keep the moisture from seeping through the clay, because it will ruin the painting on the outside.

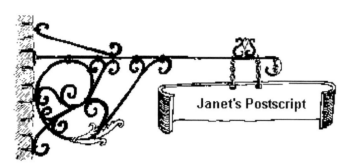

Janet's Postscript

The experience I had with Natasha during the pot painting was wonderful. We discussed and debated techniques, we talked about her Mommy and what her Mommy liked, what colours she liked and how we could please her, and I know that my daughter-in-law also feels that the pot is special because her mother-in-law and her daughter both worked on it together. Pots can be decorated with Christmas themes for Christmas, boats for Daddy on Father's Day – the choices are endless.

We work hard at finding the balance between our relationship with our grandchildren and that with their parents. There must be no competition or hint of it . . .and that's a fine line because when the kids go home, the smallest comments (e.g., I don't have to do that at Grandpa's house . . . or, Grandma says you should . . .) can set a parent's teeth on edge. The only solution is to set clear boundaries as to who's responsible for what, and open communication between parents and grandparents.

I have a prime example: I had Tasha's bangs and hair trimmed last week – just a little something, I thought – turns out her father wants her hair to grow to ponytail length. Things have been cool (chilly) lately between us, and I owe an apology to him as soon as the temperature warms up. Live, learn and be careful!

WHAT ABOUT BIRTHDAYS, CHRISTMAS AND OTHER HOLIDAY EVENTS?

Many kids make cards at school or on their own as gifts for parents. Gifts can mean so much more when you work with your grandchild to create a gift for parents from both of you. Yvonne's (Tasha's mother) face was a picture of delight when she realized that I had spent most of my day working with Tasha to make her the Mother's Day pot. Symbolic, isn't it?

TRY THIS #30

EGG CANDLES

You Will Need:

an egg carton
a clean, large, sharp needle or pin
a can
a small pot
vegetable oil
a ruler
oven mitts

eggs, any number
a bowl
candle wax, in bars or shredded
candlewick
a crayon with its paper removed
scissors
a spoon or stick for stirring

If you want to leave your candle in its shell, don't oil the inside of the egg or peel off the shell. You can also make smaller egg candles this way, using shells that have been cracked in half. You may even want to decorate the shells with water paints or acrylic craft paints, or try dyeing them. For shiny egg candles, polish the finished candles with a little vegetable oil.

1. Place an egg in the carton, pointed end up, and poke a hole in the shell with the needle. Chip away some of the shell to make a hole about 2 cm (3/4 in.) across. Break up the yolk with the needle and then pour the white and yolk into the bowl. Remove the whitish lining from inside the shell. Thoroughly rinse out the shell and place it upside down to dry. Repeat this process with all the eggs you are using.
2. Two bars of wax or 500 ml (2c.) of shredded wax will fill about six eggs.
3. Keeping this in mind, place as much wax as you'll need in the can, along with a crayon.
4. Shape the can to form a spout.
5. Place the can in the pot and add water to the pot until the water comes about one-third of the way up the can. Heat the pot on medium-low.
6. While the wax is melting, thoroughly coat the insides of the dry eggshells with vegetable oil. Place them upright in the egg carton.
7. When the wax has melted, turn off the heat. Remove the pot from the stove. Ask an adult to very carefully dip the length of wick into the wax. Hold it above the can until it stops dripping.
8. Hold one end of the wick in each hand, pull it straight and hold it as it cools. Cut it into 8 cm (3 in.) pieces when it has hardened.

40

TRY THIS #30
continued

EGG CANDLES continued

9. Ask an adult to carefully pour the wax into the prepared eggs. As the wax begins to set but is still soft (after about ten minutes), poke a prepared wick into each egg.

10. As the wax cools it will shrink and leave a hollow in each egg. Heat more wax to fill the hollow spaces. When the wax is hard and cool, peel off the shells. If areas of the shells are difficult to peel off, firmly tap them on the countertop.

(Source unknown)

Happiness is
being and doing together!

TRY THIS #31A

CLAY-POT CANDLES

This project is a candle and holder all in one.
Make it as plain or as fancy as you like.

You Will Need:

- a clean, dry clay pot, 5 to 9 cm (2 to 3 in.) in diameter
- newspaper and acrylic craft paint and a paintbrush (optional)
- a can
- candle wax, in bars or shredded
- a crayon with its paper removed
- a small pot
- candlewick
- scissors, a pencil, masking tape, wax paper, oven mitts

1. If you are going to paint your pot, spread newspaper over your work surface. See "Other Ideas" (following) for some suggestions on how to paint it. You don't need to paint the inside of the pot, except for the rim. Allow the pot to dry completely.
2. Place one or two bars of wax or 25 – 500 ml. (1 to 2 cups) of shredded wax and the crayon in the can.
3. Shape the can to form a spout. Place the can in the pot and add water to the pot until the water comes about one-third of the way up the can. Heat the pot on medium-low.
4. While the wax is melting, stick at least two layers of masking tape inside the pot, across the hole in the bottom. Cut a piece of wick about 5 cm (2 in.) longer than your pot is tall. Tape the wick to the center bottom of the pot.
5. Place the pencil across the top of the clay pot and tape the top of the wick to it so that the wick is straight. Place the prepared pot on a sheet of wax paper.
6. When the wax has melted, turn off the heat. Wearing oven mitts, remove the pot from the stove. Gently stir the wax to mix in the colour.
7. Ask an adult to carefully pour the wax into the clay pot to about 1 cm (1/2 inch from the top. If the wax shrinks as it hardens, fill in the hollow with a bit more melted wax. Trim the wick to about 1.5 cm (5/8 in.).

TRY THIS #31B

OTHER IDEAS FOR CLAY-POT CANDLEHOLDERS

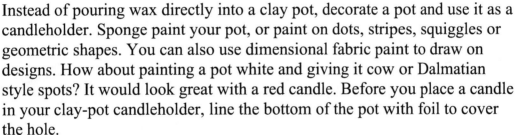

- When you add colour to your candle, choose a colour to match the paint or decorations on your pot.
- For a festive clay pot, paint the pot gold on the outside and around the rim on the inside. Add colour and a scent, and sprinkle a little gold glitter on top of the wax as it hardens.
- Instead of painting the pot, tie on a bow or other trimmings. Make sure the decorations will not be near the flame.

Instead of pouring wax directly into a clay pot, decorate a pot and use it as a candleholder. Sponge paint your pot, or paint on dots, stripes, squiggles or geometric shapes. You can also use dimensional fabric paint to draw on designs. How about painting a pot white and giving it cow or Dalmatian style spots? It would look great with a red candle. Before you place a candle in your clay-pot candleholder, line the bottom of the pot with foil to cover the hole.

(Source unknown)

A GRANDCHILD'S REFLECTIONS: CHRISTMAS 1991

Grandma, Uncle John and Uncle Bob came to my house for Christmas. They came over from Abbotsford. My Grandma is short with short straight blondish hair. She still has smooth skin. Grandma played play dough with us.

Ryan
Strawberry Vale Elementary School

TRY THIS #32

PLAYDOUGH DECORATIONS

Stretch your imagination! Try your hand at wall decorations, tree decorations, napkin rings and more!

COOKED SALT DOUGH

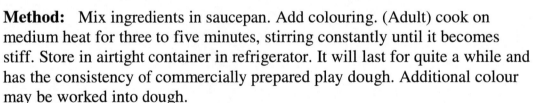

You Will Need:
1 cup salt
2 cups flour
4 teaspoons cream of tartar
2 tablespoons cooking oil
2 cups water
Powder paint or Edicol
Saucepan

Method: Mix ingredients in saucepan. Add colouring. (Adult) cook on medium heat for three to five minutes, stirring constantly until it becomes stiff. Store in airtight container in refrigerator. It will last for quite a while and has the consistency of commercially prepared play dough. Additional colour may be worked into dough.

You can dry your projects in a 250 F oven for 1 ½ to 2 hours, or let them air dry. When the playdough is dry, decorate with poster or acrylic paints. Small hooks can be put in the top of your creations and they can be hung in windows, or on the Christmas tree.

These also make terrific fridge magnets to give as personalized gifts. Just adhere a piece of magnetic tape (available at craft stores) to the back of the finished decoration.

TRY THIS #33

UNCOOKED SALT DOUGH

This is the easiest recipe: it can be made in less than three minutes.
Let children make it themselves whenever possible.

You Will Need:
- 2 cups flour
- 1 cup salt
- 1 tablespoon cooking oil
- 1 cup water
- powder paint or food colouring
- bowl and spoons

Method: Mix powder paint with
flour and salt (food colouring may be
added to water as an alternative). Add
oil and water. Knead. Children will
like to use rollers, biscuit cutters and
toothpicks with dough. Store dough in plastic bags. If it becomes sticky, add
more flour. Dough will keep for more than a week, even longer if it's kept in
a refrigerator, but it has a tendency to crumble. Small shapes of this mixture
can be baked in a 350° F oven for 45 minutes to make them hard.
Makes enough for six children.

*"Art is a personal and satisfying activity at any age, for
although the arts are responsible for a greater awareness of
the external world, it is also the arts that give vent to the
emotions, the joy and fears of life."*

Victor Lowenfeld and Lambert W. Brittain,
Creative and Mental Growth

A Lesson We've Learned

9

When grandchildren come to visit, tell them the things you have to do (e.g., vacuum, shop, cook, drive to…) and ask them how they'd like to be involved.

STUMBLING ACROSS NEW TALENT: THE FIVE-YEAR-OLD GOURMET CHEF

Many times I stumble on what my grandchildren can do with me by being open to any experience. One day my granddaughter, Natasha, was visiting unexpectedly and was going to be staying overnight. I had invited several couples for dinner and did not have the time to be actively playing or working with her on something. I pulled up a stool to the kitchen counter and suggested she might like to watch me. No sooner was she watching me than she asked if she could do some of the things that I was doing. In no time at all I had her chopping onions, slicing mushrooms – I was careful to give her a serrated knife that wasn't too sharp so she could saw away at the onions without risking her little fingers. She became the most amazing chopper! Shortly after that, as I was measuring foods, she became interested in what a quarter of a cup was, what a half-cup was, and from then on in the next two hours, every time I had to measure something, she was the one who did the measuring and dumping it into the bowl. I was fascinated with the high level of interest she had in being a gourmet chef like Grandma. The highlight of the dinner, and the highlight of my time with Natasha was the orange dessert that we made. This is a wonderful one for making with children. I found it in a local newspaper and it sounded fascinating. I've attached the recipe on page 48.

Imagine Natasha's delight as the oranges were brought out of the fridge during dinner, the lids put on them and the orange rind sprinkled over them. She really felt she had constructed this magnificent dessert herself.

"Cooking is like love – it should be entered into with abandon, or not at all."

Harriet vanHorne

Another thought: I didn't want Natasha sitting at the dining room table with us, as we had an adult-oriented evening planned, yet I didn't want to exclude her. I fed her supper early, then had her take her activities to another part of the house where she played and worked quietly by herself. We dressed her up and the agreement we made was that she would be the one to deliver each person's dessert to them. Imagine her pride as we put the finishing touches on the oranges and she was able to claim that she had been a significant helper throughout the whole meal. She did join us for her orange at the dessert table.

Janet's Postscript

By the end of the evening we were closer because we had created something together and shared in the pride of serving it and displaying our work.

Since that event we've noticed a keen interest on Natasha's part in helping to cook. They key word here is "helping". Just last week we were at Great Grandma's house for dinner and she dove right into the kitchen work, efficiently washing up. As she finished, she twirled in a happy circle and exclaimed, "I just <u>love</u> being a helper . . . and I'm good at it."

Our book puts a big emphasis on "doing and being" with our grandkids. When I first started down this path, I thought our "doing and being" had to be a plan specific to my grandchild's interests. To some extent this is what I'm suggesting: that part of the time can be them doing "our thing" and our "must-do" tasks.

Rory is 12 now. With him I offer a modest salary and give him a list of jobs I really need done. He picks the one(s) that most appeal to him. It supplements his allowance nicely. He does a good job washing and vacuuming my car, he cleans the carport, waters the flowers – he's a great helper, too. And it's best when I'm working with him 'cause we talk!

DID YOU KNOW?

In the brainstorming session with kids, we asked them what they most liked to do; cooking predominated.

- Cooking – brownies, bread, cakes, cupcakes, buns, pies – *Amanda*
- "Then we would always come home and bake bread. While the bread was baking we would be baking, we would be baking cakes, squares, cookies and other treats" – *Pamela*
- "I still like baking with my Grandma!" – *Tana*

TRY THIS #34

ORANGES EN SURPRISE

4 large navel oranges
2 egg whites
1/2 cup sugar
Fresh mint leaves

2 cups orange sherbet
Pinch cream of tartar
Dash almond extract
Candied orange peel

Cut off top quarters of oranges, discard. Turn oranges and slice off the stem ends so that oranges sit flat. Spoon out flesh, reserving for another use. Place hollowed skins on baking sheet lined with wax paper and freeze until rigid. Divide sherbet evenly among oranges, firmly packing with back of spoon.

Return oranges to freezer. Meanwhile, in glass bowl, using clean beaters, beat egg whites until frothy; add cream of tartar. Gradually add sugar. Continue beating about 3 minutes or until eggs are glossy and form stiff peaks; stir in almond extract. When orange shells are firmly frozen, remove from freezer and place on baking sheet. Cover openings decoratively with meringue. Immediately bake in pre-heated 425ºF oven for 2 minutes. Reduce heat to 375º and bake 3 to 5 minutes more or until meringue is set and lightly browned. Garnish with mint and candied orange peel. Serve immediately. Serves 4.

TRY THIS #35

PLAYDOUGH YOU CAN EAT *Make delicious sculptures and eat them*

You Will Need:

- a bowl
- two cups of powdered dry milk
- two cups of smooth peanut butter
- one cup of honey

1. Mix the ingredients together in the bowl and stir until well blended.
2. Make projects for your family and friends or create interesting edible party favours.
3. Projects can be decorated with raisins, shredded coconut or other treats
4. These projects cannot be saved. They are made to be eaten.
5. Encourage the kids to be creative!

TRY THIS #36

CORNFLAKE CRUNCHIES

100 g butter
1/4 cup honey
2 tablespoons brown sugar
2 cups cornflakes
2 tablespoons chopped glacé cherries
2 tablespoons chopped mixed nuts (optional)

Preparation Time: 20 minutes
Cooking Time: 10 minutes
Makes 24

1. Line two 12-cup muffin tins with paper muffin cups.
2. Combine the butter, honey and sugar in a small heavy-based pan. Stir over low heat without boiling until the butter has melted and sugar is completely dissolved. Bring to boil; reduce heat. Simmer for 5 minutes. Remove from heat immediately.
3. Combine cornflakes, cherries, nuts (if using) and butter mixture in a medium mixing bowl. Spoon the mixture into patty cases. Refrigerate until set, about 1 hour. Store in an airtight container in refrigerator for up to 2 days.

TRY THIS #37

POPCORN POPS

1 tablespoon oil
1/4 cup popping corn
3/4 cup sugar
1/4 cup water
25 g butter

Preparation time: 15minutes
Cooking time: 15 minutes
Makes 6

4 drops red or green food colouring
6 wooden icy-pole sticks

1. Heat oil in a large pan. Add corn, cover and cook over medium heat. Hold the lid tightly, shaking pan occasionally. Cook until the popping stops. Put popcorn in a large bowl; set aside.
2. Combine the sugar, butter and water in a small heavy-based pan. Stir over medium heat without boiling until sugar has completely dissolved. Brush sugar crystals from the sides of the pan with a wet pastry brush. Bring to boil; boil without stirring for 5 minutes. Remove from heat, stir in food colouring.
3. Pour the syrup over the popcorn. Using two metal spoons, combine thoroughly. Allow the mixture to cool until just possible to handle. With oiled hands and working quickly, press the popcorn firmly into roughly ball shapes around the top of each icy-pole stick. Serve on the day of making.

A Lesson We've Learned

10

Grandparents can be the matchmaker between a grandchild's interests and talents, and arrange lessons to invest in long term success.

THE UNTHINKABLE: GRANDMA ON A HORSE!

All my life I've been afraid of horses. I tried taking lessons when I was a child but found that horses responded to me by trying to scrape me off on a fence, so I decided not to pursue that as a young person.

Once I discovered the magic of "being and doing" with my grandchildren, Grandpa and I decided to start Natasha with horseback riding. Actually, this idea came forward as we discussed the growing levels of violence, drugs and alcohol abuse in young teenagers. We discussed ways we as grandparents could help to head Natasha down the right path in this regard. Horseback riding came up as one of the activities which young girls seem to stay with for years and well into their teenage years.

Indeed, it seemed true when we visited a couple of horseback riding stables; we discovered 17- and 18-year-old girls working with the horses and teaching young children how to ride. We believed that if we could engage our grandchildren in activities which would be absorbing to them and activities that could grow with them as they grew up, we would be making a major investment in a healthy teenage experience for them.

I decided to take horseback riding lessons with Natasha. This was a truly wonderful experience, as we were both learning together and learning the same skills together. We were able to coach each other at home, tying imaginary reins onto chairs and practising how to run the reins through our fingers and how to pull to indicate messages to the horse. We were able to commiserate about our sore bums at the end of our first trotting lesson. She was able to see the fear in me that she was feeling from time to time, especially when her horse bit the bum of my horse. This was during one of our first lessons. My horse reared up in the air. I felt like an old version of Roy Rogers. Natasha has royally entertained people with the storytelling around Grandma screaming, her hair standing up on end and her arms up in the air waving madly as I tried to keep my balance on the horse.

Janet's Postscript

By doing these kinds of things together, we are constructing our relationship a step at a time and definitely bonding. We have so many stories to talk about related to our horseback riding experience. This summer we signed Natasha up for a one-week horse camp. We delivered her first thing in the morning; she stayed in our home for the week, and we picked her up in the late afternoon. This was another way of demonstrating our commitment to her and to her growth and happiness. Her parents have gone to watch her proudly display her new equine skills. We bought her secondhand riding jodhpurs and boots and riding hat which are kept in her closet in our house. This has been a long-term investment for all of us, and we know it will pay off.

Interestingly enough, she had been very shy up to the point where she started the horseback lessons at age 6. We have seen a big change in her self-confidence, and we attribute it to the growing confidence she has as she learns to manage a very large animal and interact with the other young people who are taking riding lessons there too.

TRY THIS #38

MAKE LIBRARY AND BOOKSTORE TOURS

Haunt your local library for ideas on books to purchase. Ask the librarian for recommended childrens' books for the pertinent age. Research and photocopy information on themes of interest to your grandkids and mail it to them. Make booklets of topics to encourage learning in a specific area. Tour all local bookstores until your find the best one for your pocketbook and interest, and don't forget used bookstores where terrific bargains on classics can be found.

TRY THIS #39

HEALTH AND LEARNING WALKS

A book of interesting walking opportunities was just published in Victoria. I need to walk for health reasons and as I understand it, the author also identifies nature highlights to be seen along the way. Perfect! If such a book does not exist in your area, why not create your own? Great learning opportunities here!

TRY THIS #40

Call your local YM/YWCA for courses offered year 'round. A review of available courses in our city interested us – and note their introductory paragraph:

A COMMUNITY COMMITMENT TO KIDS

Societal issues facing today's youth are more challenging than ever before. For the adults of the future, the Y believes all young people deserve every opportunity to clarify their values, acquire interpersonal and life skills and develop positive attitudes and self-concept. Our programs and services for youth are vehicles through which youth increase their sense of self-worth and respect for community.

Computer Classes

- Introduction to Computers
- Introduction to Windows
- Introduction to Internet and E-mail
- Computers for Older Beginners

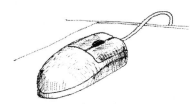

Introduction to Meditation

Using a 'smorgasbord' approach, focus is on exploring more deeply the meditative process and connecting with the "Joy of Now". You will explore grounding, centering and quieting of the mind through the use of movements, sounds, positions and meditation tools. A combination of short, "Use-anywhere" and longer more detailed techniques will be used. Some meditation experience or Intro to Meditation I, a prerequisite.

Children's Meditation: A Workshop for Parents

An opportunity for parents to experience meditation options that they can share with their children. Simple meditations and visualizations will be explored that can help children to sleep peacefully, develop concentration, awaken creativity and quiet fears. Childminding is included if you wish.

Developing Capable People

This highly acclaimed program teaches adults how to assist children and teens to acquire the seven Life Principles to help prepare them for the challenge of the 21st Century. Who should attend? Educators, school counsellors, parents, social workers, child care workers, coaches and any other adults interested in helping kids.

Youth Basketball Skills and Drills

Come and shoot hoops, practise your skills or enjoy a pick-up game with your friends.

"Children reinvent your world for you."

Susan Sarandon

TRY THIS #40
continued

Youth Gymnastics

The gymnastic program provides an opportunity for children to engage in enjoyable and challenging activities at a recreational level. Our focus is on improvement and personal achievement allowing individuals to progress at their own pace.

Youth Floor Hockey

Fun for everyone – beginner to intermediate. Boys and girls. (. . . wonder what they'll think when grandpa gets on the floor!) Learn the basic of shots and techniques. For absolute beginners or those with some experience.

Creative Dance for Children

Ballet and jazz techniques will help to develop creativity with movement to music. This class is geared towards the development of coordination and spatial skills while focusing on the enjoyment of dance.

Karate

A martial arts program for kids and their parents that teaches self-discipline, self-confidence and self-respect through karate. There will be a strong emphasis on self defence.

Youth Squash

Get ready for this fun squash club at the Y. Become involved in developing your squash skills under the guidance of a qualified coach.

Youth Racquetball

Youth Fencing – 12 years and older

Beginner: basic footwork, simple attack and defence, group lesson. Intermediate: practise with an opponent, individual lessons.

Creative Clay

This after-school program lets kids discover their creative abilities while building a solid foundation of pottery skills. Build, glaze and fire your own creations, even try your hand at the potter's wheel.

Herbal Gifts to Make For Christmas

Learn to make your own Christmas gifts using herbs and natural ingredients. Make a variety of gifts ranging from massage oils, lip balm, bath salts and salves.

TRY THIS #41

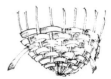

PHONE BOOK FUN

Crafts

When we "let our fingers do the walking through the Yellow Pages",
as our telephone company suggests, we find a wealth of things to learn and do:

- adventure games (e.g., paintball)
- art schools
- baseball clubs
- birdwatching, nature lessons
- canoeing and kayaking
- ceramic instruction
- Christmas decorations
- cooking instruction
- dance schools
- dramatic art schools
- fitness centres
- glass blowing
- hiking
- music instruction (vocal, accordion, guitar, piano, etc.)
- photography lessons
- sailing instruction
- skateboarding lessons
- skydiving lessons
- swimming/diving lessons
- wildflower collecting

- aircraft flying schools
- ballet schools
- beekeeping
- boating instruction (sailing dinghies)
- carving
- charm and modelling schools
- computer training and instruction
- craft lessons
- diving instruction
- equestrian services
- gardening lessons (e.g., herbs)
- golf instruction
- language schools
- pet training
- puppetry
- self-defence lessons
- skating (figure skating, hockey lessons)
- weaving, knitting, other kinds of handiwork
- youth organizations

Wow! this could be a lifetime of learning together!

Birdwatching

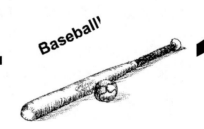

Baseball

Let's Make Memories:
Being and Doing Together

Conclusion: THE VOICES OF THE GRANDCHILDREN

There were so many important things people said in our interviews about "being and doing" together that weren't entire stories, but it would be a shame to leave them out.

MONOPOLY MARATHON WITH GRANDMA

Grandma and I used to play Monopoly, and we would play for the entire weekend. We would start Friday night and we would just move the game over and eat at the table, but we would play that all weekend long, off and on, all the time. And it was a time that we could sit and talk, and that's what was really neat about the game. Because we could sit and talk while we were playing it. The same with Scrabble and Nana. Nana loved Scrabble and crosswords, and we talked while we played, and that was neat.

Wendy Holob

"GRANDMA SWAM BESIDE ME"

In the summer we would go to the beach for the whole day and we would have lunch then we would go swimming and I was always in the water and my Grandma would swim beside me. After that we would walk down the beach picking blackberries and then we would go out for dinner.

Once I was going to cross-country races. After the race my Grandma took me and Lacy out for ice cream and about one year after that my Grandma died. When I told Lacy she said that she liked my Grandma because she was so nice, and she said, "I will miss your Grandma because every time after a race she would buy me and you ice cream." My Grandma was "Very" nice.

Rochelle Weitman
Strawberry Vale Elementary School

"MY MEMORY IS BRAIDING BULLRUSHES"

He (Grandpa) would come and spend summers with us, probably several summers, and we'd rent a cottage in Northern Minnesota and they would come and they'd have their own little cottage but he and I would go out in the boat, like, little power boat, motor boat, and we'd go touring and exploring. He also taught me how to braid. I must have been five. And not only did he teach me how to braid in threes, he taught me how to braid in four, five, six, that kind of braid. Dozens of bullrushes together, you know those bulrushes growing. He could find things to do with whatever was around you.

Oh, and I've got pictures of him when he came up to here they had fruit trees in the back of the yard and he was the kind of grandfather that would load all of the grandchildren in the wheelbarrow and wheelbarrow them around and then we'd pick the fruit. He was always doing stuff with us but he never sat us down to tell us a lesson, it was always his actions. That's very much my family, that actions speak louder than words. You don't try and tell people what to do but you show it by example.

Elsa Swain vanVliet

COMMUNING AND PLAYING WITH GRANDPA

I think one of the things that I remember most with one of my grandfathers would be the long walks we took each day as I was growing up as a two and three year old. Because I didn't have a father figure at the time, he was my father figure. And that was probably one of the first times that I experienced the connection with another human being where you don't have to exchange words, there's just a sense of well-being and connectedness with another human being just by the look in their eyes or their gestures, the spontaneity and the playfulness and that sort of thing. Again, the spontaneity of a lot of the things that he did. There was a playfulness, and that's one of the things probably that he passed on to me is that playfulness, that spontaneous playfulness, to be in the moment and it doesn't matter whether you're five years old or 55 years old, sort of let it all hang out there and have a good time and just enjoy that time and play.

Michael Swain Todd

TIME!

The thing I like about my Grandma is she is nice, she cares about us and she always gives us food to eat.

My Grandma is special to me because she takes me many places, she teaches me how to knit and crochet. My Grandma tells me what kind of stuff is what.

The lessons I learn from my Grandma is how to pronounce Chinese letters and how to pronounce the letters in Chinese sentences.

The things my Grandma does that mean a lot to me is she spends a lot of time with me.

Denise
Lake Hill Elementary School

"MY GRANDMA IS THE WISEST, NICEST PERSON I KNOW"

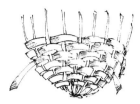

My most memorable moments were always on January first. My Grandma and I would always go to the water slides and have a lot of fun. Then we would always come home and bake bread. While the bread is baking we would be making cakes, cookies, squares and all other treats. It would take the whole day. Some days I would sleep over at her house. The next day my Grandma would come to our house for a turkey dinner. I would always play games with her and have a lot of fun. We would make crafts (baskets, dolls). But one year ago my Grandma left and made me really sad. She came back one day but I don't know if she enjoyed it. She might come back in the fall but I don't think she will. I get upset thinking about it so I hope she will move back soon. My Grandma is the wisest, nicest person I know.

Pamela Sheehan
Strawberry Vale Elementary School

GRANDMA HOGS THE MIKE!

My Grandma in Saint John was real nice, too, and very special to me. The only problem on karaoke night at Uncle Walter's house was she was a mike hog. There was not one song she did not sing alone or with somebody. But besides that, she was great. She'd do anything for you. Example: she would take the kids (including myself) to the river to swim every morning and unless you know something different, she's the greatest grandma in the world.

Jonathon
Lake Hill Elementary School

NEW THINGS TO EXPERIENCE

On Saturday we mostly go to our grandparents' house because there's no time on Monday to Friday because we have school to do. Our grandparents are special because they sometimes take us to places we've never been before. This has happened since I was around six years old. It was fun. They do things I've never done before, like they do horseback riding, then I tried it. It was a little scary riding on the horse. My grandparents are in Victoria.

My other grandparents are from Regina. They are great, too. They teach us some Math, Chinese and art.

David Lui
Lake Hill Elementary School

"Play and physical activity are inextricably linked – not as a task, but as a reward; not as a question, but, as an answer; not as a prescription, but as a lifestyle."

Dr. George Sheehan, *Because They're Young:*
(Active Living For Canadian Children and Youth, Blueprint for Action, October 1989)

"THEY LIVE IN MY BACKYARD"

I think that one of the ways my grandparents are special is because I can always go over to their house because they live in my backyard. In other words, they live behind me. I think I'm lucky I can do that. Lots of people can't do that.

I like it when I come over and my grandma has just baked cookies or an apple pie. She bakes them real good. I also like it when my grandparents bring me to Elk Lake.

The most significant time was when I went to Elk Lake. It was very fun. I want to go there next summer. I also like to go there and just have a cookie or two and a drink, and just talk about stuff. I like having them over for Christmas dinner. We talk for about half an hour and then I get bored and go play on the computer. I also like going outside and talking to my Grandpa while he picks berries and other food. Usually I get a couple of strawberries or raspberries if he or she is picking them. I like their berries.

Alex McLean
Lake Hill Elementary School

Snapshots

"There is a universal truth I have found in my work. Everybody longs to be loved. And the greatest thing we can do is let somebody know that they are loved and capable of loving."

Fred Rogers (of "Mister Rogers' Neighbourhood")

Chapter 2

Treasures and Traditions:
The Connection to Family Values

Cousins!

Treasures and Traditions:
The Connection to Family Values

Introduction: OUR GRANDCHILDREN, OUR TREASURES

Everything we do in our lives - our choices, our decisions, our problem solving - is based on our values and our belief systems. Whether the issues are minor or more important, like the choices about entertainment, friendships or schooling, each choice is a reflection of our attitudes, belief systems and ultimately our values.

Simon, Howe and Kirschenbaum in their book "Values Clarification" point out that "rarely in the school curriculum is attention paid to crucial educational experience of the examination of values, ideals and goals, even though the value systems which students develop are directly related to the kind of people they are and will be, and to the quality of the relationships they will form."

They continue: "All of us, young or old, often become confused about our values. But for the youth of today, the values conflicts are more acute. They are surrounded by a bewildering array of alternatives and the complexity of these times has made the act of choosing infinitely more difficult."

So what can we as grandparents do to contribute to the exploration of the notion of values in these treasures, our grandchildren?

- Moralize? Not likely to be effective…it didn't work on us, did it?

- Take a laissez-faire attitude? "They'll figure it out." We've seen the results of this approach: left alone, children experience a great deal of conflict and confusion. 1999 will be remembered as the year that teen violence and massacres became commonplace.

- Modelling? Ideally, it might work; have limited time with them and they are bombarded with role models - some of them undesirable from our perspectives.

For the purposes of this book we propose the values clarification approach. It is based on "the approach formulated by Louis Raths and is concerned not with the content of people's values but on the process of valuing."

In a recent news article on the Denver massacre called "So, What Are We Going to Do to Help Today's Kids?," Ellen Goodman says: "We need fewer guns and more adults. We need parents to be brave....There is no one thing (to do). There is everything."

We say, "Grandparents, let's do our part by starting the conversation about values *today*."

To accomplish this, we need to use strategies to help our grandchildren become aware of the beliefs and behaviours we prize in ourselves and others by engaging them in experiences which lead them to consider what *they* prize. They need to learn to weigh the pros and cons of alternatives, because only when they begin to make their own choices and evaluate consequences will they develop their *own* values.

An effective way to accomplish this is to tie the conversations to a topic which will capture their interest and engage the two of you together. We found that students were enthusiastic about searching for, exploring and speculating about the treasures and traditions in their families through interviews. Senior members of families were delighted to reflect back on the most memorable moments with their grandparents. This experience became fertile ground for engaging discussion and debate.

This chapter explores traditions and treasures and the "why" of those choices, as well as activities to engage grandparents and children in focused discussion about beliefs, behaviours and values.

A Lesson We've Learned

11

Powerful family values wait patiently to be explored.

A GRANDPARENT PROJECT: TREASURES

We gave a homework assignment to over fifty Grade Six and Seven students to explore the memories that they and their parents hold dear to their hearts. They were to interview their parents, using the following instructions.

Think of four or five things (objects) that were passed on to you from a previous generation.

- Try to put them in order of preference; then decide if you could only keep one, what would it be?
- Why does that one become first choice?
- How does it connect for you?
- Who does it remind you of, and why?
- What was this person like, what were his/her most admirable qualities?
- If you could thank him/her for the treasure, what would you say to them about what it means to you?

Be sure to take careful notes, then create a written report. Review it for accuracy with the person interviewed.

As you will see by the stories highlighted in this chapter, some interesting trends emerged:

- jewellery was a favourite treasure for many
- the last contact, or the last message dominated several stories
- old things, multi-generational keepsakes were frequently identified
- memories and feelings meant the most to some

"We must always have old memories and young hopes."

Arsène Houssaye

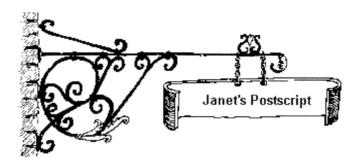

Janet's Postscript

Many of the children were highly impacted by the process of interviewing their parents, and showed an intense interest not only in the treasures or traditions, but also in values that inevitably became part of the discussion. Descriptors such as dignity, gentleness, loving, supportive, "everybody's friend," sense of humour, kind, caring and respect were a few of many.

As well, we held a public contest to gather adult recollections of their grandparents. Most of the stories featured traditions, treasures and related values.

The suggested activities in "TRY THIS" focus on ways to nurture and document memories so that our grandchildren's lives will be rich in memories we can create together. When we're gone, those memories and the values they express will be a lasting legacy, not just for them but for the generations that follow.

As James M. Barrie says: "God gave us memory that we might have roses in December."

Snapshots

TRY THIS #42

BEGIN YOUR AUTOBIOGRAPHIES WITH A TIMELINE

Timelines are a fun and interesting way to start thinking about life stories. We recommend starting with simple things like:

- the life of a pet
- a birthday party
- a walk in the park
- a summer vacation

- a baby's day
- the school year
- a craft project
- an upcoming family event (timelines can also be used for planning)

When you've had enough practice, draw a timeline about a part of your life discussing the events you chose to enter on your timeline. Keep this first one short and simple. Then help your grandchild draw a timeline about a part of their life. You'll probably have to ask probing questions like "What happened next?" or "Who was involved at that point?" or "What month or day did that occur?" to ensure all connections are included in the timeline.

More complex timelines are included in Lesson 18.

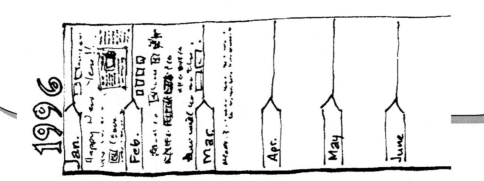

"Like all creatures, one of the family's first jobs is to persuade its members they're special, more wonderful than the neighbouring barbarians. The persuasion consists of stories showing family members demonstrating admirable traits, which it claims are family traits. Attention to the stories' actual truth is never the family's most compelling consideration. Encouraging belief is. The family's survival depends on the shared sensibility of its members."

Elizabeth Stone

TRY THIS #43

START YOUR AUTOBIOGRAPHY

Choose two or three events from your writing partner's timeline that you think might be interesting to document and both of you write your story separately or together if they need help. Tell it orally first.

A few guidelines:

- autobiographies are told like a story
- they may feature only one event from your life, or one year or one day. We encourage you to start small so the task seems manageable
- they often include dates and names of people and places
- they are told from the writer's vantage using "I," "me," "we," or "us"
- they are usually written in the past tense

Decide who you are writing for. The writing may be for only each other or it could be to share with the rest of the family.

TRY THIS #44

TIMELINES THROUGH PICTURES

Timelines can also be told through pictures and mementos. You can use a photo album or an ordinary notebook with sketches instead of pictures. Today's smaller photo albums are a perfect size for saving special events and are more manageable for saving.

Sometimes we don't foresee the possibilities in the future. In my interview with Daphne, she presented me with a notebook journal compiled by her Great Grandmother in the early 1900's. Mementos such as ticket stubs and candy wrappers were pasted in and delightful discussions about the first car experience and the day her cart and pony arrived on the train were captivating. I wonder if it ever occurred to her that it would become a treasure for Daphne?

TRY THIS #45

SIMPLE JOURNALS

Introduce your grandchild to the concept of journals by reading journal entries by other writers so that you can see how people write about the events in their lives. Point out that archaeologists, explorers and scientists often kept personal records of their work and the discoveries they were making.

Some journals are written with sharing in mind. A journal can even be a joint activity to compile both of your thoughts and feelings about trips, excursions or projects you have undertaken.

Some journals are very personal and are meant for your eyes only, unless you decide to share it. It will be very important to clarify together what kind of diary you are writing and what its purpose is. Who will you share it with? Will you read each other's?

Snapshots

Four Generations
1991

A Lesson We've Learned

12

Treasures and traditions are simply eloquent memories of the feelings we felt in the best times.

"...BY GIVING THE LOVE YOU'VE GIVEN TO ME"

My dad taught me a lot about my great grandfather. My great grandfather left my dad many things when he died. He left him a gold railways watch on a gold chain. My dad also got a small silver cigar box he now uses to put card decks in and a wooden cigar box that he now uses to hold pictures, papers, and other things. My great grandfather left my dad a portable wooden desk too. My dad also received a "sporran", a furry pouch worn on the front of a kilt.

If my dad could only keep one of these things it would be the gold watch because it reminds him of how his grandfather and his father always had to be on time because they worked on the railway and the trains couldn't be late. It's also the most valuable of the possessions that he was left by his grandfather.

My dad says his grandfather was a very good husband, father, and provider for his family. He had six children and took care of his niece and nephew when their parents were killed in a fire. He lived with his mother-in-law and father-in-law and after his wife died he remarried and had another child. When his son-in-law was killed from gas in World War I he also had to help provide for his daughter's two young sons.

If my father could thank my great grandfather for the things he has given him, he would say: "Thank you very much but I would give it all away for one more day with you."

by Christa McCowan
Lakehill Elementary School, Victoria, B.C.

"The only genuine love worthy of the name is unconditional..."

John Powell

"...BY GIVING THE LOVE YOU'VE GIVEN TO ME"

The four things my mom chose that were passed on to her were:

- love
- necklace
- dish
- rings

My mom said she would choose to keep love because so much love has been passed on. It connects for my mom because she passes on the love to everyone. The love reminds my mom of all the things she's learned. My mom would thank her parents by saying: "I love you and I will give the love you gave to me."

Jyoti Banga
Strawberry Vale Elementary School

Snapshots

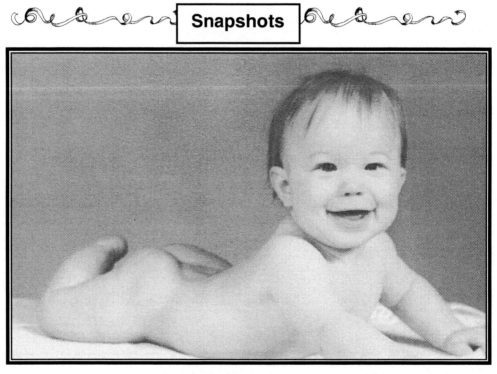

Anonymous,
1967

"I want you to get excited about who you are, what you are, what you have, and what can still be for you. I want to inspire you to see that you can go far beyond where you are right now."

Virginia Satir

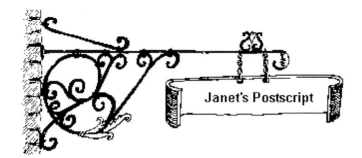

Janet's Postscript

How proud I would be if my grandchildren were to say this about me when I'm gone.

The values in these two stories are powerful ones:

- work ethic on the trains
- responsibility within the family
- commitment to family members
- strength and courage in adversity
- a belief in the power of love

What an investment these grandparents have made, and how enriched are the lives of those who remember! Now the next generation of children can inherit that legacy.

I had just reached this point in my writing when the Oprah show featured 17-year-old Rachel's family who were grieving over her death in the Columbine tragedy. Each member of the family described how important their last talk and touch with Rachel was:

- the last "I love you"
- the last touch
- the last interaction
- the last conversation with her dad about her future kids and what they'd be like.

Rachel's father said about that talk: "Now I know it was a Divine appointment."

We need to cherish every minute we have with them.

Snapshots

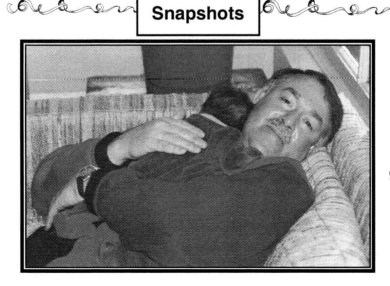

Grandpa with newborn granddaughter 1991

TRY THIS #46

PHOTO ESSAYS AND CAPTIONS: A GREAT WAY TO TELL THE STORY

Photo essays are a series of photographs and, sometimes, information. Captions usually appear under the photographs to explain the photograph. The photographs and words are supposed to work together to create a feeling about the story. The photographs and words are organized to tell a story with a beginning, middle and end, or they can be a collection of images on a theme and can be viewed in any order.

TRY THIS #47

RECYCLING OLD PHOTOS WITH HISTORY AS A FOCUS

Go through old boxes of photos, buy scrapbooks or photo albums and create photo essays about family members or special events in your family. Each of you could choose an idea that is important to you and work on your scrapbooks side by side or you could choose joint topics. For example:

- collections of favourite clothing through the decades
- a collection of family pets, including your grandchild's existing pet(s)
- family look-alikes
- family hairstyles through the years
- family cars
- family members who have passed on
- family get-togethers
- old hats and shoes

These can even be presented as a series of collages. Recently, I saw a beautiful collage of all the babies in the family – a great conversation piece!

"We can love completely without complete understanding."

A River Runs Through It (screenplay)

TRY THIS #48

SHARING PHOTO STORIES

Who will you share your photo stories with besides each other? If other members of the family who are involved are far away, you could send it to them. You could do a number of scrapbooks or photo albums, each based on different topics, and circulate them through the family inviting others to add their photos on the same them – a progression photo story. You can use cutouts from old magazines to supplement your own collection.

TRY THIS #49

CHECK YOUR TIMELINES TO GUARANTEE ORDER

Before committing your photographs and captions to the album, be sure to lay it out on the table so you can ensure that your layout makes sense. If your layout tells a story, be sure the photographs are clustered with a beginning, a middle and an end. If you have empty spots in your collection because photographs are missing, one of you can draw in what your ideal photograph would have looked like had you had one, or cut out magazine pieces to create the collage that represents your idea.

A Lesson We've Learned 13

We can discover powerful family values as we reflect on "beginnings" and "endings".

"...GIVEN TO HER AT BIRTH..."

This past weekend I learned a lot about my grandma's heritage and the relationship she had with her mother. Her mother was very kind, she always put everyone else first, worked very hard and never expected anything in return.

My grandma's relationship with her mother was very solid and she wishes that she could tell her mother how much she appreciated the way she raised her. I learned that my Oma emigrated here from Austria, to Wilkie, Saskatchewan where my grandma was born and raised. When my Oma came to Canada she brought with her a few treasured belongings. Some of the things that she brought with her were:

- her parents' wedding picture
- her mother's gold wedding band
- several old china pieces

Above all, my grandma's most cherished item was her mother's opal earrings which were given to her at her birth by her mother. My grandma has always had a love for jewellery and having these earrings make my grandma feel that her mom will always be a part of her.

My grandma wishes that she could thank her with all her heart, and would like to tell her that they will be hers until she passes them on to one of her daughters and that she will always be in our hearts.

by Kelsey Kuebler
Lakehill Elementary School, Victoria, B.C.

"...IT WAS THE LAST THING HIS MOTHER GAVE HIM..."

My dad has four treasures: he has a clock from his mother, World War II medals from his grandfather, old pictures from his Ukrainian grandfather homesteading in Peace River, and an organ also from his grandfather. Out of all the treasures he likes the clock the most because it was the last thing his mother gave him. It reminds my dad of how kind and caring she was to him and her grandchildren. If my dad could thank her he would say: "Thank you, it reminds me of you every time I look at it." The clock sits in our living room and always gets compliments.

by Kyle Petrunik
Lakehill Elementary School, Victoria, B.C.

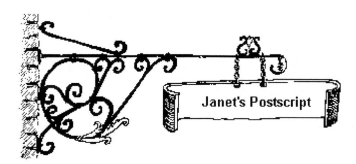

Janet's Postscript

As I read these children's stories I found myself wishing I had given something special (besides my heart) to my grandchildren at birth....It seems to me that the messages in these stories feature treasures that can be talked about. We need to position treasures in our lives so that the conversations come naturally. The clock attracts compliments and memories on a daily basis, the earrings are passed through three generations. The memories are satisfying for us, but very powerful lessons when the stories are told to young children.

"Treasure the love you receive above all.
It will survive long after your gold and
good health have vanished."

Og Mandino

TRY THIS #50

TOURING THE TREASURES: LOOKING FOR QUALITIES

Take a tour through your house with your grandchild and pen and paper in hand. Make a list of everything you see that brings back memories. Be sure to include things your grandchild is curious about.

Stick it on the fridge or in a special place. Whenever you visit together, they can choose the items they want to hear about. As you tell the stories, share the qualities you admired in the family members you refer to. This same activity can be used long distance, through e-mail or in letters.

TRY THIS #51

EVERY FAMILY HAS HEROES

A hero is sometimes someone who lives in the same house as we do. Today we try to encourage children to look around them for heroes they rub shoulders with every day so that they can begin to identify role models in their lives. It is important to remember a hero is not perfect. A hero usually:

- is a female or male with special traits such as intelligence, courage or kindness
- has a problem to solve or a goal to achieve
- makes wise choices and decisions
- overcomes obstacles
- is loved by people

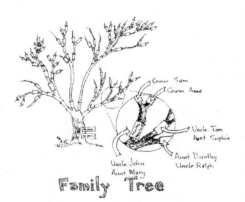

Hero stories often reveal a lesson. Here are some things to think about before you decide on your hero. Together you can write a story about a hero in your family. It could be someone in the family you admire or someone who has done something great. Be sure you identify their special characteristics, the problem they have to solve, their choices and decisions that you admire, the obstacles they faced, and how people love them.

TRY THIS #52

BABY TREASURES

Create a collection of 8½ x 11 photos of all members of the family when they were babies or getting married or teenagers…your choice. (I have a dandy of my 35-year-old son, bare naked on a lace blanket with his little bum in the air.) Gather the grandkids round for stories about when each of them was young. Use sticky office labels to write key words from the stories you tell. Decide together what personal qualities you will write on the labels, e.g., brave, strong, honest. This activity can be repeated over and over with each new story. Invite the kids to decide who they admire and why...a great way to bring the discussion of values out in the open naturally.

TRY THIS #53

CONNECTING TO YOUR FAR-FLUNG FAMILY

Together, make a list of all the family members you can think of. Consider different parts of the country, different parts of the world. Sketch your family trees and include great aunts and uncles, second cousins and maybe even adopted family members. Send a special message, even to the family member your grandchild has not yet met. There is nothing more exciting than young children receiving their own unexpected mail. This may be a way to start making connections between far-flung members of the family, and may also give your grandchildren a sense of the extended part of their connections.

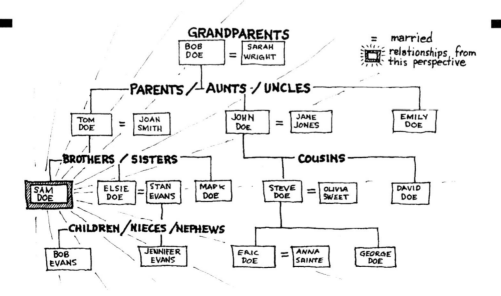

A Lesson We've Learned

14

Handwritten messages from the past can speak volumes to future generations.

"...SENTIMENTAL CARDS FROM GRANDPA..."

When Grandma moved in with mum and dad almost three years ago, she downsized significantly and either sold many items or gave many things away. Among the treasures she kept, we've discovered sentimental cards from Grandpa, icing roses from their 50th wedding anniversary cake and photographs of the two of them - he in black tie and she in a long gown she'd made herself, attending formal occasions. These items speak volumes about Grandma. She had always missed Grandpa and made no bones about it. Grandma loved a social occasion and birthdays. She celebrated her 88th birthday on Christmas Day and three days later attended Elizabeth's wedding. It was important to her that we were all settled down and married. These were events that added to her satisfaction.

An excerpt from Grandma's (Millicent Forrester) eulogy
by Alison Giles

"...THE LAST PIECE OF HANDWRITING..."

My grandmother's favourite items that were passed on to her were:
- a china tea set
- a recipe
- a gold locket
- a penknife
- an old wrinkled story book

The order she put them in was: the recipe, penknife, locket, dishes, then the book. Her first choice was the recipe because it was the last piece of handwriting of her dad's that was in her possession and it reminded my grandmother of what type of work he did. His most admirable qualities were that he was gentle, loving, fun and supportive. He was everybody's friend, he always saw the good in somebody, and he gave great cuddles. If he was still around to thank, my grandmother might say that this piece of paper was one of the most valuable pieces of paper she ever owned.

by Dylan Martin
Strawberry Vale Elementary, Victoria, B.C.

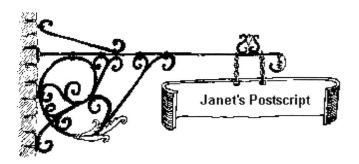

Janet's Postscript

These two stories had quite an impact on me. My dad has been gone ten years. Whenever I flip through something and see his signature my heart swells with affection but I have nothing from him in handwriting, in fact no messages at all. I would love it if I had notes meant specially for me so I'm going to start this week. I'm making up a postcard format that can be glued onto the backs of photos and mailed. Every week I'm going to mail the grandkids photos of them or us or a special time we had together. They don't get much mail....I'd love to see the excitement on their faces at the mailbox.

P.P.S. Postcards had their 'hey day' in the forties when post-war travelling was accessible to more than just the rich, and died off in the seventies when phone connections became affordable.

P.P.P.S. A postcard is a great way to send a quick message. Six months after I wrote this piece, I was sorting through old photos with one of the grandkids and found a postcard from my dad to my son. Tears welled up in my eyes, and my heart swelled. Now we have a new treasure!

TRY THIS #54

TRIED AND TRUE TRADITIONAL POSTCARDS WITH A NEW TWIST

Turning regular pictures into postcards is an easy thing to do. Be sure to document each of your visits with your camera, you can usually have them developed the same day. Take some of the special pictures from your day: it could be making supper, it could be horseback riding, skating, playing hide-and-go-seek...whatever makes up your fun. Divide the back of the snapshot in half to separate the message from the address; use the left side of the postcard for the message and the right side for the address and stamp. You can send joint postcards; you can send ten postcards, one to each member of the family, tailoring the picture to them. Be as creative as you like.

"I love thee for a heart that's kind –
not for the knowledge in thy mind."

W.H. Davies

TRY THIS #55

CREATIVE POSTCARDS FROM THE KIDS

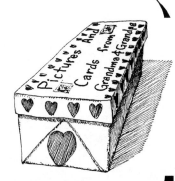

- Purchase a recipe card box with colourful recipe cards.
- Order a roll of personalized address stickers with grandma/grandpa's address.
- Position the stickers on the recipe cards, leaving ½ of the card for a message from the grandkids.
- Package it all up with 25 postage stamps and sent instructions to the grandkids
- ask them to draw you a postcard once a week and mail them to you.
- Possible weekly topics could include their proudest moment, something they did that was most exciting, something about someone else in their family or their pet, how school was, when they were sad, etc.
- Ask them to write their story on the message side or have an adult transcribe it for them.
- Keep a recipe box on your end to collect their cards. Later make the collection into a scrapbook.

TRY THIS #56

PICTURE TREASURE CHESTS

Create a special storage box so that the grandkids can save the postcards over time. Use one of the painting strategies in Chapter One to decorate any old box, or purchase a special carved box or visit your local "dollar store" for a wide variety of interesting and colourful boxes.

*"The family you come from isn't as important
as the family you're going to have."*

Ring Lardner

(Author's note:
how true, and what a good reason to work on it!)

TRY THIS #57

THANK-YOU NOTES

Thank-you notes in our e-mail society are fast becoming extinct, but writing a thank-you note is one of the most thoughtful things we can do for each other. We can send one to thank special friends or relatives in our family for dinners that they held for us, for special treasures they have given us and for continuing the traditions that are important.

As grandparents, we can play an important role by writing thank-you letters together with our grandchildren for family members.

Another tradition reinstated!

Together, you can practise sending thank-you notes to family friends or family members who have done something nice. Be sure to consider many of the topics that can naturally come up during this process:

- how to decorate your thank-you letter
- how the mail system works in your part of town
- how to make change for the purchase of the stamp
- an understanding of the postal code system

"There are more treasure in books than in all the pirates' loot on Treasure Island…and best of all, you can enjoy these riches every day of your life."

Walt Disney

A Lesson We've Learned 15

What we learned from our parents needs to be put into words.

"...SOME THINGS MY DAD LEARNED FROM HIS PARENTS..."

My parents are both very impressed with their parents. Some of the most memorable heirlooms that were passed down to my dad from generation to generation were for my dad, the pocket watch that he was given with a fob that his dad made out of one of his own Royal Canadian Air Force medals. My dad also has one of his grandfather's old cameras.

But the thing that he treasures the most are all of the memories that he got from being around his parents. My dad's parents also told him if he wanted to be someone and he is willing to work towards it, then to go for it and he would get their full support.

Some of the great advice my dad's parents gave were:
- to be his own person
- to help others and don't expect anything in return
- you don't have to be rich to be happy

If my dad were to look at his pocket watch his dad gave him he would see all of the care that he put into his work and family. Another thing my dad learned from his father is to laugh everyday, and laugh a lot. Some things my dad learned from his parents was to be practical and to be helpful, and how to cook and help out. Another great thing my dad learned from his parents and grandparents is to just be yourself.

In my dad's lifetime with his parents he would describe his parents as quiet, knowledgeable, humorous, good teachers; they let you make mistakes then teach you about it, how to love nature, and most of all to respect other things and people. So all around my dad learned a lot from his father and has still many memories about him even today. Many of these memories can make him laugh and even cry as he remembers and shares his memories with others.

by a Grade 7 student, Victoria, B.C.

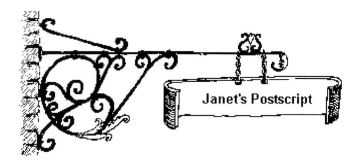

Janet's Postscript

As I read this story I paused, pen in hand....

What did I learn from:

- my mother?
- my father?
- my children?
- what did they learn from me?

Have I ever articulated the answers to any of those questions? The answer is no, yet I see in this story such powerful and important lessons for living. Maybe it's time I started...and I'd like to tell my mom while she's still here...and we'll both cry over lunch....

TRY THIS #58

TEACHING THE INTERVIEW PROCESS

As indicated earlier in the chapter, we had classes of Grade 6/7 students interview their parents about their grandparents. We discovered that the experience was as enlightening and exciting for the students as the information they collected.

We suggest that grandma or grandpa teach the interview process to their grandchild by helping them interview other members of the family for the family record.

Planning ahead makes the interviews go more smoothly. Here are some steps that will help.

Decide who you want to interview and why.

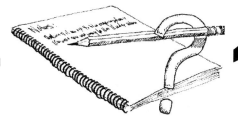

TRY THIS #59

PREPARE FOR THE INTERVIEW

- research the topic or issue you are investigating and develop a list of questions
- make an appointment, arrange a time and place for the interview
- explain to the person you are interviewing what you want to talk about (you might decide to use a tape recorder)
- ask a family member to check your planned questions and practise reading them

TRY THIS #60

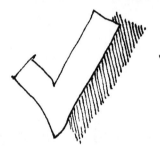

DURING THE INTERVIEW

- remind your subject of the purpose of the interview
- make sure your guest is comfortable
- look and act interested and make eye contact
- take careful notes
- ask follow-up questions. If you think of a question that goes further than the one on your list, jot it down and then ask it at the end of the interview or when your guest has finished talking.
- if you don't understand something, ask for an explanation

"History is the ship carrying living memories to the future."

Stephen Spender

TRY THIS #61

AFTER THE INTERVIEW:

- thank your guest
- check any spelling you might need to, or ask someone to edit it for you
- organize your notes as soon as you can. You might have questions later and may have to call; ask if that is O.K.
- write out what you learned, and then write out your interview
- give a Draft to the person(s) you interviewed to ensure they are comfortable with the results
- encourage your grandchildren to collect interviews, add photos and begin the development of a family history, featuring traditions and treasures

Snapshots

The Christening,
1970

A Lesson We've Learned

16

The best relationship with our grandchildren will be built on history, strength, love, kindness, time, teaching, storytelling and safety.

"...THAT WAS THE SAFEST PLACE IN THE WORLD"

The things that were passed on to my mom were:

- a ring
- rocking chair
- cat
- pictures

She says she would keep the ring because the cat is very old and the rocking chair flips when you sit in it, and the pictures are old and falling apart. Besides, there are too many pictures and she couldn't pick just one. The ring was a personal choice because I always told my grandmother that I wanted the ring. She said that she would give it to me when she died and I said: "I never want you to die."

She says she gets to wear it all the time and see it and feel it. It reminds her of my grandmother. Her brother made it for her when he lived up in Whitehorse. It's made of gold nuggets and it's very strong.

Her grandmother was a very strong woman but she was soft and she loved people and animals. She always had a lot of cats around and you knew you were loved when you were around her. It has been eleven years since her grandmother has died. But if she could talk to her and tell her how much she loves the ring. I would, and I wish one day when I die one of my girls will love it as much as I did.

"Memory is the treasury and guardian of all things."
Cicero

It's not because it has gold in it that I love it so much, it's because it's a nice strong ring and it reminds me of a nice strong woman.

I love my grandmother as much as I do because she never got angry with me no matter what I did. She taught me how to sew on a treadle machine, she taught me about botany and planting bulbs. She taught me what it means to have a relationship with animals and how to really enjoy the beach.

I remember when we went up to Whitehorse and I flew in an airplane for the first time. I remember when we went to the beach and we would stay there for the whole day and swim and look at rocks.

My grandma and grandpa had a huge bed and when my grandma and grandpa went to bed I would crawl in between them and that was the safest place in the world.

by Rochelle Weitman
Lakehill Elementary School, Victoria, B.C.

Snapshots

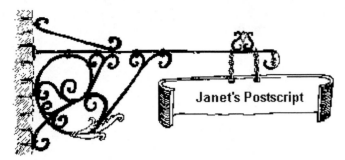

Janet's Postscript

As I reviewed this story and considered my own experiences with our grandchildren, I gave myself a passing mark in a number of these areas and a "needs improvement" in the areas of 'history' and 'storytelling.' I need to develop some systematic plans in these categories which in fact could be combined.

As I read Rochelle's eloquent words, I also felt a twinge at my raised and impatient voice during Natasha's last visit. I rarely do that, and I saw the surprise and hurt on her face. A quiet firmness would have sufficed.

Sorry, sweetheart.

TRY THIS #62

WRITING POEMS TOGETHER

Gather together as much poetry by other people as you can to help you think of ideas for how to write various kinds of poems. Consider these steps as you write:

1. Research various styles of poetry before trying this with children.
2. Collect some poetry by and for kids.
3. Decide what kind of poem you want to write.
4. Introduce the styles best suited to the child's age and ask them to pick the style they prefer. (Kids love Haiku.)
5. Select a topic or subject for your poem.
6. Build poems together before trying one on your own.

Think about your topic; what ideas and pictures come to mind, what details can you pick out. If you are having trouble thinking of words to describe your topic, create a web to help you develop ideas.

"On with the dance! let joy be unconfined;..."

Lord Byron

TRY THIS #63

WEBBING

Webbing involves the creation of a type of knowledge map. It is generally used to record many ideas and to show initial connections among concepts. When beginning the study of a theme, story or poem, webbing is ideal for identifying parameters and central components.

- Have your grandchild record the core topic or idea in the middle of a sheet of paper, drawing a circle around the word. Instruct them to write three to six main concepts that relate to the circled word. Circle these as well and connect them to the centre circle with a line (often called a link).

- Encourage your grandchild to write down ideas that relate to these main concepts with links to each circled concept. Do not draw any shapes around these words. (This allows for easier reading of the main concepts.)

- Decide which words and ideas from your web you can use in your poem.

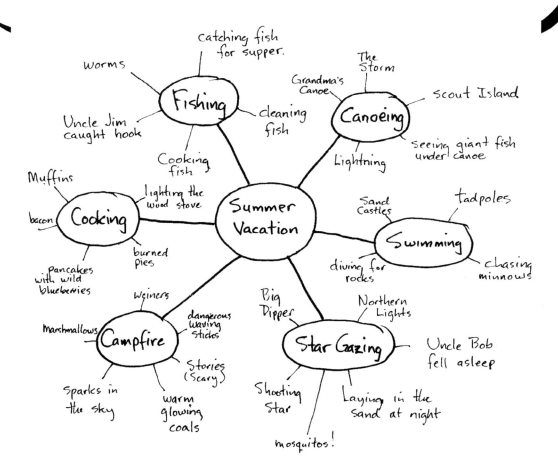

TRY THIS #64

A SCRAPBOOK OF VALUES

Most families like to collect things and then don't know what to do with them. Perhaps you have the beginnings of a scrapbook. Scrapbooks are places to report information or store memories.

It can be fun to keep mementos of trips you've taken, or to collect newspaper and magazine articles about your favourite people or hobbies. Perhaps there is a scrapbook about you at home with your cutest baby picture, a lock of baby hair, or your hand print at one day old. Scrapbooks can also contain factual information about something that interests you. One page from a scrapbook could include:

- the title
- a photograph
- captions
- a poem
- coins

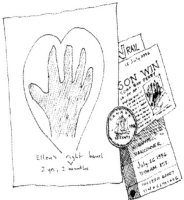

Some scrapbooks store memories while other scrapbooks report and store information.

Scrapbooks are meant to be shared, so they should be interesting. Different kinds of writing can be used, such as titles, captions, stories, reports, charts, maps and explanations. A variety of items can be included photographs, cards, ticket stubs, etcetera.

Scrapbooks can be organized by time and titles, and headings are usually used to help organize the information.

- Start a scrapbook about a hobby or interest you share together.
- Start a personal scrapbook about one of you. It could be a keepsake and highlight special times in your life. Give it as a gift to the person you created it with.
- Make a scrapbook for a parent or grandparent. What a thrill it would be for them to look back at events of their lives organized by the two of you.
- Tell a story you've heard about the traditions in your family and think about the item that would represent the family's life of the times they shared that tradition and values. Then build a scrapbook around it.

TRY THIS #65

COLLECTING FAMILY RECIPES

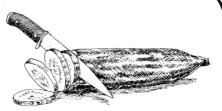

Recipes are a wonderful way to share treasures and traditions with family and friends.

- Interview each family member, send them a postcard or a letter or use any other of the information gathering strategies we have mentioned in this chapter. Collect a recipe from each member of your extended family; then a joint project between the two of you could be creating a family recipe book with all the family recipes.
- You might also want to consider including the traditions in the family that use specific recipes and include those recipes in the family cookbook.
- You might also include holiday menus for favourite family holidays.
- You could collect recipes for perfect days, such as picnics.

Note: Your family recipe collection could become the root of creating your family tree and further family traditions.

...and why is cooking with our grandchildren so important?

"Nothing we learn is more important than the skills required to work cooperatively with other people. Most human interaction is cooperative. Without some skill in cooperating effectively, it is difficult (if not impossible) to maintain a marriage, hold a job, or be part of a community, society and world."

D.W. Johnson, R.T. Johnson and E.J. Holubec, Cooperating in the Classroom

A Lesson We've Learned

17

We need to create opportunities to discuss our values, family values, and the emerging values of our grandchildren.

"...BECAUSE OF THE LITTLE NOTES IN THERE FROM HER DAD"

My mom's five most special objects that were passed on to her from previous family are:

- a rose bowl that is about 90 years old
- a whole bunch of silver bracelets that are about 75 years old
- a silver compass that is 100 years old
- five leather-bound books that are about 100 years old too
- a handmade jewellery box that is about 100 years old

These are all very special treasures to my mom. My mom's first choice of those five things are the five leather-bound books. After that comes the rose bowl, the jewellery, bracelets, the jewelry box, and then the compass.

The five leather-bound books come first because they are from her family. Also because of the little notes in them from her dad. She says they are very beautiful old books. The books remind her of her grandmother because she was a school teacher and she loved books and reading. My mom likes reading and that's how she can connect. My mom was named after her grandmother. She was a very interesting grandmother since she was from Ireland, also she talked to my mom and her sister about Ireland a lot. My mom says she had a great interest in gardening and loved gardens. She developed that interest in my mom.

My mom says she would thank her grandmother for passing the books along to her and keeping them in great shape. She would also thank her for the respect and love of books that she passed on.

by Lia Robbins
Lakehill Elementary School, Victoria, B.C.

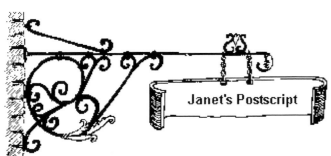

The Three Bears had their porridge…

Cinderella had her slipper…

Seven fairies were always godmothers to a princess…

The magic mirror always answered to "Mirror, mirror on the wall, who is the fairest one of all?"…

The Mad Hatter had his teapot, the March Hare had his watch… and Aladdin had his lamp.

Our childhood stories are rich with descriptions of treasures and tradition. Fairy tales and fables raised important lessons. Biblical stories reinforced values; our parents used some or all as examples of right and wrong.

Before Lia interviewed her parents, she reported she was unaware of the significance of some of these items, yet so many connections arose in this short story about the five leather-bound books:

- notes from grandfather
- love of books
- her aunt
- respect

- grandmother, a school teacher
- family roots in Ireland
- gardens

The grandkids are coming for the weekend and this story has prompted me to consider how little they know about their roots. I've asked my mom for the family movies dating as far back as the 1940s (...hope we can find a projector to show them...).

What will be really important is the conversation we have about the memories, the qualities and characteristics of family members we have admired, and of course the values that emerge. For long-distance grandparents, turn this into an e-mail, or regular mail, back and forth.

TRY THIS #66

SEARCHING FOR CHARACTER

Using a stack of your daily newspapers, start a contest in motion. Ask your grandkid(s) to launch a timed search for examples of characteristics they would admire in the following categories:

- bravery either physical or emotional
- examples of people who have made mistakes and handled it well
- examples of people who have used money wisely
- risk takers
- sports heroes who have demonstrated self discipline
- respectful behaviour
- politicians who are honourable
- new products which will make a positive contribution
- responsible behaviour

Time the activity with an alarm clock. See who can collect the most examples. You play too. At the finish of the race, introduce your examples to each other and explain why you chose them.

Present your top five choices to another member of the family and ask him to put them in order of characters he would most admire.

This activity can be modified for younger children by using the same approach, simpler language and story books instead of newspapers.

It also can be adapted for use with television shows.

…a great way to keep those conversations about values flowing and prominent.

TRY THIS #67

KEEPING PEERS IN PERSPECTIVE

It's never too soon to start kids talking about desirable and undesirable characteristics of their friends. Unless these conversations are started early we can lose them to peer pressure by the time they're in their teens.

Try the following strategies to explore kids and their peer relationships. Conduct your search in newspapers and TV to keep the discussion objective. When the door is safely open, shift the conversation to focus on real family members and/or their friends in school or the neighbourhood.

Talk about and find:
* samples of cliques that exclude people
* examples of exclusions that violate a person's rights
* people who are popular their positive and negative qualities
* samples of negative peer pressure and positive peer pressure
* examples of drug or alcohol incidents where people may have been pressured
* ads that use peer pressure
* examples of violence that could have been prevented by positive peer pressure

Work on this one together…it's a difficult topic. This activity is best used by pre-teens but could be modified for young children by using their storybooks and the characters in them with a focus on which characters demonstrate positive qualities and which characters demonstrate negative qualities.

A few ideas to share with your grandkids about handling peer pressure:

* *Don't put yourself in situations where you have to make an on-the-spot decision. If you know the kids are heading into a house to do things you don't want to do, don't go with them.*
* *Express your feelings honestly. People usually respect someone who speaks up to say, "I don't feel good about this."*
* *Say a flat "no". Don't feel you have to give reasons or defend your answer.*

TRY THIS #68

IT ALL BOILS DOWN TO RESPECT!

No matter what the behaviour, the age or the circumstances, universally we all want to be treated with respect and we'll have a better chance of that happening, if we also treat others with respect. Young and old need to talk about what that means.

Search newspapers, magazines and television shows for signs of respect between people. Look for signs of respect in the following areas:

- politics
- sports
- theatre
- movies
- money
- attitude
- personality
- employers
- history
- inventions
- advertisements
- women

Then look for signs of *disrespect*. Once you have finished with this objective approach, ask the same questions about family members using sentence stems such as:

- Today I showed respect for _____ by…
- I was disrespectful to my _____ once. I …
- I respect my _____ because…
- When I am disrespectful I _____…
- We show respect in our family when we…_____
- We show disrespect in our family when we…
- I'm going to set a goal to be more respectful by…
- On a respect scale of 1 to 10, I would rank myself as ___ because…
- The person I respect most in my family is _____ because…

"Becoming responsible adults is no longer a matter of whether children hang up their pajamas or put dirty towels in the hamper, but whether they care about themselves and others – and whether they see everyday chores as related to how we treat this planet."

Eda Leshan

TRY THIS #69

GETTING TO THE ROOT OF THEIR PROBLEMS: THE FISHBONE

Now for my favourite way to find out what the real problem is. If your grandkids seem to have a problem, it won't get resolved until they understand and consider all of the possible causes.

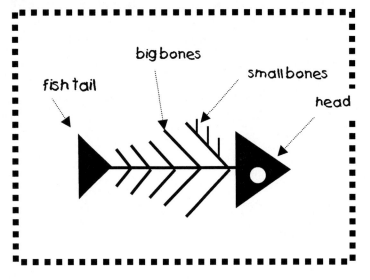

Too often, even we as adults jump to solutions to the perceived problem, only to find that ninety percent of the problem still exists! What we need to be able to consider is all aspects of the problem so we can isolate the ***root*** causes of the problem. Only then can we confidently determine the solution that will give us the "biggest bang for our buck"…and it's fun, too!

When you see the grandkids a bit down in the mouth, use this strategy to help them sort it out. It will work well in your life as well.

Step 1: PROBLEM STATEMENT
First you need the problem statement. It is very important that:
- your grandchild agrees it's an accurate description of the problem
- it implies no solutions
- it is brief

For example:
"My dad seems to be always mad at me," not "my dad is mad because I'm messy," which would imply a solution…be tidy! Dad might be mad about a number of things.

TRY THIS #69
continued

THE FISHBONE CONTINUED!

STEP 2: DRAW FISHBONE
Put the problem statement at the top of the page. Draw a large fishbone on the paper – as big as you can (you can be creative, I've seen hilarious ones.)

STEP 3: DO BIG BONE CAUSES
Draw 6 or 8 big bones, then ask, "What might be the cause of the problem?" Write each of the responses on the big bones.

Problem Statement: Dad seems to be always mad at me.

What might be the causes?

Big Bones:
- my messes
- he doesn't love me
- bad report card
- mom's sick
- dad's tired
- I'm noisy
- lose his tools
- dog died

There's no limit on the number of big bones but 6 or 8 is usually enough. Write them along the "big bones" lines.

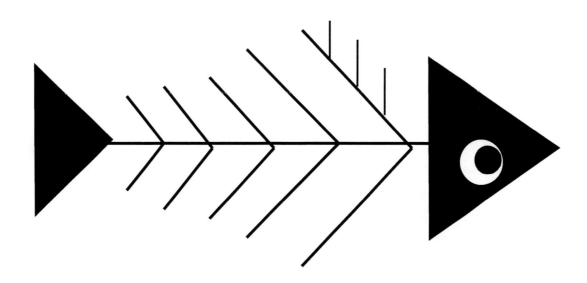

TRY THIS #69
continued

THE FISHBONE CONTINUED!

STEP 4: DRAW SMALL BONE CAUSES

Now ask the questions, "Why might we say this is a cause?"

No you are starting to flesh out the big bones (see diagram in Step 2). The big bones start to look like this:

(WHY) **MY MESSES**
- ① clothes on floor
- ① dirty dishes in sink
- ① paint spilled
- ① hamster cage stinks
- ① school notebooks messy

DAD'S TIRED
- ② working two shifts
  mom snores
- ③ four kids to look after
  watches late movie
- ③ ② worried about mommy

HE DOESN'T LOVE ME
he yells

LOSE HIS TOOLS
- ① forget to put them back
  use them everyday
- ① get rusty
- ① he can't find them

MOM'S SICK
- ③ ② he has to look after us
- ② he does her work
- ② medicine costs a lot
  etc.
  etc.

"No problem can stand the assault of sustained thinking."

Voltaire

TRY THIS #69
continued

THE FISHBONE CONTINUED!

STEP 5: ANALYZE THE FISHBONE

Now ask the questions, "Why might we say this is a cause?"

No you are starting to flesh out the big bones (see diagram in Step 2). The big bones start to look like this:

At this point, you start to look for themes on the whole bone. For example:
① messes/bad habits
② too much pressure on dad
③ family worries

Put a number beside all those that fall into the themes.

In this case, "messes and bad habits" is a prominent cause so you would want to take action right away. "Mom snores" is probably something the child can't do anything about. "Family worries/money" would be difficult for a child to impact.

TRY THIS #70

MAKING THE ACTION PLAN

STEP 6: ACTION PLAN

Here's where the grandparents come in. Help your grandchild(ren) analyze, come to agreement on what the "root" cause(s) is, and then set goals for themselves.

You can also develop a plan for encouraging and reinforcing the planned changes.

Won't the parents be grateful to you when the messes are a thing of the past!

P.S.: I'd suggest in this case that you also slip in a proposal that the kids plan some special treats for dad to relieve him of some pressure – maybe you could take the four kids once a week for a sleepover!!!??! Remember Lesson 8? We need to take care of their parents, too.

A Lesson We've Learned 18

Whether we've met them or not, our ancestors can teach us important values through stories of their past.

"...SUCH TREASURES AS HIS NAME..."

In this project, I interviewed my dad because his grandparents were around longer in his life. My dad received such treasures as:

- his name
- picture (photos)
- his dad's baseball uniform
- his dad's and grandfather's watches
- his great grandfather's lead toy soldier
- a clock that was given to his grandmother by Buffalo Bill Cody
- a car blanket from one of the first cars ever to be driven in Victoria

The order that the items are listed, is the order that my dad values most. It is obvious how his name is connected to him from previous generation. It reminds him of his ancestors, but especially of his dad. His dad (my grandfather) was a great, loving fun-loving guy. He was the type of person who would put you first and never put himself first. He wouldn't expect anything from anyone. He was a great guy and his death was a great loss to the family. I wish I had met him.

by Chris Hepburn

Janet's Postscript

Each of the items Chris mentions has itself a story yet untold:

- How do the pictures demonstrate values?
- How did cars impact the structure or order of families in the early 1900s?

Chris has emerged from the discussion with his dad clear on the importance of love, heritage through names, fun and the concept of selflessness and generosity. If these are lasting memories, the impact on Chris' way of being may be lasting!

TRY THIS #71

MORE SOPHISTICATED DIARIES

Try one of these ideas:

- keep a diary for a week and then share it together during your next visit
- keep diaries of special trips or vacations when you are away from each other, so you can share it when you return
- keep your diary in a notebook or a loose-leaf binder, on a cassette, on a computer or on videotape
- interview other family and friends about whether or not they keep diaries, and what they might look like
- keep your diary in ink rather than pencil so your ideas and words won't fade over time. It may be your great grandchild who is reading your entries decades from now!
- write as little or as much as you want to each day

TRY THIS #72

MORE CHALLENGING TIMELINES (CONTINUED FROM LESSON 11)

Try one of these suggestions.

- Draw a timeline to record the life of a pet in the family or of another grandparent or of your mother or father. If a grandparent is telling the story of the parent by drawing a timeline with the child, it might be important to include funny and/or special moments on the timeline. Think of other ways to make it interesting to read, for instance, you might include pictures or photographs.

- Choose ten important events in your life or the life of a family member, and put them on a timeline.

- Choose an object or a treasure to research, showing how things have changed over the years. Mark any major changes on the timeline.

- Choose a time period in the history of one of the family members, and plot important dates and happenings on the timelines.

Timelines take us from where we were,
to where we are,
and to where we want to be.

*"To forget one's ancestors is to be a brook
without a source, a tree without a root."*

Chinese Proverb

TRY THIS #73

HINTS FOR ENCOURAGING YOUNG WRITERS

When we work on projects together with our children, we have the opportunity to encourage or discourage them by our responses. Young children want to write but often cannot write as well as they speak. Some hints for encouraging the young writer:

- appreciate attempts, not just the final product
- taking a relaxed attitude
- being supportive, providing help when they need it, reading or writing the hard parts
- accentuating the positive – acknowledging what he/she does right rather than emphasizing mistakes
- keeping a focus on meaning being selective when pointing out errors rather than over-correcting

When a child doesn't know a word, give him time, you may choose to tell him or encourage him to make a prediction. Either way, have him read and re-read the sentences to maintain the flow.

It may or may not be important to have all the spelling correct depending on the audience. Make the decision together and explain the editing process, so that they know that eventually all finished work needs an edit, not just theirs.

"Education is an ornament in prosperity and a refuge in adversity."
Aristotle

TRY THIS #74

GRANDPARENTS: BUILDING ON EARLY WRITING

We know that most of what children learn about writing occurs without instruction.

Their writing is enhanced by regular usage, through experimentation, from having audiences to respond to, and from demonstrations. That's why significant adults at home can play an important role in "teaching" writing because it isn't actual teaching.

We can help them by enhancing their knowledge of:

- the world – ideas related to topics
- language – words and their meanings, grammatical patterns
- stories and other forms – beginnings, middles and ends
- print – left to right and top to bottom, relationships between letters and speech sounds, spelling patterns, punctuation

The focus must always be on making meaning. Refer to Chapter 5 for more detail on age-appropriate writing skills.

"Her manner of storytelling evoked tenderness and mystery as she put her face close to mine and fixed me with her big believing eyes. Thus was the strength that was developing in me directly infused from her."

Maxim Gorky

A Lesson We've Learned 19

Let them know they have a special place in your home as well as in your heart.

"... WITH HEART AND HOME..."

It was a very special little red suitcase – just big enough for me to carry – all the way down the lane to my Grandad's house. That was a special place in my life. Whenever I wanted, I could pack my little red suitcase and go to visit my Grandad who lived just four houses away, sleep overnight, have big cuddles, lots of stories, and then return home the next day.

I did this so often my Grandad made me my own special room in his house. We picked out the wallpaper which was sunny yellow flowers, and that was my bedroom when I came to visit.

And, one of the best parts was when years later I visited with my own children, lo and behold inside the medicine chest in my room was the flowered yellow wallpaper!!

Grandma Wendy Graham

"By the time the youngest children have learned to keep the house tidy, the oldest grandchildren are on hand to tear it to pieces."

Christopher Morley

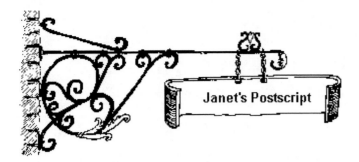

Janet's Postscript

Grandad's house was a special place, full of love and a feeling of safety and belonging. Grandad's heart and home had a special place for his granddaughter and grandson. The special place need not be so grand as a room for a grandchild, but can be a drawer filled with special items you share with your grandchild, or a box coloured with your grandchild, that holds special things you two can share. It can be a certain chair you always sit in when your grandchild climbs up on your lap for a story. It is something only the two of you share, and your imagination can be the limit.

TRY THIS #75

MAKE A PLACE IN YOUR HOME AS WELL AS IN YOUR HEART

Give your grandchild a special suitcase which can be theirs for when they come to visit you. Mark it with their name to take home each time they leave and bring it back when they come to visit. Give them a drawer or corner of the closet for them to unpackin. Keep an extra set of clothes for accidents or to dress up in. They need to feel they belong.

TRY THIS #76

HOW TO RESPOND TO A CHILD'S WORK

Instead of trying to interpret art work, ask questions or talk about the effort that has gone into the work. Try:

- "What bright colours you used!"
- "Look at all the different kinds of lines!"
- "I can see you've been working very hard!"
- "Can you tell me what is going on here?"
- "This picture makes me feel so…!"
- or, write down their story about it

TRY THIS #77

YOUR CHILD'S CRAFT CORNER FOR CREATING TREASURES

Art sessions can be easy and ongoing if you create a craft corner that can be used independently. The following ideas will help you get organized:

- shoe boxes and plastic buckets can be filled with crayons, paints and glue
- markers, pencils, scissors and paintbrushes can stand upright in coffee cans or plastic jars, or lie in plastic silverware trays
- egg cartons hold buttons, stickers, and glitter
- cardboard boxes hold feathers, cones, yarn and collections for a collage
- paper supplies, old magazines, paper plates and craft books are a staple

"The man with imagination is never alone."

Unknown

TRY THIS #78

TIPS FOR SAVING YOUR GRANDCHILD'S ART TREASURES

1. Appreciate the best. If it is great, save it or wait a day and quietly dispose of it. Save items that show a developmental spurt such as shapes, lines, people, self-portraits.
2. Stow away masterpieces. Make a cardboard flat file that will slide under a bed or behind a couch. Take pictures of three-dimensional work and save the photos in a book.
3. Label art with name, age and artist and the subject, as told by the artist.
4. Give some away, to other grandparents who live afar or other family members. Frame special ones as gifts to their parents. Create a museum in the garage or hallway wall. Celebrate their work!

"Two boys arrived yesterday with a pebble they said was the head of a dog until I pointed out that it was really a typewriter."

Pablo Picasso

A Lesson We've Learned

20

When generation after generation in our family repeat celebration in ritual ways, the family ingredients must be worth studying.

"… BIRTHDAYS WERE VERY SPECIAL…"

In our family, birthdays were very special. I remember how my mother always put a lot of effort into preparing for special birthday celebrations for us children. I continued these special traditions with my children and now, today, also with my grandchildren.

This is how it was and how it is still today:

A birthday table with presents on it, decorated with flowers on a white tablecloth, and a birthday cake with lit candles as a centerpiece are set up in the morning while the birthday-girl or birthday-boy waits in another room. Then, when everything is ready, a sister or brother (or even mum or dad) rings a cow-bell which has been in the family for many generations. As the bell rings, the child can then come (or, most often "run") into the room. Each surprise on the table is examined with glee, while the rest of the family sings "Happy Birthday." Then, she or he blows out the candles while making a special wish for the next year.

To make sure the other children are not left out, a special "Pot-Hunt" game is then played after the cake has been devoured. Each child in turn is given a wooden spoon and blindfolded, and then spun around a few times. A small toy or surprise is put under a large pot. The search then begins for the pot, with the spoon tapping out the way along the floor (or on the grass in the garden) until the pot is hit with a loud "clang", signalling the hunt is over! The blindfold comes off in a flash and then they enjoy their surprise as well!

Without this game it would not be a real birthday!

Later on in the afternoon, friends and playmates arrive for a party with more games and good food. Happy music plays in the house throughout the day. Talented and not-so-talented family members alike play their instruments and everyone sings along in between the festivities. Taking a lot of photographs (and videos too) ensures that everyone knows that celebrating this birthday is definitely a special occasion.

These pictures mark the occasion for our family as the years go by and as the family grows – so that future generations can also share these simple yet important ingredients of family fun, celebration, music and laughter together!

Helga Bruecki

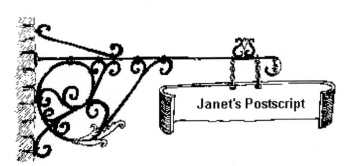

Janet's Postscript

I found this story captivating. Up until now I would have considered our family birthdays to be quite acceptable – usually a family dinner, the obligatory balloon, the cake, a card and gift thoughtfully selected, and sometimes more.

This story made me think about the many celebrations in our family, but none quite so carefully planned, nurtured and a promise to future generations. We think a lot about the future these days, and this story seemed like the perfect one to end our chapter on Treasures and Traditions.

Helga describes so many special moments:
- the birthday starts with lit candles in early morning
- the birthday child waiting and waiting
- the cow-bell – in the family for generations
- a surprise for all in the "Pot-Hunt" game
- happy music and sing-alongs throughout the day

Happy Birthday to you
Happy Birthday to you
Happy Birthday dear darling
Happy Birthday to you!

I paused to imagine the year 2050 and the future generation who pores through the family videos of the previous five generations.

What stories, what personalities, what lessons, what pride and what a legacy!

Thank you, Helga!

TRY THIS #79

A SCRAPBOOK OF FAMILY TRADITIONS

We all have them! But do we pay attention to the detail and do we embellish them as our own family's uniqueness enters the picture? Do we record them as a contribution to our future family's understanding of our time and history? Do we even notice some that are so embedded in family culture that they are taken for granted?

Why not interview family members to collect a record of all traditions, including recipes, events, celebrations, holidays and passages, and then put them together as a special gift for all members of the family at Christmas. Be sure to include photos of the traditions. If you don't have many, this might be a good time to start.

TRY THIS #80

CREATE A NEW FAMILY TRADITION

Choose your favourite time of year, your favourite event or a special person achieving a new accomplishment, and plan the celebration with your grandchildren. Most likely they'll be far more creative than you! The challenge might be to let your imagination soar, even while you monitor the logistics. Document the first time you use it and plan modifications to make it even better next time.

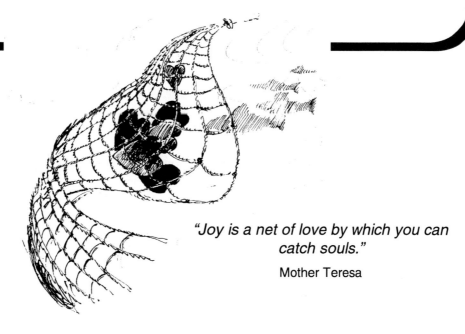

"Joy is a net of love by which you can catch souls."

Mother Teresa

TRY THIS #81

START A LIFELONG TREASURE CHEST

The "Dollar Store" has some great colourful boxes. I've seen some magnificent carved ones recently or…then there is the old and a bit tawdry doll's clothes trunk my grandpa made for me. Maybe we could fix it up, sand and paint it then decorate it with the shells we've found together.

Maybe we could start a treasure box to keep here at Grammy's house and, on each visit, we could explore to find old family treasures - a photo, a book, a keepsake. Once we've shared the stories we could wrap the treasure in tissue and tuck it in the chest for unwrapping and retelling in future visits and eventually one day to go home with her, for her to share with her son or granddaughter.

TRY THIS #82

WHAT IS FAMILY FUN?

It will be different in every family. I think of key words like:

balloons, balloons, balloons! art, paint, pens, hugs, teasing, jokes, yes, healthy touching, feelings, safe, tears, honour, dance, sing, love, kites, read, kooky, silliness, giggle, brag, joy, twinkle, compassion, nature, toys, play, jeans, hobbies, gifts, celebration, holidays, homemade, organized, music, creativity, process not product, and so on and so on!

Remember Helga's tip:

Be sure that whatever you do to nurture
traditions in your family, the key ingredients
are always:
family fun
celebration
music
and
LAUGHTER!

CONGRATULATIONS

Treasures and Traditions:
The Connection to Values

CONCLUSION: So Many Different Choices

We thought it might be interesting to compile the list of treasures identified in our stories – published and not published. Repeats indicate the frequency with which the item was a chosen treasure.

- a china tea set
- a gold locket
- a recipe
- a penknife
- an old wrinkled story book
- furniture
- jewellery
- stories
- pictures
- a chair
- a guitar
- mother's wedding band
- father's carving set

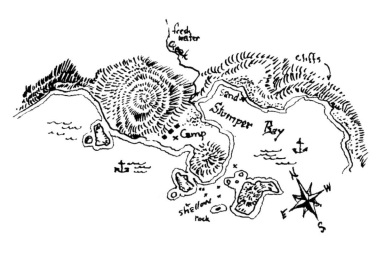

- love
- necklace
- dish
- rings
- mom's wedding ring
- paintings of grandfather when he was young

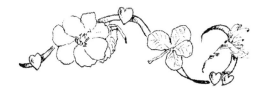

- her baby book
- photo album of really old family pictures
- watch fob made of Royal Canadian Air Force medals
- grandfather's camera
- memories from being around parents
- a ring
- cat
- rocking chair
- pictures
- cigar box
- gold railway watch
- portable wooden desk
- a sporran
- a clock
- World War II medals
- pictures of homesteading
- lady's hat pin
- a hymn book
- a 100-year-old music box
- parents' wedding picture
- mom's opal earrings
- rose bowl (90 years old)
- silver bracelets (a whole bunch)
- silver compass (100 years old)
- handmade jewellery box (100 years old)
- fine leather-bound books
- his grandfather's name
- his dad's baseball uniform
- his great grandfather's lead toy soldier
- a clock given to his grandmother by Buffalo Bill Cody
- rocking horse
- antique plane
- silverware

Maybe these will give us some hints about what we might pass on to future generations.

"Today, see if you can stretch your heart and expand your love so that it touches not only those to whom you can give it easily, but also to those who need it so much."

Daphne Rose Kingma

Chapter 3

"I Am Lovable": Nurturing Their Self-Esteem

"I Am Lovable": Nurturing Their Self-Esteem

Introduction: BUILDING A CLIMATE OF LOVE

Most of us will take grandparenting very seriously. We are determined to do a good job and we will find many ways to do so: caring, time, energy, educational toys and games, good books, and financial support, if necessary. We have dreams of what/who this child will become.

How can we make their dreams and ours come true?

In her landmark book, "Your Child's Self-Esteem," Dorothy Corkille Briggs describes it in a nutshell:

"You want life's positives for them: inner confidence, a sense of purpose and involvement, meaningful constructive relationships with others, success at school and work...and most of all, happiness."

Today, enough evidence has accumulated to give us just such a formula: if your child has high self-esteem, he has it made. Mounting research shows that the fully functioning child (or adult) is different from the person who flounders through life.

The difference lies in his attitude towards himself, his degree of self-esteem.

What is self-esteem? *"It is how a person feels about himself – how much he likes his particular person."*

She goes on to say *"high self-esteem is a quiet sense of self-respect and self-worth. When you have it deep inside, you're glad you're you."*

"In fact," she says, *"self-esteem is the mainspring that slates every child for success or failure as a human being."*

As grandparents who care, along with their parents, we must discover or create ways to help our kids to a firm and wholehearted belief in themselves.

Strong self-respect is based on three main beliefs:

"I am lovable", *"I am worthwhile"* and *"I have something to offer others."* These are needs we continue to have as we become adults, and they are critical to our emotional well-being.

As Dorothy points out, oddly enough almost all parents would say they love their children, but somehow young ones sometimes don't get the message. She says, *"It is the child's feeling about being loved or unloved that affects how he will develop."*

Where does self-esteem come from? It does not come from family wealth, education, geographical living area, social class, or father's/mother's occupation.

It comes instead from the quality of the relationships that exist between the child and those who play a significant role in his or her life.

In this chapter we will explore how we can build a climate of love for our grandchildren. The lessons in this chapter reflect the views of Dorothy Corkille Briggs' tried, true and scholarly examination of "Your Child's Self-Esteem."

We thank two very special people who provided us with "Letters to Our Grandchildren," which are the focal points of the chapter. Margaret Swain (my mom) wrote to her eight grandchildren, who will see these letters for the first time in print…and Don Prentice, who wrote letters to both newborn great grandchildren, and one to each of his two grandkids. They will all feel cherished!

"Now, with God's help, I shall become myself."
Kierkegaard

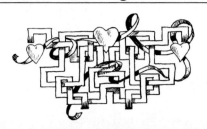

A Lesson We've Learned

21

Being cherished as a person nurtures the feeling of being loved.

Our neighbour, Don Prentice, wrote this beautiful letter to his new great grandchild.. Clearly, he cherishes her already.

A LETTER TO HALEY

Hello, Haley:

Welcome. I am so very, very happy that you have chosen your Mom and Dad to come to, and to share your life here with them and through them with me and other family members.

Now, I've got a big, big lead time on you, and on your parents too, in number of years in this old world. And I want you to know this. I want you to know that what has meant, and means, more to me than anything else in my life is the relationship with, and the time spent, with my sons and daughters, and their sons and daughters. And of course, with their wonderful Mom. Who unfortunately you will not get to know here. Unless of course, you stopped and spent some time with her enroute to this place. I wouldn't be a bit surprised. Perhaps that's why you arrived a bit behind schedule.

But now here you are. Safe and sound and oh (according to the feedback I am getting from all who have seen you) so very lovely. Thank you, little sweetheart. Your being here is one of the richest of blessings for every member of your Mom's family and your Dad's family. And especially so, of course, for your Mom and Dad themselves.

How do I know all this? Well now, young lady, I know it all because I have been there. Four wonderful, wonderful times I have been there. And I remember it all as if it were yesterday. All times, full to the brim and running over with never-to-be-forgotten feelings and things and happenings and excitements and joy.

Oh boy! How I remember the feeling of small arms about my neck. And the feeling of tiny hands pulling at my pant legs for attention and to be picked up.

And the touch of my own child's lips on my face. The sound of child laughter. The sound of child crying, and the relief and sense of fulfillment over the quietness that comes with cuddling and comforting.

And too, it's so much fun to remember 'jig-a-jig-a-jig-a-jigging' my kids on my knee. And singing rousing renditions of 'Little Brown Jug.' And holding them tight to my chest and close to my nose, and smelling their special and very exclusive baby smell.

And walking, and walking, and walking with my arms wrapped about them. Back and forth. Back and forth. I swear I must have walked the equivalent of around the world with each one of them.

And the heart-tugging sadness at having to leave them for a time, and the inexpressible joy upon returning to them.

All the greatest of happy experiences. And now happy recollections.

So you see Haley, little so loved one, why I can be so happy for your Mom and your Dad because you have joined them here. You are going to add to their already rich store of blessings. And you are going to add to their bulging bank of precious memories. I know, as I have said, because I have been there, and I am there.

There is something else I must talk to you about. It is about your name. I want you to really feel the significance of it. Not just for you, but for all of us. You are the namesake of a very special lady; your Grandmother on your Dad's side. She was no ordinary person, and she had a deep and abiding influence on all she shared her life here with. We are then, all of us, greatly better off and better people because of her.

So while it is sad that you will not meet her here, she has left the best of all possible gifts here for you that you will enjoy and will benefit from all of your years. She left you a Dad, and Aunts and Uncles, and sisters and cousins and 'me' – we all took on some of her qualities and nature, and her wonderful love, we are and living them.

What a fortunate one you are. Combine all that with all the good stuff from your Mom's side, and you are living and will continue to live an exceptionally good life. And you will help others have more good in their lives than would be so without you.

And that's my wish for you. A really good life. A life knowledge that lifts you up and sees you living in a wondrous light that detaches you from and protects you from the dark side of this world.

I wish you an abundance of all good things: happiness, joy, loving and lasting companionships. I wish you the capacity to give unconditional love to those who are worthy of it.

Of course I will be seeing you one of these days. I could have sat beside you and said all this to you. But no, I couldn't wait. It had to be done now. And too, I think your Dad and Mom may want to put this letter to you away and bring it out and let you read it yourself at the right and appropriate time.

I am a long way away from you. But love knows no distance or time, and thus I am sure you are feeling the love I am adding from way out here to the mountain of more local love already around you.

Don

Snapshots

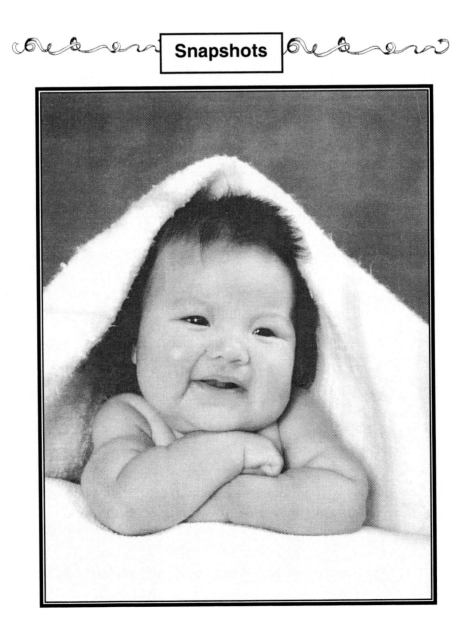

TRY THIS #83

CELEBRATE THE ARRIVAL

- create an event of the special day or year they were born and make a book of it
- collect newspaper articles about world events of the time, horoscopes for her
- write a letter about where you were and what you did when you heard of the new arrival
- describe your feelings, dreams, hopes for his future
- make a list of promises you intend to keep
- include some treasures and explain why they are treasures
- tell her why you cherish her

TRY THIS #84

A "CHERISHED" PHOTO SHOOT

Give a gift certificate for a professional photo of babe, and maybe mom and dad too. Suggest the photographer be creative to create the ambiance of the baby in the context of "being cherished." Have it enlarged and framed for all first family members.

We have a beauty of Tasha at three days old, tucked into her Mom's terry bathrobe. Mom's hair falls over her as she gazes lovingly at her new daughter. Tasha's seven now, but the photo still holds a place of honour. Tasha knows she was cherished from the day she was born.

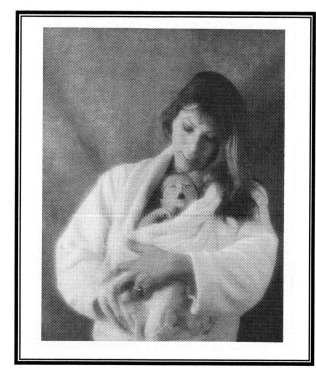

TRY THIS #85

CELEBRATE THE ARRIVAL: VIDEO VERSION

Make your own video the day he is born. Tell him everything or anything that seems important – like Don's letter, but a video version of it.

Ideas?
- your welcome speech
- where and how you heard
- what you thought and what you did
- hopes for his future
- promises you make to him
- memories of his mom or dad's birth
- family treasurers that will be his someday
- a tour of your house and garden
- a place that will be his when he visits

TRY THIS #86

CELEBRATE THE ARRIVAL: HOW TO CHERISH

Key to cherishing our children is enlarging our own capacity to cherish. Now would be a good time to start practising.

- make a list of your special qualities
- what makes you different from other people?
- what capacities and sensitivities are uniquely yours?
- what are your specialties?

Dorothy Corkille Briggs says, *"When you prize your own uniqueness (even though you are aware of your shortcomings), when you respect yourself and focus on your positive qualities, you are freer to cherish children."*

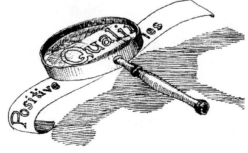

A Lesson We've Learned

22

Our young ones will feel cherished when we take the time "to find each other."

A LETTER TO BRAD

It was at school, at noon hour in the staffroom, when I was called to the telephone, which was in the cloakroom to provide some privacy. Closing the door behind, me I picked up the receiver and heard the message I had been expecting daily...We had a grandson! I was filled with such joy and relief...followed by frustration and despair, for Bradley was a world away in Port Alberni, British Columbia, and I was in Northern Ontario. It would be months before I could hold him and count his toes. But we did come, Grandpa and I, at Easter, Brad...and you fulfilled all our hopes and dreams. (Little did we know that five more grandsons would follow!) During our years in the Bahamas, your Mom and Dad kept us up-to-date with pictures and tapes...and brought you to see us at Kama in the summers. You and I were the early risers those wonderful sun filled days; we would have breakfast together, and then wander the beaches, finding treasures...and more importantly, finding each other. Now you have a home of your own not far away, and best of all...you have given me another wonderful granddaughter, and two "great-grands," as the Bahamians would say. You have always made me proud...and I love you,

Grandma
(Margaret Swain)

"The only gift is a portion of thyself."

Ralph Waldo Emerson

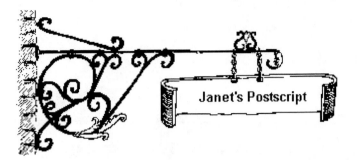

Janet's Postscript

I remember those times, I was only 20 with a new babe, and so far away from Mom and Dad and family. Phone calls were expensive and mail was slow, and I was so lonely. Brad was the first grandchild for six or so years, and now is the oldest at age 35, and he feels special in my mom's eyes. Whether near or far, mom is always there for her eight grandkids. She consistently marks every event, celebration and holiday with letters, cards, baking and a phone call, and she hasn't let up at age 85. Her grandkids are spread across the country now –did that slow her down?

No! At 83 she bought herself a computer, determined to stay in touch through e-mail, and now she shares her stories, her love and even her recipes. She's taught me a great deal about the importance of my maternal and now grand-maternal presence in our family, and I'm so grateful for that.

Grandma Margaret and Brad loved finding each other at the beach. Try a few of these ideas:

TRY THIS #87

BEING OBSERVERS TOGETHER #1

Just go for a walk together in nature. Look for:
- shapes clouds make
- signs of different seasons
- delicate patterns
- hard-to-see life
- unusual shades of one colour
- beautiful stones
- something you've never seen before

Share and compare!

TRY THIS #88

BEING OBSERVERS TOGETHER #2

Choose something from the world of nature. It could be an animal, a bird, an anthill… something living.

Each of you can observe the same thing without speaking, then share your observations.

- does it do anything unusual?
- what are its habits?
- how does it eat?
- what does it look like?
- do you see patterns?

You can record your observations using drawings, photos or videotapes, which could be the start of a scrapbook.

The most fun will come when you have your follow-up conversation.

- which human(s) did it remind you of?
- would you want to be a _____? Why or why not?
- if you were a _____, where would you want to live? Why?
. . . and so on!

TRY THIS #89

CELEBRATE BEING TOGETHER #3

- kick off your shoes and run in the grass
- play ball in the rain
- be a frog hopping, a lamb bleating, a crane stretching, be crazy!
- try kite-flying, even if you never could before
- buy balloons for your walk and watch people smile
- get dirty
- pile autumn leaves on each other
- press leaves in wax paper
- be an angel in the snow

CHERISH EACH OTHER!

TRY THIS #90

SPYING UNDERWATER

Cut the bottom out of a large can. Cover it with clear plastic wrap and secure it tightly with a large elastic. You have created a form of spyglass and you'll be able to use it to peer into the underwater world of creepy crawlies.

Whether your hunt is in a saltwater tide pool or freshwater, take some books about water creatures with you. Find a flat rock or log to sit on.

- plan a hunt for a particular creature
- make it a contest
- make a list of what you already know and what you want to find out
- look up information about your finds
- most important of all . . . talk!

Use open-ended questions and put "why would you say that?" at the end of each.

Be sure to share your memories and stories about days at the beach with their mom and dad. They particularly love to find out that their parents were naughty!

Remind them about eco-rules. Put everything back gently, and leave things the way you found them.

A Lesson We've Learned

23

The cornerstone of the love that nurtures is psychological safety.

"...WITH A SON OF YOUR OWN"

Snapshots

Dear Justin:

And now to you, Justin...a special young man who has always marched to a different drummer...Even before you were born, twice you sent your mother off to the hospital in labour, only to change your mind and refuse to follow through. I was there keeping brother Brad company, so your parents would be free to be together, and to rush off whenever you sounded the alarm...You finally decided to venture out into this world, and we were all so

happy with this new little person. I thought I'd be able to help with night feedings...and at the same time steal a little time to rock and cuddle you. So when I heard the first whimper and snuffle from the nursery, I rushed barefoot to quiet you so your parents could sleep on. A few seconds later there were three heads bent over the crib...so I went back to bed...Same scene the next night. I gave up that race and went back to day duty in the kitchen.

From the day you first discovered a grassy lawn and crawled around on it, you had a special affinity for all the little inhabitants who lived in that miniature world...ants, spiders, beetles and caterpillars...they were all your friends. And on the beach and in the tide pools at Gordon Head, you knew all the little water dwellers; visitors were always amazed at the extent of your knowledge.

Do you remember the shrimp party your parents hosted one moonlit September night? You joined the rest of us on the rocks with your shrimp net, and helped fill the pail. You may even have carried the pail back to the house. You had been taught that it was acceptable to bring water creatures back home for a few hours to observe them; then they

were to be released back where you had
found them. We all were witness to your
horror...and sympathized with you...when
you saw the pot of boiling water on the stove
and realized that we intended to eat your
friends. I think we all felt a little guilty.

I have been so happy that we have lived in the same city for the past twenty years. It has
made it easier for us to see each other often, especially when you were younger. I have
watched you mature from toddler to teenager; and now to a sensitive, loving young man
with a son of your own. I enjoy the evenings you and Trevor come to dinner, and we
watch him develop and grow. He is a handsome, captivating little boy, and you are a
good father. You have always been very dear to me, and you know that I love you very
much.

Grandma
(Margaret Swain)

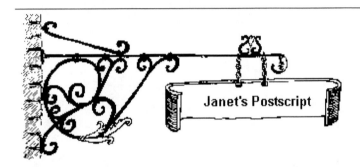

Janet's Postscript

Our son Justin is now 25 and proud
father to our great young grandson,
Trevor, who is three now.

Justin had a very difficult time with
relationships with his peers during his
school years, often the victim of
teasing or bullying. A gentle, loving
kind of guy, it was not his way to fight back. He tells us now that he has recognized that
his self-esteem is low, and he has made a plan to learn about it, read about it and centre
himself.

My mom has played a pivotal role in this transformation. Since his son was born (Justin
is a single parent), an incredibly important bond has built between him and his grandma.
He has a regular date for dinner with her and Trevor, every second Thursday.

My mom is Justin's psychological safety. He talks about everything that's on his mind:
his new girlfriend, money issues, his future, his job, Trevor, Trev's mom. He pours it all
out, some things I know he doesn't share with me. Why? He trusts her implicitly, and the
bedrock of psychological safety is trust.

The single most important ingredient in a nurturing relationship is honesty. So Justin can
be honest with his grandmother and trust she will not judge him for it, but rather listen
and provide gentle guidance where appropriate.

It's such a relief to us, his parents, to know he has her to turn to. She has been his anchor
and his lifeline. Thanks, Mom. I love you.

How can we create a haven of psychological safety for our young people? How we talk to them and how we listen to them will make an important difference.

The following guidelines written by grandpa and counsellor Michael Mort provide some useful tips:

TRY THIS #91

ABOUT ENCOURAGEMENT INSTEAD OF PRAISE

1. Encouragement is a key to high self esteem.
2. Encouragement is not about achievement; rather, it's about effort, contribution and appreciation.
3. Encouragement emphasizes willingness, not worth.
4. The child is valued, whether she achieves or not.

Tips for encouragement:
- recognize effort, rather than accomplishment
- value a child *as he is*, not as he could be
- show appreciation for contributions
- acknowledge what the child *can* do
- demonstrate faith in the child

Samples of encouragement:
- "I appreciate what you did"
- "You're getting it"
- "It looks like you worked hard on this"
- "I have faith in you"
- "I like the way you tidied up"
- "I notice all the colours in your picture"
- "You sure are improving"

Remember, it takes nine positive comments to undo the damage of one negative comment.

TRY THIS #92

SETTING LIMITS

Setting limits and using *choice and consequences* can help to avoid child/adult power struggles and also establish an effective framework of decision-making for children.

Remember:
1. Setting limits for children provides them with structure and predictability.
2. Children can then function with safety and some independence.
3. The limits which have been set change over time as the child grows.
4. Limits have to be reasonable, have purpose, and be applied fairly.
5. When an adult is not involved in setting limits, children feel uncertainty, anxiety and sometimes afraid, which can lead to "acting out" and misbehaviour.

Tips for setting limits:
- Set limits which are most important for the welfare of the child. Too many can confuse them.
- discuss the limit setting with parents first, to ensure cooperation and collaboration
- discuss the limits with the children, seeking their understanding
- review limits briefly with each new visit

"If I can ease one life the aching,
Or cool one pain,
Or help one fainting robin
Unto his nest again,
I shall not live in vain."

Emily Dickinson

TRY THIS #93

CHOICES AND CONSEQUENCES (not punishment)

Remember:

1. Choices and consequences provide a way to make the child responsible for his/her own behaviour
2. All of us are always learning how to make better choices which have desirable consequences. *This is an important life skill.*
3. Children need to understand that each decision has a consequence: sometimes positive, sometimes negative.

Tips:

- the adult becomes advisor, coach, information giver
- celebrate and discuss wise choices, and empathize with them as they experience the consequence of an unwise choice
- the adult needs to apply the concept of **unconditional love** throughout; the child is neither "good" nor "bad" as a result of their decisions

Note: Punishment is *way* down on the list of methods effective in encouraging positive behaviours. Resulting resentment or fear can set the stage for disrespect and abuse.

TRY THIS #94

SAY "NO!" TO BULLYING

In a recent school survey, one out of four children indicated they were victims of bullying. This is a major issue for youth today. How can we help?

Remember:

1. Bullying occurs when there is an imbalance of power.
2. Victims cannot defend themselves, and feel helpless as a result.
3. Bullies will keep on bullying, unless an adult intervenes.
4. Victims deserve adult protection.

Tips:

- bullies are sometimes within our own families…cousins, sisters, brothers, even parents and grandparents
- adults need to be alert for the signs
- it takes an adult to intervene
- we can help by encouraging children to say no to bullying and to seek help from an adult such as a counsellor, teacher, parent, or grandparent

The bully, not the victim, is the person with the problem.

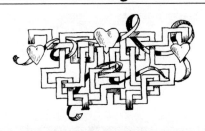

A Lesson We've Learned

24

Children survive on acceptance but they blossom on love.

LETTER TO MY UNBORN GRANDCHILD

Your Dad was a wonderful baby and child, and is now a terrific young man. He is loving and caring and has a great sense of humour. Your Dad was much loved and anticipated when he was in my womb, as you are much loved and anticipated as we patiently wait to meet you.

I look forward to holding you, smelling your new baby skin, snuggling your warm little head on my shoulder, which are my fondest memories when I reach way back to my own wee baby, many years ago. As each year passes and you grow up so quickly, Papa and I look forward to spending much time nurturing you and teaching you as we did our two boys. I have many things I want to show you, tell you about and look forward to with you.

I will love you unconditionally as I did your Dad, and your parents will be the greatest. I am excited about the prospect of your Dad being a father, for I know he has no idea how head over heels he will fall when you are born. Your Mom and Dad have great expectations for parenthood, as your Papa and I had, and I know you will grow up in a loving family who will guide you through life in the best way they know.

Love, Nana
(Nancy Swain Smeltzer)

"Some people come into our lives and quietly go; others stay for a while and leave footprints on our hearts and we are never the same."

Anonymous

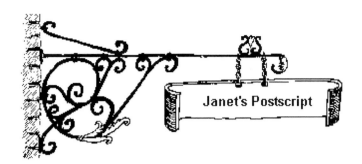

Janet's Postscript

When I asked my sister if she'd like to write a letter to her unborn grandchild, her eyes filled with tears even before her mouth formed the word "yes".

Nancy is a person so full of love, "her cup runneth over," as the saying goes. She's exactly what every grandchild deserves. She's the difference between surviving and blossoming. She's the difference between a cup half empty and a cup half full. She's the difference between lemons and lemonade.

Nancy will do all that she promises in her letter. She will hold and snuggle, she will nurture and teach and she will love unconditionally. She will be so great as a grandparent, largely because she has the experience for the job. We all do.

We can all look back at our parenting and identify what we did well, what we could have done better, and what we would change if we could "have another crack at it."

Well, we do have another chance – a chance to invest our experience and wisdom about parenting in our grandchildren.

Snapshots

Gizella & daughter Judy
1968

Granddaughter Julia
1992

133

So what can we do to help the "blossoming" along?

TRY THIS #95

CREATE MATCHING GARDENS

Plan a special garden – herbs, vegetables, shade, perennial or annual. It could be one large patio pot, or a corner of a garden. Fence it in with a decorative one-foot fence (can be bought in any garden store) so that your "grandparent garden" is landmarked for all to see.

If you're lucky enough to live close to each other, shop together at your local nursery, choose your plants or seeds. Make a paper plan for your garden first.

If you live far apart, make your plan by proposing ideas in colour photocopies from a garden book – great topic for ongoing letters via fax, e-mail or post.

TRY THIS #96

STORE THE MEMORIES OF YOUR GARDEN

- press blossoms and leaves in between wax paper with an iron. Remember when we used to do that? Hint: put a cloth between the wax paper and the iron.
- take pictures of yourselves and your sweeties with the changes in your garden
- make a scrapbook

TRY THIS #97

WINTER FLOWER CANDLES

Take any old store-bought pillar-type candle. With a glue stick found in any stationery store, rub glue on the outside of the candle, then carefully lay on flowers, petals or leaves which have been pressed in a book.

Melt regular paraffin wax in an old pot or can, and carefully dip the whole candle once or twice to seal the flowers in.

If you live far apart, you can send one to each other.

TRY THIS #98

DECORATE YOUR GARDEN

Build a scarecrow for the garden. Use grandpa's old fishing hat or grandma's favourite dress from the Sixties. Old fur coats look great on scarecrows, and don't get spray painted there!

Instead of the seed envelope marking each row, cut the end off an envelope, glue your grandchild's photo on it and attach it to a stake with a title, e.g., "Rory's delphiniums."

Remember: Children survive on acceptance, but blossom on your love.

Cherish your blossoms!

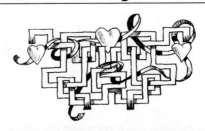

A Lesson We've Learned   25

A hundred years from now all that may matter is that the world will be a better place because we were important in the life a child.

A LETTER ABOUT MY GRANDMA
(excerpt from a eulogy)

Homemade Items Were Treasured

Grandma (Millicent Forrester) had a huge capacity to love. If she could have had half a dozen children, she probably would have. Mom and Grandma didn't always see eye to eye on a number of issues but in spite of this, Grandma would have done anything for Mom. She absolutely adored babies, flowers, social occasions, and Elvis. I'm not talking about the rock star who lived in Memphis but the Siamese cat who lives on Beaufort Road. Grandma was the first to admit she wasn't really taken with pets but when it came to Elvis, she was smitten. When Dad used to threaten to pitch Elvis outside because he'd been up to one of his howling and yowling episodes (and he really is a yowler), Grandma was quite convinced Elvis was simply communicating and she, in turn, would threaten Dad right back.

It goes without saying that we are growing up in a generation vastly different from Grandma's. Ours is an instant generation. We want everything, and we want it now. Hers was a generation where you saved until you had enough money to buy things, where you never took food for granted, where you never put off 'til tomorrow what you could do today, and where home-made items were treasured because they represented time spent on something worthwhile that spoke from the heart.

In spite of this generation gap, Grandma strived to be contemporary. She found computers baffling, but she would nevertheless get on a keyboard and have a go at computer golf anyway. She knew how to handle Automatic Teller Machines, self-serve gas stations, and long-distance dialing. She was a champion of the balanced chequebook. She had a strong work ethic and always inquired about our work. She was among the pioneers of women who worked outside the home, having worked as an office manager for a general contracting firm in Stoke-on-Trent, England.

Alison Giles

P.S.: The full text of this touching eulogy can be found in the conclusion of this book.

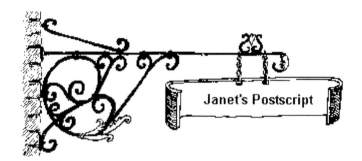

Janet's Postscript

This eulogy (in total several pages long) was delivered at Alison Giles' grandma's memorial service in April of 1998. Her name was Millicent Forrester. The lesson is a reworded version of an old familiar saying, but Alison used it in the eulogy because she says, "…that's what it all boils down to."

I particularly liked the part about homemade items being treasured "because they represented time spent on something worthwhile that spoke from the heart," so our *Try This* section features the opportunity to make things together.

TRY THIS #99

PERSONALIZED PILLOWCASES

Make a collage of your favourite photos of your grandchildren, or of the two or three of you together. Glue the photos on to paper which is less than the size of a pillowcase. Take your collage and a light-coloured pillowcase to a photocopy shop with a colour copier. Ask them to photocopy your collage onto the pillowcase.

Decorate the edges of the pillowcase with tassels or fancy trim or a ruffle. This will decorate their bed and snuggle them at night or during their naps.
Sweet Dreams!

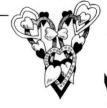

TRY THIS #100

GRANNY-IN-A-BAG

Wendy Holob had her whole Grade 2 class do this for parent's night. It was eerie to walk into her room and see a class of life-size dolls dressed in real clothes – certainly a well-behaved and attentive group!

You could make a set of the family or, if you live far away, you could make a pair of dolls – grandma and grandpa, dress them in your clothes and send them to the grandkids – they can then cuddle with you every day or read a book with your arm around them.

I'm going to try this with my grandkids and ask if they'll leave them at my house to keep me company when they're gone.

Have fun shopping for the stuff for hair, etc.

Materials Needed:
- large sheet of paper to trace their body
- large piece of light-coloured fabric for the body (a sheet would do, or a pink/beige/brown fabric)
- sewing machine or needle and thread
- polyester filling or nylons or . . . for stuffing the body (try craft stores)
- yarn, buttons, etc., for hair, eyes . . . be creative . . . check possibilities at the craft store

Fold the fabric in half. Pin the body cut-out pieces on the fabric, and cut to create front and back of the body. Leave a margin for stitching (slightly bigger than their body). Stitch around the edges of the body with a one-inch seam. Leave an opening at the head for stuffing. Turn it inside out and stuff. Glue on hair with glue gun, sew on button eyes. Use your imagination for the mouth. Fabric paint could be used for bright cheeks.

"Joy is the serious business of heaven."

C.S. Lewis

TRY THIS #101

SAVINGS PIGGY BANK

Alison learned to "save 'til you
had enough to buy things" from
her grandma. The other day when
one of the grandkids was here, she
had a pocket full of money; I said
she needed a piggy bank. She
asked what a piggy bank was. I
was amazed – we always had one
as kids (remember using a knife in
the slot to get the coins back out?).

Why not make one together? You need:
- a balloon for the pig's body
- lots of newspaper ripped in strips
- toilet paper rolls for feet
- paper maché paste

Combine paste with 2 cups of cold water in a bowl. Add it to a pot of 2 cups
of boiling water and bring to a boil. Remove from heat and stir in 3
tablespoons of sugar. Let it cool to thicken.

Blow up the balloon and knot the end. Dip newspaper strips into the paste and
cover the balloon with several layers. Let dry between layers (sometimes
requires 2 days) Use several layers or strips to form pig ears and snout.
(You'll need a picture for ideas). Use toilet paper tubes for feet and nose.
Attach with wet strips.

Use your imagination to finish the pig:
- something curly for tail
- acrylic paint to decorate – flowers, stripes, stars

Cut a slit in the top for coins . . .and remember to talk.
While you make the pig, talk about values related to money. Take them to the
bank and teach them how to open their own savings account. What a great
investment!

TRY THIS #102

MAKE A CHRISTMAS TREE SKIRT

I found this idea in a family magazine, I believe it was "Family Fun."

Cut a large circle, big enough to surround the bottom of your tree, out of your favourite fabric. Edge the circle with lace or another printed fabric or finishing ribbon.

Each year have the grandchild print their hands on it with fabric paint. They can also write their names and the date. This makes a wonderful annual tradition.

Snapshots

The Special Christmas Dress

A Lesson We've Learned

26

We can learn to appraise our potential, then set goals to achieve it.

GRANNY WENDY'S LETTER TO HAYDEN:

You are my firstborn grandchild – and what a joy you are in my life!

When you were only minutes old, I held you tightly wrapped in my arms, and wondered whether I could hold you forever, protected from all the evils of the world, and keep you safe forever. I cried. And I also not only loved you at that moment, but I fell in love with you.

The joy I feel when being around you is comparable to nothing in my life. It is so heartwarming to have a little one in my life, to see you grow and become a little boy. I realized when I held you in my arms when you were minutes old, that I could not protect you from the world, but rather I would be a better Granny for you if I had time and energy for you forever.

There are so many things for you out in this world, and I would like to help you learn about some of them. I would like to teach you about the ocean and all its magic. I would like to teach you how to ride your two-wheeler, to ski, and to see the world through your eyes with all the wonderment of a young child.

I want to be part of those experiences with you and part of many other things in your life. Education is a lifelong ongoing process, and I want to encourage you to keep your

curiosity and interest in all things – never to be complacent about what the world can do for you and what it can provide you – and I want to share this with you.

I want to take your hand whenever I can to share whatever I can with you. Maybe just watch the clouds in the sky, or go for a walk in the park – I just want to have some time with you.

I want you to grow into a man who has a sense of self-esteem, to know that whatever you choose to do can be done, and to know that whatever you want to be, you can be. I will offer you my guidance, both financially and emotionally, while you do this, and I will try to know what to do when the time comes.

Mostly, I want you to find your Granny and Paca's house a place where you can come whenever you want, however you want, and feel it to be a place of safety. As you grow up, you will find there are times when the world does not seem fair, or even equal, and please just know we are here with open arms to love you and accept you for what you are and who you are.

You have brought a new kind of joy into my life, Hayden, which is hard to describe to anyone else. It is the kind of joy that swells my heart when I see you, that makes me burst with pride when I see how clever you are, and that makes me fall in love with you all over again when you say, "Love you, Granny."

Thank you for coming into my life and bringing me such joy.

Granny
(Wendy Graham)

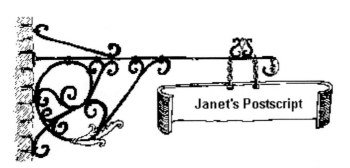

Janet's Postscript

Wendy is a close friend of mine and I've seen her in the joy she describes. In fact, our friendship has been built on since the moment she told me Hayden's arrival was imminent. I had two grandchildren at the time, Rory and Natasha, and few friends or acquaintances had yet to know this joy. It was wonderful to have someone who understood.

I thought Wendy's use of "I fell in love with you" is so accurate. I remember the first time I fell in love . . . several words come to mind – euphoria, a full or swollen heart, an unmistakable joy, a longing when distanced from them, a sweetness, an ecstasy.

What would your list of words look like? Be sure to tell your "grands" how you feel, or write them your own letter. They'll feel cherished!

The following are ideas we developed in Rick Hansen's BC Life Skills Program. They all focus on goal-setting – a critical skill for children to get to where they want to go.

What Is a Goal?

Children should be able to:

- define the term "goal"
- identify personal learning goals
- imagine what it is like to experience success

TRY THIS #103

PAST SUCCESS WITH GOAL SETTING

Ask them to think of times when they decided to learn to do something that was important to them. Encourage them to recognize that they have been able to achieve many different goals. Ask them:

- How do you feel when you decide to learn something new? (set a goal)
- How do you feel when you are able to learn what you set out to learn? (meet the goal)
- Ask them to complete the following sentence stem with as many different endings as they can. "I have learned to . . ." Discuss their responses.

Have them brainstorm examples of the difference between a wish and a goal.

TRY THIS #104

POSSIBLE SUCCESS WITH GOAL SETTING

Brainstorm the many areas in their lives where they could set important goals:

- school work
- house/yard work
- saving money
- a sport

- relationships
- being a helper
- pets
- behaviour

- family
- recreation
- good deeds
- collections

Help them to set priorities, and choose one or two or three of the areas where they want to set a goal.

TRY THIS #105

PLANNING SUCCESS BY GOAL SETTING

Using the attached Goal-Setting Model, have them record the chosen goal on it. Ask them to choose some specific things that each can do to help achieve the goal, and record these. As they discuss their goal and the plan for achieving it, watch for evidence that they are beginning to generate strategies on their own. Can they adjust the plan or goal as necessary? Can they use the strategies they have learned to achieve other goals in their lives?

TRY THIS #106

GOAL SETTING THROUGH PROBLEM SOLVING

Frequently we find ourselves, children and adults, having to set goals as a result of an emerging problem. In this case, we need to be able to guide our children through a problem-solving process. The following is a useful and fun model to use.

Problem Solving Model

Step 1: **Identify the problem and possible causes of the problem.**
Tip: *Be sure to seek out all potential causes and agree on the most serious cause before taking the next step, or you will be solving only a small part of the problem.*

Step 2: **Determine potential solutions**
Tip: *Brainstorming is effective here. Allow time to explore all possible solutions and consider for each whether it is a solution within your/their control.*

Step 3: **Select the best solution and one you all agree on.**

Step 4: **Create an action plan and follow it.**
Tip: *Address questions like, "who?" "how?" "when?" "what?"*

Step 5: **Evaluate the effectiveness of the solution.**
Tip: *Set a date to check on whether the solution worked or not, and whether further solutions are needed.*

Once children learn this problem-solving model,
it can become a critical tool to use throughout their lives.

"Keep away from people who try to belittle your ambitions.
Small people always do that, but the really great make you feel that you
too can become great."

Mark Twain

A Lesson We've Learned   27

**We must dream our dreams with them,
then pave the way for the dreams to come true.**

A MESSAGE OF LOVE FROM GRANNY

Dearest Cody:

You bring a smile to my face each and every time I see you. With your laughing eyes and bright smile, you warm my heart, and I thank you for being a part of my life.

When you were so very small, I looked upon your face and saw a kind of gentleness like your mother when she was small, and as you have grown I have watched you mirror your mother in so many of your ways. Always the gentle little one, your mother, you have taken that wonderful part of her and made it part of you. As I watch you, I remember the days when she was little, and see you in her.

The gentleness in your soul is so heartwarming. I want to be able to nurture that softness and gentleness in you, to ensure your life does not take that from you, and to be able to see you grow into a strong, capable and intelligent young man. I want to be able to provide every opportunity for you to do these things, to be able to take whatever path you may choose, and to be one of the people in your life who will make a difference.

I want to take your little hand and run through the grass and across the fields and hear you laugh and see you smile. I want to blow dandelions into the wind and talk about where they go and what they become. I want to encourage your love of animals, and of people, and to teach you that everyone has both good and bad in them, and it is important to look for some good in everyone in this world.

I want you to learn to trust your instincts, and be brave about your convictions. The world is here for you to enjoy and embrace, and I want to hold your hand as you gently try to become an adult. I want you to have fun.

I want to be able to help you decide your life's dream, to help you to make that dream come true, and to be someone in your life you can come to for help and wisdom and, most of all, unconditional love.

My arms held you so many times when you were little and very colicky, and somehow or other, the quietness of my heart and the love of my soul would calm your fears. Please know that the quietness and calmness will be there for you forever, and I want to be a part of your life forever.

I love you very much, Cody.

> *Granny*
> *(Wendy Graham)*

Janet's Postscript

My husband Michael and I were having our usual Sunday brunch together shortly after I had completed the first goal-setting lesson.

Michael is a very insightful person. We were discussing how we might help our grandkids through this kind of strategy, when Michael made a critical comment. He suggested that perhaps we needed to be setting goals for ourselves as well, with respect to how we cherish our "grand" ones so that "our dreams for them come true." If our dreams are carefully planned and successful, theirs will be, too.

Wendy's letter to her second-born grandson provided the perfect story thread for Michael's insight. To quote Wendy, "I want to be able to help you decide your life's dream, to help you to make that dream come true and to be someone in your life you can come to for help and wisdom . . ."

The following strategies may provide you with guidelines to help you make your plan.

"In youth we learn; in age we understand."

Marie von Ebner-Eschenbach

TRY THIS #107

THEIR DREAMS, OUR DREAMS

Consider age categories and what your dreams might look like with respect to their lifelong success. Add your own values and priorities.

Ages 0 – 5
- building your bond
- considering pre-school activities
- building book collections
- giving gifts which are educational
- beginning college funds
- beginning recreational activities
- establishing your communication plan with them
- celebrating progress

Snapshots

1998
Santa's
Anonymous
Fashion Show

Janet with her
granddaughter
Natasha,
who dreams of
being a model

TRY THIS #108

OPENING DOORS

Ages 6 – 10

- exploring special skills and interests
- teaching them goal-setting skills
- talking with them about career opportunities
- furthering all activities developed in the 0–5 age range
- "talking while being" with them (Chapter 1)
- exploring values (Chapter 2)
- nurturing their self-esteem (Chapter 3)
- supporting their school learning (see Chapter 5)
- celebrating progress along the way

TRY THIS #109

SUPPORTING TEENS

Ages 11 – 18

"Yikes!" Rory is only 13, but I'll give it a whirl. These are the most difficult years for kids and their parents. We could make a big contribution here!

- listening
- listening
- listening
- active listening
- just being there
- reading the latest books on teens
- helping their parents by explaining their teen's viewpoints to them
- being a middleman
- providing time out for everyone
- continuing activities developed in the 6 – 10 age range
- listening
- listening
- listening and *not* withdrawing approval

TRY THIS #110

STAYING CONNECTED

Ages 19+

- listening as in age range 11 to 18
- providing career path guidance
- being more of a friend than a caregiver
- sharing your wisdom as wanted and/or needed
- gently guiding
- being another ear
- loving unconditionally
- passing on family heritage, history
- celebrating their achievements
- celebrating their lives
- celebrating them
- celebrating family
- welcoming their own families and the next generation

SUMMARY

As you make your plan for your dreams for them, remember to:

- keep your plan "in synch" with plans their parents are making, and engage parents as partners throughout
- make the goals achievable
- learn from mistakes and overcome obstacles
- develop implementation plans, including initiating, organizing, completing and evaluating progress
- celebrate small and big successes along the way!

A Lesson We've Learned 28

Self-esteem blossoms when we are clear on our belief system, learn new skills and are supported by those around us.

A LETTER TO A GRANNY IN WALES

My first grandchild, a grandson, was born prematurely, just as my daughter and son-in-law were moving house. In this letter, the baby "tells" his other grandmother, who lives in Wales, about his homecoming.

Ruth Chudley

Dear Grandma Dolly,

Today I am five days old, so I asked my Grandma Ruth to write to you all about me and the exciting time everyone is having because of me, especially because I gave everyone quite a surprise by arriving a few weeks early.

My mom just stayed quietly in the hospital and looked after me, but my dad and my grandma were in a flat spin for a few days trying to do their regular jobs, becoming acquainted with me, and trying to sort out the new house, which was all higgledy-piggledy, I can tell you. They tried to distract me by putting the lovely flowers that Mom and Dad's friends had given them, here and there around the house, but I could see that there was furniture all over the place, and books and laundry. I could not even go into my own little room, except to have my diaper changed.

The new carpet they had put down especially for me looks really nice, so I am a very lucky boy to have such a nice home.

The first night I was at home, I slept in the laundry basket. What do you think of that? It was okay because I didn't sleep much. It was so quiet around here. I was used to a lot of babies in the nursery, all of us crying at one time or another. Dad was really tired when he went to work the next day. Mom was tired, too. I slept all morning and felt fine.

Grandma was out around the town early doing errands, buying me things like nighties and Vaseline and some small, small diapers. She had made some out of a flannelette sheet to do me over the night. They had blue stripes on them but nobody cared about that.

I guess Dad has been telling you over the phone what I look like – a dear little face, dark eyes, lot of dark hair (straight as a straight stick), and, for my small size, big hands with long fingers, and feet that are long and skinny. In other words, I am just perfect!

Dad and Mom and Grandma love me and cuddle me, so life is just wonderful for all of us. I wish you were here, too, to cuddle me, but I know you are thinking about it and loving me from way over in Wales.

I'm sending you my love, and Grandma Ruth sends you her congratulations because you both have me for a grandson.

Janet's Postscript

This premature baby already has his support team established around him – one grandma writing to another who is out of the country.

I hear so many stories of grandparents in competition with others in the other part of the extended family. There is such richness, however, when various family members can come together to celebrate grandchildren and family. We have started to invite Tasha and Rory's other grandpa, aunt and uncle to our house for Christmas dinner and the grandkids' birthdays, and it has worked very well. The grandkids love it – so many cuddles, so much laughter, so much love as they bounce from one to the other's laps for hugs.

Each of us has something different to offer and they know it. What a family support system we are, all in one room. One of the best parts of it all is watching the cousins build their relationships, and family events such as the one described are one of the special ways they connect – another support group as they grow up.

"Today, see if you can stretch your heart and expand your love so that it touches not only those to whom you can give it easily, but also to those who need it so much."

Daphne Rose Kingma

BUILDING POSITIVE FAMILY FEELINGS

These activities are great ideas for family fun during extended family get-togethers.

TRY THIS #111

GETTING TO KNOW YOU BETTER

Pair family members so that two people from families who don't live together can interview each other.

Give them a topic to discuss that will help them to get to know each other.

- a favourite pet
- a favourite relative
- an accident
- a hobby
- a goal they are setting
- their best day
- their job or their school
- favourite TV show and why
- most important value

This can be done before or after dinner, or even at the table before dessert. It will only take a few minutes. Ask each person to share something new they learned about the other person.

TRY THIS #112

YOU'RE A GREAT FAMILY!

Distribute a recipe card or paper plate and pen to each person. Each person writes his or her name on it at the top of the card, or centre of the plate, then the cards or plates are circulated throughout the group Each person writes a positive comment about the person named. At the end of the event, each person goes home with a keepsake to remember.

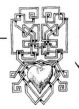

TRY THIS #113

DEVELOP A FAMILY SLOGAN

In old England it was common for a family to have a coat of arms, a flag and a slogan. In his book "The Seven Habits of Effective Families", Steven Covey promotes this same strategy as a way of giving the family a philosophical base for family problem-solving and planning.

- have family members brainstorm words that might describe this family to the rest of the world
- if the family group is large, you might choose to split them into groups for this activity
- in smaller groups, ask each group to use the brainstormed words to create a slogan they could use if they were advertising the family
- share the slogans
- discuss which one is best and why
- choose one
- have it professionally designed to be hung in each household

Snapshots

Liam
born 1996

TRY THIS #114

DEVELOP A FAMILY COAT OF ARMS

Pair family members so that an older family member works with a younger one.

Ask each member to create their own coat of arms, using the attached form.

- in Section 1, each person puts something they do very well
- in Section 2, each person puts something about themselves that other family members might not know
- in Section 3 they put how they spend their spare time
- in Section 4, something they want to learn, and
- in Section 5, a drawing of how they see their family

Share the various Coats of Arms.

Try developing a Family Coat of Arms that all could agree on.

TRY THIS #115

A FAMILY CHAIN LETTER

Years back, chainletters were considered to be illegal operations since money was often a key ingredient. Why not take this old idea and start a chain letter to gather family views on history?

The initiator of the letter would make:
- a list of family members who will be invited to participate, and their mailing address
- a list of questions to be asked and a form for each family member to complete. Questions may include topics such as history, hobbies, personal characteristics, travel experiences, education, feelings, perceptions on recent news events, goals, favourite books and magazines, recipes or any combination of the above; invite them to include photos as well.

Include instructions for each person receiving the package to complete the forms, and mail them to the next person on the list.

29

A Lesson We've Learned

LONG-DISTANCE GRANDPARENTS
"There are only two lasting things we can hope to give to our children. One of these is roots; the other, wings."
Hodding Carter

EXCERPTS FROM A GRANDMOTHER'S LETTER TO HER GROWN GRANDCHILDREN

Story #1

Dear Glen:

One day, a year or so ago, my doorbell rang in the late afternoon. I opened the door to find a smiling young man in suit and tie, briefcase in hand; before I could tell him I didn't want to subscribe to any magazines...I realized it was you, Glen, and I was speechless. I had never before seen you in business garb, and it was a bit of a shock! You come from a sport-loving family, and your wardrobe has always consisted mainly of track suits and sweatshirts. From the time you could tie on your skates, or hold a bat, you were involved in community sports. Seeing you that afternoon, I realized how quickly the years slip by, and how far you have come.

Story #2

Dear Brent:

And now, last on the list...but only because you were last-born!...is Brent.
What confusion and consternation you caused when your birth date was a few weeks away. You had your mother in hospital in Victoria for a month prior to your arrival; you signalled,
"All hands on deck...I'm on my way!"...which caused your Dad to cut curves and corners all the way from Port Alberni and arrive in no shape to coach a birth...only to find you

had changed your mind! Your Mom and I decided you really needed a Dad, so there was no way we were going to have him making another trip flying at low level...and we decided not to tell him until you were here. And that's how I happened to be there for your introduction to the world. And that's why you have always been my special lad...I was there!

❧ Story #3 ❧

Dear Michael:

Michael, you came into our lives as a four-year-old, blond, blue-eyed bonus when Bob and your mother were married, and our relationship has always been a long-distance one. With your home in Montreal or Toronto, our yearly visits kept us in touch, but we missed your growing-up years. That saddened me; but we have come to know and love each other in your adult years. When I spoke at your wedding reception a few years ago, I earned spontaneous applause when I referred to you as a "unique young man"...for that is what you are. The lovely thing about having six grandsons is, if the gods are with you, you will eventually have six lovely new granddaughters...without the complications and terrors of seeing them through their teenage years!

Story #4

Dear Chris:

In March of 1993 I sat in the auditorium of the RCMP barracks and watched, with my heart swelling with love and pride, the graduation ceremonies of a group of fine-looking young men and women. They had completed the months of grueling training and came out winners. In their dress uniforms, complete with red coats, they were a picture I'll never forget. Among them...a head taller than most, was Chris. Your whole family was there...parents, sister, and two set of grandparents; though one grandfather was not present in body, I knew he was not missing this party...he would have been so proud of you, Chris, and I was proud for both of us.

Story #5

Dear Marianne:

We have a granddaughter! And oh! how welcome you were, Marianne...It was fun to think in terms of pink and frilly dresses, instead of track suits and overalls; but that phase was short-lived. You established your independence before you were three, and have maintained it ever since! You were sweet and sassy...lively and full of giggles...with a sense of humour that kept your Dad on his toes, and your Grandfather wound around your little finger. From grade school through university, you have set lofty goals for yourself and achieved them. When you decided it was time to look to the future, Darren didn't have a chance! A year or so later you were married, and East-met-West in a great family gathering in Ottawa.

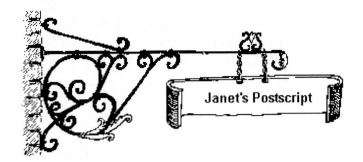

Janet's Postscript

My mother has been such an incredible mother, grandmother and matriarch for our extended family.

She's amazing and she lives this lesson. She has given all of us roots. Together with my father, who passed on ten years ago, she has, through love and support, created a richly textured family mosaic. Her seven grandchildren are thriving, and the source of our family's health and success can only be attributed to their parenting, which in turn we have passed on to our children and now their children as well as, of course, the life partners we have married along the way.

She maintains close connections with her four kids, their seven kids and now four great-grandchildren spread from Vancouver Island to Toronto.

What is so special about Mom?
- She encourages each of us when we dare to dream. She knows we can do what we set our minds to.
- She always gives us as much time as we need.
- We can trust her with our deepest secrets, our wildest dreams and our tears – she doesn't judge.
- She supports each of us. They say that if you look into the lives of heroes, our role models, you will find an important support person, someone who cares, understands, believes in them and, above all, supports them.

That's my mom and that's my dad, too . . .and we can be that for our children and grandchildren through our love, support, and connections.

*"It is as grandmothers that our mothers come
into the fullness of their grace."*
Christopher Morley

Once again the letters and reflections in this section lead us to consider the significance of time with and for our grandchildren, through which we have an opportunity to support them. The following strategies are designed to enhance communication with young people. We are proposing that when families come together for a dinner or celebration, that ½ hour be aside at the beginning or end for a focussed time to share. In the speed of the last few decades, we seem to have lost the ability to stop in our family groups and to listen to, and learn from, each other. Do we really know each other? These proposed activities could be a start.

TRY THIS #116

FAMILY ROOTS

Collect a variety of photos from the family – any age, any stage of life, including some of family members in the present.

At the next gathering, display the photos and take turns identifying/sharing the following information about family members:

- careers and career changes
- role models and why you would choose them
- challenges faced
- proud accomplishments
- hobbies/interests
- connections between young and old
- similarities and differences

Conclude by listing words or characteristics that would describe your family overall.

"If your baby is "beautiful and perfect, never cries or fusses, sleeps on schedule and burps on demand, an angel all the time..."
you're the grandma."

Teresa Bloomingdale

TRY THIS #117

THEIR SUPPORT NETWORKS

The purpose of this exercise is to understand the support networks that could be available for the child, with a focus on family and other friends.

1. Brainstorm the meaning of the word "support." (Might include: love, acceptance, assistance, information, friendship, protection, advice.) Depending how young your grandchild is, you might need to coach and teach. Make a list on paper.

2. Brainstorm feelings we have when we feel supported (might include positive, valued, appreciated, understood, trusted, less vulnerable, safe).

3. Brainstorm our different people who can be called on for support (might include parents, guardians, siblings, friends, schoolmates). Make a list on paper and be sure to include names of family members.

TRY THIS #118

SUCCESS IS...

Share with each other what the meaning of success is:
*   share all the things you are successful at
*   add to each other's lists in case you've been shy
*   make a list of people you know who are successful
*   make a list of adjectives that describe successful people
*   describe what your life will be like if you have a successful future
*   choose an area where you want to be more successful. Set your goals. Be sure to include a start date, an implementation plan, a time to evaluate progress
*   check in frequently to cheer on your partner's progress

TRY THIS #119

I TRUST YOU, YOU TRUST ME

Do a trust walk – it can be at home, in a park, be sure it's somewhere safe.

We recommend Grandma or Grandpa go first. If the children are young, it would be advisable for both grandparents to be present, with one acting as observer for safety's sake.

The leader takes the blindfolded one on a trust walk. The two hold hands during the walk. The leader could take them:

- to things that smell
- to things that have texture
- to touch shapes of things
- to hear things

The blindfolded person guesses what they are experiencing. After 4 or 5 minutes they reverse roles, take a different route and repeat the process.

After, discuss:

- how did you feel when blindfolded?
- did you trust the leader? Why?
- what did you need when you were blindfolded?

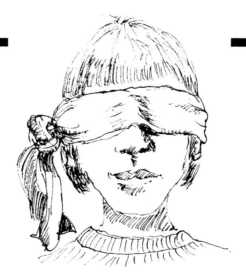

"One touch is worth ten thousand words."

Harold Bloomfield

A Lesson We've Learned 30

FOLLOW YOUR BLISS
Over the years our strong and deeply felt love and encouragement can help them find hope and purpose forever.

A LETTER FROM A 26 YEAR-OLD GRANDDAUGHTER

Dear Don (Prentice):

I thought I would write you a real letter, as opposed to an e-mail. However, I do think it would be fun to send e-mails to each other, too, now that I have my own e-mail account. Don, let me tell you, I am in serious trouble now that I have access to the Internet . . . .

. . . .I'll be the next to sign up for IAA – Internet Addicts Anonymous. I am just the type to get hooked on the "Web"! My Dad has already given me a warning as to how much my new hobby is costing him per hour! Oops! Well, I say, I *have* to write to Joelle in Australia, Dad!

So how are things in the beautiful West? My Dad had a great time, and has the pictures to show it! I'm sure he will send you them via e-mail. I have been missing my wonderful Stuie lately, as it was about a year ago that he left us. I often think about what you would say to make me feel better, as you have always been the one to do that. When I think about school and the uncertainties I see in front of me as I "follow my dream," I try to remember what you told me: "Follow Your Bliss," even though, at times, it is the most difficult thing to keep in perspective.

Even though we are miles apart, I want you to know that your love and encouragement that I feel so strongly and deeply, helps me in so many ways. I feel very closely connected to you now, as I always have, and as I know I always will, no matter the distance. I think of you all the time, and of all the "words of wisdom" you have shared with me over the years. You are the one who has *always* been able to see the hope and purpose in everything. That has always meant a great deal to me – I hope that I am learning to see life that way. I miss you and hope to see you soon!

Love always,
Kelly (Prentice)

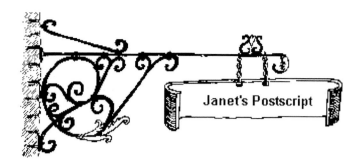

Janet's Postscript

Early in this chapter we read letters from Don to his great-grandchildren. Don (kind of shyly) shared this letter from Kelly. The words in "this lesson we've learned" are direct quotes from Kelly's letter. This is a young woman whose grandfather is "the one who helps me feel better," who advises her to follow your bliss, whose "love and encouragement that I feel so strongly and deeply, helps me in so many ways." She then describes how "closely connected" she feels now and always, and how many "words of wisdom" have helped her "see the hope and purpose in everything." All of this in spite of the great distance between them.

So, what is the importance of Kelly's letter, and how is it relevant and can it be replicated? We need only to go back to Chapter 1, Lessons We've Learned #1 and think about what Dr. Gordon Neufeld has to say about attachments and connections and the critical role they play for today's youth.

A Vancouver *Sun* article headlined "Children Lost Among Their Peers," written by Karen Gram, makes the point eloquently.

The Introduction to the article uses a Kindergarten dismissal to bring it home.

Snapshots

CHILDREN LOST AMONG THEIR PEERS
by Karen Gram, Vancouver *Sun, (reprinted by permission)*

Inside the kindergarten classroom of an elementary school, the children gather at the door, ready to go home. Some quietly wait for the teacher to dismiss them. They wave to parents from the threshold and hold up artwork, eager to show what they have made.

Others ignore the adults. They play and push each other into the hall. They chase each other in circles, oblivious to admonishments of teacher and parents.

The second group perfectly demonstrates the early stages of what a Vancouver-based clinical and developmental psychologist fears is a trend destroying the psychological health of an ever-growing number of people. Dr. Gordon Neufeld calls it peer-orientation. It is rampant among juvenile delinquents, but is also evident in every school and on every playground.

He says the children in the first group above take their cues from adults. They are "adult-oriented" and are most closely attached to parents or other adults responsible for them. But those in the second group try to win attention and approval of peers – not parents. They are "peer-oriented."

He identifies signs of peer orientation:
- is your child emulating classmates, or one particular friend, to the exclusion of your own modeling?
- is your child bored when not with peers?
- is your child no longer seeking closeness and approval from you?
- is your child constantly demanding to be with friends?
- is school work deteriorating?
- are behavioural problems increasing?

He described "What Parents Can Do."

***We submit that grandparents can fulfill the same role
in support of the children's parents.***

What parents and grandparents can do:

- Make the relationship between you and your grandchildren sacred – not dependent on achievement or good behaviour. Make sure they can trust you.

- Have faith that your grandchildren will learn proper behaviour as they develop. They don't need lessons; they need nurturing and security.

- Woo your grandchildren by providing closeness generously and spontaneously before it is demanded, and without making the child work for it.

- Don't create attachment vacuums. In your absence, transfer your authority and connectiveness to the person substituting for you.

- Matchmake between your children and their teachers or care-givers. Tell the teacher all the nice things your child says about her and viceversa. Help them develop a good relationship.

- Limit your children's time with peers. Provide lots of family fun.

That's what this book is all about.
A passion for our grandchildren.
Our families need us now.

They need:
- trust and nurturing
  - security
  - closeness
  - connectiveness
  - family fun
- a sacred relationship

Snapshots

"They may not need me, but they might,
I'll let my head be just in sight.
A smile as small as mine may be
Precisely their necessity."

Emily Dickinson

TRY THIS #120

"I LIKE ME BECAUSE..."

The objective here is to explore our views of ourselves in an enjoyable and positive manner. Start with yourself to role-model the process with your grandchild.

Before you start, you might want to make a list of categories that will prompt ideas.

Since self-esteem is ownership of a viewpoint, no contradictions are permitted, but each of you can add your viewpoint to the other's list at the end.

Categories to consider:
- schoolwork
- crafts
- games
- relationships
- family

TRY THIS #121

"WE KNOW EACH OTHER, DON'T WE?"

Divide the family into groups of two.
This will work even if there are only two of you.

Make a list of categories:
- jobs
- school
- childhood
- hobbies
- friends
- babyhood
- family
- something funny

Take turns picking a topic. When you pick the topic, the other person has to tell what they know about you. When they finish, you add two more things (they didn't mention) which are important to you.

TRY THIS #122

"I'M REALLY OKAY"

Both of you think about three stages in your lives. For a grandchild it could be:

- Before I could walk…
- Before I went to school…
- After I started school…

Yours could be the same or different.

- The objective of the exercise is to reinforce self-esteem and to practise empathic listening.
- Recall something from each stage that you did or that happened to you of which you are proud.
- Each of you express three things.
- The other person then describes what the speaker meant (not said) and adds a compliment, giving praise to the speaker on their accomplishments. Record these in your journal or on sticky notes for the fridge door.
- Discuss how comfortable you were with praising yourself.
- How did it feel to be an empathic listener?

TRY THIS #123

HELPING THEM MAKE POSITIVE CHANGES

When you want a child to change their behaviour, help them view themselves differently by:
- looking for opportunities to show the child a new picture of self
- put the child in a situation where he/she can see themselves differently
- let the child overhear you say something positive about him/her
- model the behaviour you'd like to see
- be a storehouse for the child's finest moments
- when he or she behaves according to the old label, state your feelings and expectations.

Source: *"How To Talk So Kids Will Listen and Listen So Kids Will Talk"*

"I Am Lovable": Nurturing Their Self-Esteem

CONCLUSION: "The Proof is in the Pudding", as Grandma used to say

We chose the words "I am lovable" as the sub-title for this chapter on self-esteem as the simplest definition of what self-esteem is all about.

A quick review of the interviews we held demonstrates the power of the feelings grandparents have left behind:

- "how sweet they treat me"
- "they call me just about every Sunday"
- "she writes me long letters about four times a month"
- "my Granny was so excited when I was born she rushed out the door to the ferry and left the door open!"
- "the kind of guy who would dig up his garden just to find me fishing bait"
- "being with them was a whole different world"
- "she is always telling me what a good job I am doing"
- "she makes me feel good about myself"
- "as long as I held his hand nothing could hurt me"
- "we would play Monopoly all weekend so we could sit and talk"
- "he was always doing stuff with us"
- "he'd say, "this little kid is going to be smart!""
- "she loved to do things with me"
- "she always looked out for my best interests"
- "she would let my sister and I cut her long white hair as we played hairdresser, as long as it could still go in a french roll so no one would know"

In the hundreds of pages of stories and interviews, the recurring theme is one of feeling special and feeling loved. My favorite quote is **"Grandparents love us as we love our teddys"** by Melissa at Lakehill School. Says it all doesn't it? No matter how we accomplish it, each in our own way, this feeling is the best legacy we can leave them.

A Reminder:

Seven Ways to Nurture Self-Esteem in Others

Appreciating everyone's wroth and acting responsibly toward one another are important components of self-esteem. Here are some ways we can foster self-esteem in others:

1. **Give Personal Attention.** To provide this, we need to learn to listen respectfully.

2. **Demonstrate Respect, Acceptance and Support.** Human beings need to be treated with respect from the first moment of their lives.

3. **Encourage Healthy Achievement.** Living with expectations creates meaning in people's lives.

4. **Provide a Sensible Structure.** To explore and grow, human beings need limits, guidance, and rules that are enforced consistently and fairly.

5. **Appreciate the benefits of a multi-cultural society.** Diversity is a source of strength.

6. **Negotiate Conflicts.** It is never appropriate to inflict injury, shame or humiliation on another human being.

7. **Encourage Autonomy and Competence.** We act responsibly when we encourage people to grow beyond dependence; to struggle – and succeed in order to develop a sense of competence.

New Woman, March 1991

 **Snapshots**

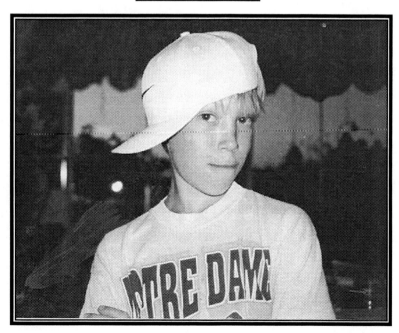

Chapter 4

Unconditional Love

Unconditional Love

Introduction: A JOY THAT BRINGS PEACE TO THE SOUL

Unconditional love – we all want it for ourselves, we all want to give it to others. We all know what it feels like, but what is it? How would we describe it?

In pursuit of creating a definition of it, we found that each person we interviewed had his or her own unique way of describing it. The following are some of the definitions presented:

- without any personal motive
- giving love for the sake of giving it
- expecting nothing in return
- tolerance, freedom for the recipient to be what they are
- not having to make themselves into anything to get approval
- love that's always there and they know it
- love that exists, that does not depend on being returned
- "I love you just because you are you"
- you can't take it back, you can't take it away
- it's non-negotiable
- loving them the same way all the time
- even when you don't like the things they do, you let them know you love them
- always being there for them, always listening, always being available
- a joy that brings peace to the soul

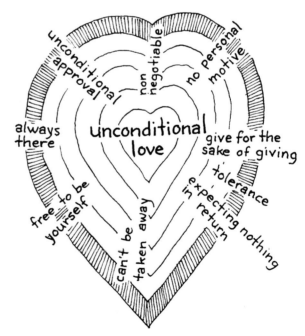

My favourite metaphor was one expressed by Michael, my husband. He said, "It's a cashier's cheque and you can spend it anytime you need it." I like the notion of prepaid, money in the bank, a guarantee.

So how do we provide it, display it, make sure they know it without relying on material things, without "spoiling them"? How do we make it real?

That's what this chapter is all about. While we celebrate the joy of our unconditional love, both the giving and the getting of it, we can use it as the basis for continuing the work of the first three chapters:

1. Making Memories: Being and Doing Together;
2. Building Family Values Through Treasures and Traditions – Celebrating Old Ones and Creating New Ones; and
3. Nurturing Self-Esteem Through Values.

Celebrate your unconditional love and the joy in your hearts. You'll know you have it when you feel the peace in your soul.

Snapshots

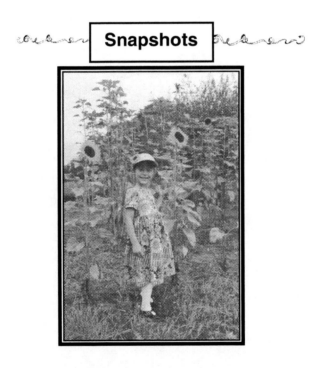

"There is no vocabulary for the love within a family,
love that's lived in but not looked at, love within the light of which
all else is seen, the love within which all other love finds speech,
this love is silent."

T.S. Eliot

A Lesson We've Learned 31

Unconditional loving is the best feeling in the world, the deepest form of joy.

s

...AND THEY KNOW IT!

Our love for our grandchildren is unconditional and they know it! When I first learned on January 3, 1995 that we were going to become first-time grandparents in August, I wondered what I could do to make a difference in my grandbaby's life. I remembered from my own life, and the joy I felt when a story was related to me of my own childhood. With that in mind, and because we live in close proximity to our children, I decided to write a journal for this Little Stranger. I obtained a hard-covered, lined, 8 ½ " x 11" book from the local stationery store and began.

Our son Craig and his wife, Christine, came to see me at work to tell me the exciting news of our grandbaby's beginnings. From then on, I wrote to Our Little Stranger when I had something to share – a family event, Chris's doctor visits, who comprised our family, what we all felt as the "big event" moved closer, etc. The Journal follows the birth process right up to that exciting day, August 3, 1995, when our Kayleigh was born.

On August 4, 1997, Kayleigh was blessed with a baby brother, Ian, who also has his own separate Journal. As it is with most siblings, they are as opposite in nature as they could possibly be, and their bonding processes are now duly noted and recorded in each of their books.

After three and a half years, Kayleigh's Journal now occupies one and half books, and Ian's one book is nearly half filled. Both Ian and Kayleigh have amused, cajoled, entertained and tickled our heart strings. I have recorded these events in their books as they have happened, intertwining them with stories from my childhood or stories about their daddy's antics when he was their age.

These Journals also serve as a record of family traditions and histories, world events, special holiday events and the people who have been in our grandbabies' world to this point.

In addition to Ian and Kayleigh's written Journals, I have taken hundreds of photographs, which serve as pictorial recordings of their lives. The stories recorded in the Journals match up with the photographs in their private albums. A highlight of a visit to Grandma and Grandpa's home is to jump up on our laps and listen intently to stories told to them from the photographs displayed.

I feel very blessed to have this opportunity of recording the lives of our grandbabies for their future use and pleasure. These Journals will be presented to each of them later in their lives – maybe on graduation nights or on the eve of their weddings. I trust they will serve as a record to show them how much they were loved as children and will add much to their self-image and esteem, as well as their sense of belonging.

Grandma Gwen Thomson

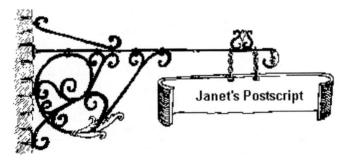

Janet's Postscript

Gwen was a secretary at one of the schools where I was working. In a quiet coffee moment, we discovered we were both grandmothers. Each time I visited, we shared a little more and one day Gwen told me about her journal for her "grandbaby" begun even before Kayleigh was born. When I started this book, I asked her to describe it in more detail.

What an amazing gift of time she is giving, and how valuable that gift is and will be as Kayleigh and Ian are continually reinforced by the loving visits and storytelling in the laps of grandparents with their very own photo albums.

Gwen doesn't mention what the experience feels like to her, but I could tell by the sparkle in her eyes and the love in her voice that she has found "the deepest form of joy."

"What feeling is so nice as a child's hand in yours? So small, so soft and warm, like a kitten huddling in the shelter of your clasp."

Marjorie Holmes

TRY THIS #124

FACE PAINTING PREPARATION

Over my many years of working with kids and staging events for them, face painting has always been a guaranteed success. Just last week when Trevor and Tasha were over, we got out the face paints and had a ball. I'd never done it myself, but it was a snap. The best part was the "zone" that the kids got into as I worked on their face canvas. Their eyes got dreamy; I'm sure they could feel the love pouring out of the brush directly from my hand.

Tips:

- buy water-based paints specifically designed for face art (craft stores or theatre stores)
- do not use red near the eyes (not FDA approved)
- use cotton swabs or a paintbrush and small damp sponges
- books are available with sample patterns if you're shy about making up your own
- a mirror, of course, that's the best part!

Otherwise, just copy designs from any old book.

TRY THIS #125

BOOK SEARCH

Challenge the kids to find the image they want reproduced. Explore your collection of:

- kids' books
- encyclopedias
- garden books
- kids' videos
- magazines

They have to do their homework before you face paint. If they're old enough, have them draw the design they want with felt pens first, so you have a good idea of what they want.

TRY THIS #126

FACE PAINTING CLOWN FUN

Clowns are popular; after all, face painting originated there. Whiteface with a damp sponge over the entire face, and let it dry before continuing with other colours. Find clown faces in their story books for ideas.

Snapshots

Grandpa
Michael
and
Baby
Trevor
1995

"If I'd known grandchildren were going to be so much fun, I'd have had them first."

Anonymous

TRY THIS #127

BODY PAINTING BRAINSTORM

Trevor was a bit shy, being only three, so we did his arms instead of his face and we did Natasha's cheeks.

Ideas:

- seasonal themes
- TV show characters
- cultural themes
- weather signs
- toys
- tattoos
- dress-up makeup

- favourite book
- flowers
- animals (whole face)
- fruits
- balloons
- jewellery
- monsters

Don't forget other parts of the body:

- toes
- finger faces
- feet (socks and shoes)

- wrists
- knees

A few more hints:

- outline designs in a contrasting colour
- wipe off mistakes with Q-tips
- encourage grandkids to work on each other
- put sequins or glitter on wet paint or use eyelash adhesive (keep away from eyes)
- add costumes if you like to complete the fun
- take pictures, of course!

"Everybody should try to have a grandmother, especially if they don't have a television, because they are the only grown-ups who have time."

Source Unknown

A Lesson We've Learned

32

When someone over time shows they care about us, we feel a strong and lasting connection to them.

"NO WORDS NEEDED"

I think one of the things that I remember most with one of my grandfathers would be the long walks we took each day as I was growing up as a two-and three-year old. I didn't have a father figure at the time, he was my father figure. And that was probably one of the first times that I experienced the connection with another human being where you don't have to exchange words. There's just a sense of well-being and connectedness just by the look in their eyes or their gestures, the spontaneity, the playfulness and that sort of thing.

The week prior to his death we spent together and it was the same thing. There was no wishing that things had been different along the way. Not too many words had to be exchanged. It was as if our two souls were totally intertwined. Those last few days of his life, I knew what he was thinking and feeling. We didn't have to say anything. It was an incredible experience.

Michael Todd

Snapshots

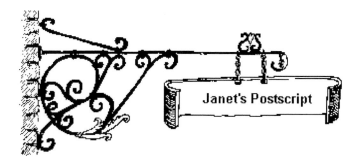

Janet's Postscript

Michael is our nephew and has lived his life in Toronto. For a while he lived with his grandparents; other years they were just around the corner, and he spent weekends and holidays at their summer place. His story rings of the connection built over time.

It reminds me of the connection I have seen between my dad and our sons Justin and Brad. When they were young the grandparents came for supper on Sunday nights. Supper was prefaced by screams and shrieks of delight as my dad played tag and hide-and-seek with our boys and any neighbourhood kids who were around.

Our house was surrounded by cliffs over the ocean, and I remember how we'd all roll our eyes as dad would spring out of a bush, run past the cliff edge and grab the closest unsuspecting child – and he was in his 70's. He was the most popular and fun grandpa around.

In his later years I saw the same connectedness that Michael Todd describes between dad and the boys. Brad, as an adult, would stop by and work in dad's garden with him, and we'd see that contended, quiet togetherness and connection.

Playing is a new way for me to be; just last week I tried to play soccer with Trevor – in high heels – and I have skinned knees and elbows as my trophy. I'm learning how to play with the grandkids like dad did. The results are very rewarding. Just like with dad, I'm finding the grandkids laugh hysterically as I join them in crazy play. I highly recommend it to you . . . it's a great excuse to be young again.

TRY THIS #128

KOOSH FOOTBALL

This is a great one for older kids and younger grandparents – it's just like playing catch, but you do it with the side of your foot, your knee, your toe or anything below the waist. Start by throwing the ball up in the air, then try to catch it on the way down with the side of your foot, knee, etc. I recommend you practice before you play with the grandkids because they're going to take to it like ducks to water!

Check out the Rosie O'Donnell show for her Koosh ball target practice. She uses a sling-shot to aim at a moving target. Why not make a slingshot like we did when we were kids – you only need the fork of a tree branch, and a large, heavy elastic. Set up tin cans and have a target practise competition.

TRY THIS #129

PLAYFUL KOOSH GAMES

Almost any of the old tried and true games that use balls can be adapted and become a great Koosh game.
- Basketball – same rules, use garbage cans for the baskets.
- Dodge the Ball – a Koosh ball instead of a bouncing ball.
- Racket Ball – catch and toss the ball with rackets.
- Volleyball – no catching or throwing, but try to get it in the other court.

There's a book on the market, "The Official Koosh Book" (listed in Appendix), if you really want to become an expert.

Or play variations of the above games with badminton birds (also light), or bean bags, sponges or….we leave it up to your imagination!

"The time to relax is when you don't have time for it."

Sidney Harris

TRY THIS #130

RELAY HYSTERIA

Relays can be so much fun even with only two people, although more is merrier! A few ideas:

- Balloon Relay: bouncing balloons in the air for a specified time span, then returning, without touching the ground (points for each successful trip)

- Spoon and Marble: using a variety of sizes of spoons, depending on age, to carry marbles a specified distance and back again for points. If more than two people are playing, marbles have to be transferred without falling – if a marble falls, the person starts over again.

- Simon Says: This time, the old standard child's game is adapted to focus on values and love; for example:
  - Name the three characteristics you admire most in your heroes, then take three steps forward.
  - Who in your family is your hero? then take two steps forward.
  - What kind act did you do for someone this week? then take ____ steps forward, and so on.

If the person can't answer, they take a step back. To make the game easier, you might want to brainstorm a list of key characteristics of heroes and favourite role models.

Other ideas? You make up the rules!

- bobbing for apples
- eggs on spoons
- balloons between the knees
- Wheelbarrow race
- Three-legged Race
- Sack race

Add interesting challenges such as what the person does when they reach the end, or add handicaps for older competitors to slow them down. The crazier the better!

TRY THIS #131

PLAYFUL TAG AND HIDING GAMES

Again, the rules don't matter as long as everyone is clear on them. We'll provide the concept, you create the rules. This leaves you free to tailor the rules specifically for the age levels and number of people participating.

Some ideas:

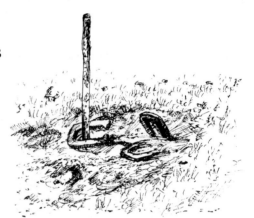

- ball tag with koosh balls, bean bags or tennis balls
- frozen tag
- Kick-The-Can
- paintball tag
- super water squirted tag
- break the balloon tag (everyone has a balloon)

Complicate any game of tag by changing body rules such as run backwards, one arms, one leg, hands behind back/over head, etc. Also, don't forget these favourite games:

- horseshoes
- badminton
- goofy golf
- checkers

- croquet
- jacks
- frisbee
- marbles

Create innovative rules for them, too!

"It's more than the shoes, the racquet or bike
It's more than your swing, the fish, or the hike
It's more than the skis, the skates, or the snow
It's ignoring the work and deciding to go."

Kristen Sheldon

A Lesson We've Learned 33

The Greatest Love of all Lies Inside of Me.

SPOTLIGHT ON SPECIALNESS

We had a long wall in our kitchen that needed some kind of decoration but was long and on a narrow side of the room. We tried a couple of large pictures and the usual things you would do with a kitchen wall, but none of it seemed to work. It occurred to us that it would be a good place to honour our family and our family members, and a small thing grew into something very big.

We painted the wall pink, a very soft pink which matched the wallpaper on the other sides of the room. We purchased a number of brass frames – the emphasis here is on all the frames being made of the same material so that there is an automatic connection between the frames – and then we set about to do blowups of any pictures that were particularly inspiring of any and all of our grandchildren. Sometimes the photo was of the grandchild with a significant adult – great-grandma, grandparent, parent – and sometimes the photo was of the child themselves. We did not focus on trying to get a balance of pictures or types of pictures; rather, each time a roll of film came back if there was one that was particularly captivating, in other words, catching a glimpse of their soul and their being, we had that particular photo enlarged.

In our choice of frames, although they were all brass they were all different shapes and proportions. A particular one was heart-shaped, of Natasha with her father during his cancer. Others were brass with a bit of wood or other adornment.

We enhanced the wall by using ribbon which we curled on scissors. We used a variety of colours, including pink, red, gold and silver, and attached these ribbons to the picture hanger mounted into the wall. Some of the ribbons hang down below the picture, some of them come up over the top and are short and curly. We made approximately 20 to 30 clowns which were only two inches tall from the clay bake (page 44). These were baked in the oven with little hangers coming out of their heads, and we tied each clown to one of the ribbons on each of the pictures so that they hung down below the pictures as well.

Overall, this has became a celebration wall. It is a focal point for visitors who come to the house and to see the children who are prominent in our lives. These pictures also display our relationship with them through the photographs; but, more specially, these are a statement to our grandchildren of the priority they hold in our lives. I don't remember where I read it, but I read several years ago that one of the ways to express to children your valuing of them is to display their pictures in prominent places. In our house, the kitchen is the most prominent place.

This is not a static display. Once the wall was full (up to 25 pictures from two feet from the floor to a foot from the ceiling), we began to substitute new pictures for old, although some of the pictures have been there throughout the life of the wall.

Many times my husband and I simply stand in the kitchen and talk about the different pictures and the qualities of members of our family that are displayed there. Often during family dinners I'll find one of them all alone quietly viewing these special photos...a great esteem booster!

"Becoming a grandparent is a second chance.
For you have a chance to put to use all the things you learned the first time
around and may have made mistakes on."

Dr. Joyce Brothers

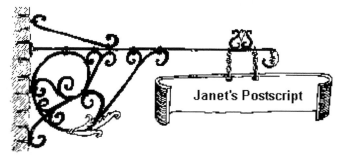

Janet's Postscript

Somewhere in our career and education training, we primary teachers learned that displaying work and pictures of young children is a stepping-stone to the development of self-esteem. In Kindergarten and Grade One, children are encouraged to draw self-portraits with sentence stems such as: I am…, I can…, I will…., all in an effort to support their evolving sense of self.

The photos that Michael and I choose to display are all about love. It's either shining from their eyes, evident in their body posture in solo photos, or demonstrated in the connection between the two people in the photo.

Our wall of specialness just grows and grows. Taking one down is difficult!

We love our grandchildren, we're proud of them, and we want them to know they're worthy of our love. We want them to know and love themselves. It's a crucial ingredient in the process of learning how to love others unconditionally.

TRY THIS #132

A MORE ORDERLY DISPLAY

Visit your local "finished wood" store and explore the varieties of molding they display. Our ribbons, clowns and photo display is getting kind of tired, and we'll try this idea soon as an alternative.

Choose a long piece of molding that can be attached to the wall horizontally. The idea is to lean photos against the wall with bottoms of the frames resting on the molding. Choose one that has a bit of a lip so the photos can't fall off.

You can paint the molding the colour of the wall, or a bright colour of other accessories in the kitchen or stain and varnish it.

This strategy provides you with the opportunity to move and rearrange pictures effortlessly. It is also a more tidy display.

TRY THIS #133

SO MANY WAYS TO SAY THEY'RE SPECIAL!

During my educational research years, I came across some significant research about the emotional impact of displaying children's photographs in quantity, quality and in meaningful places in the home. It has a very positive impact on their self-esteem and their sense of being loved and valued.

More ways to show they're special?

- Choose a time of year and place where the family is most likely to be together (Christmas, summer cottage, etc.) Take group or individual photos of whoever is present, then hang the photos in a row on a long wall to track family changes.
- Make an album of the grandkids about their parents growing up. Leave a place for the grandchild's photo to be inserted so "looks" can be compared.
- Put photos under a glass coffee table top
- Laminate photos onto coasters or placemats (either one photo per placemat, or try a collage)
- Make CDs of collections of photos rather than albums (local photo shops can do this now)
- Put photos on T-shirts
- Hang a colourful clothesline along a wall with decorated clothespins which hold up photos. The photos can be photocopy colour blowups (8 ½" X 11") for only 99 cents and can be changed frequently.

If you live far away, make a video of yourself giving advice you would give if you were closer, or teaching them a new skill. For example, for older kids, you could talk about careers, makeup, cooking, drugs and alcohol, dating, driving, golf or other sports; for younger kids, try subjects like gardening, painting, skills from Chapter 5, riddle and jokes, any activities in this book, projects underway, a series of questions for them to answer and return, a video of songs to play at bedtime.

I saw this done on the Oprah show by a mother who was dying. It was very beautiful and light and loving.

TRY THIS #134

YOUR LOCAL PHOTO PLACE

Most photo supply shops have a colour copier. Call around to find the closest one. These machines are able to do many interesting things.

- They can produce large and extra-large blowups of any photo for as low as 99¢.
- The blow-ups can be mounted onto cardboard for inexpensive displays.
- Many can use 12 normal photos and turn them into a full-size calendar with photos organized seasonally.

TRY THIS #135

FRIDGE FUN

We are all familiar with fridge magnets and displays, but the Smith family has taken that one step further. Their fridge is one massive collage of family. The entire side of the fridge is a mass of photos of family celebrations that spread over decades and which includes the birth of three new grandchildren – four generations on one fridge wall!

They have increased the number of photos by cutting out the part of each photo they want to display, and overlapped others. We recommend mounting a cardboard backing on the fridge, then using a quick-dry glue to attach the photo pieces.

Take a walk through your house, scouting for likely or unlikely places for your display. Be creative!

A Lesson We've Learned 34

We need to listen as they "ramble on and search for answers."

"THANK YOU FOR YOUR LOVING" LETTER

The initial letter Kelly wrote to her Grandfather, Don, can be found in Chapter 3, Lesson 30. When I asked Don for permission to publish Kelly's letter, he sent her an e-mail. Her reply revealed even more about the depth and importance of their relationship – a model for all of us:

Thank you so much for your wonderful letter via e-mail. It came at the perfect time, just as I remember all of your talks and letters always coming during the times I needed them most. While I do love to send and receive "real" letters, I have to admit that the convenience of this modern technology is quite handy, not to mention addictive! It is always so great to hear from you, no matter the method of communication.

As I think I told you in my letter, I feel and have always felt that we do communicate with each other often, even if it is not on paper or in person. I know that I can feel your love, and that, I think, is the most important communication of all. It really is something special, and I feel more lucky and blessed every time I think about it, or almost "rediscover" it in a sense. When I got your message just now, it made me realize just how much that feeling of knowing you are loved can affect you. Just as I was feeling kind of lost and a little lonely, I received your message. It might sound strange, but when I feel that I am being the most honest with myself about my feelings, I often begin to feel lonely or unloved. Not unloved by my family or friends, but sometimes maybe a bit unloved by myself. Then I start to really wonder about this feeling. I wonder if this is something that everyone feels, or if it is something that most people try to ignore or cover up with material things or what I call the "fake stuff", even maybe "fake" feelings in a way. I'm not too sure.

Then I wonder if I am the only one who actually thinks about this kind of stuff. "Learn to love yourself more, and good things will come to you." This is what my mom has been telling me for years. I don't know if that is really possible, though. Can you just "try" to love yourself more?! I don't know. I know that when I do try to at least "act" more confidently, things seem to become easier, whether it is related to school, work or relationships. I just question whether "acting" my way through life is really the honest thing to do.

While it is my passion when I am creating/performing a role, I don't want to live my life as an actor. I have a difficult time relating to people in my life who do "act" their way through their daily cycle. Especially recently, I am constantly wondering about people and how honest they are with themselves and with others, at least as I perceive them.

It really amazes me when I notice how much I am changing right now and how many more questions I have every day. I guess it has something to do with the phase of life I am entering, where I have to learn to be "with myself" sometimes and be okay with that, no parents protecting every outcome of every feeling I may have; learning to be satisfied with my feelings all on my own, and without judging them. I think I am learning how difficult this is – accepting and discovering the most honest "you" you find inside.

Thank you for your loving letter, and thank you for listening to me as I ramble on and search for answers,

Love Always,
Kelly

P.S.: I forgot about what you told me about your friend Janet's book. That's really neat! I'm happy that you shared (my letter) with her, and that she could relate it to what she was writing about. You can tell her, from me, that I can give her an example of the perfect "granddad" and the importance of that relationship with him...YOU!

Love You! *K.*

*"There are flowers everywhere, for those
who bother to look."*

Henri Matisse

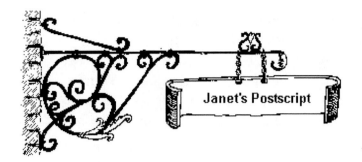

Janet's Postscript

When I shared Kelly's letters with my husband, Michael, his eyes filled with tears and he said, "If I got a letter like that from my 26-year-old grandchild, I'd feel fulfilled and, as a grandparent, I'd feel like I'd done my job. Don must be so proud."
Her P.S. is beautiful.

TRY THIS #136

LOVE NICKNAMES

Brainstorm a list of names to call them. They can be silly or fun or serious. This is a great way to let them know the characteristics you see in them.

- Trusty Justy (Justin)
- Sunny Sally
- Brave Brian
- Loving Lucy
- Super Sue
- etc.

Love names should be special, private and just between the two of you.
They tell your grandchildren that you think they are special.

TRY THIS #137

BUILDING A SPIRITUAL CONNECTION

If your grandchild lives far away, you can still build a tight connection with them, as evidenced in Don and Kelly's correspondence.

. . . and don't forget the spiritual connection. Pray for them frequently, for their safety, their protection, designate yourself as their guardian angel and tell them so. Let them know they are in your prayers. Ask God to watch over them . . . ask them to remember you in their prayers.

Build a spiritual connection, hold them in your heart and build reminders of them everywhere in your home:

- where you brush your teeth
- where you put on your jewellery
- where you shave
- in the bathtub
- on the workbench
- in the kitchen
- on the patio
- in your car

They will feel the connection, and they will feel your presence.

Tip: Remember that blowups of regular photos are just 99¢ at your local colour-copier store.

TRY THIS #138

MAKE A DATE WITH THEIR SPIRIT

By phone, fax or e-mail, brainstorm quiet places you like to be – on a beach, in the garden, on the patio, in your bedroom – and each choose one that both of you agree is a special kind of place – it doesn't have to be the same place for each of you. Select a day and a specific time that you both agree to be there.

Make a list of special things to think about such as:

- each other
- giving thanks for simple things
- why you like this place
- what you would talk about if you could be together there
- a secret you haven't told anyone

Also make a list of things you want to do there such as:

- find a gift for each other (a flower, a rock)
- draw a picture of your place
- write a letter to each other

Then communicate and share your experience by fax, phone or e-mail. Do this often. The connection will build.

TRY THIS #139

ALL FEELINGS ARE OKAY

Grandparents can play a special role here, a much more difficult job for parents who are more "on the spot".

Children often in the natural course of growing up express "not so nice" feelings. We can expect from time to time fear, anger, jealousy and varying degrees of love and happiness.

We can help by:

- being understanding of what they are feeling
- showing that we can be trusted with their feelings
- accepting whatever the feelings are
- not judging them

When children are encouraged to share their feelings and we respond in this way, they will feel the feelings less strongly and grow from the experience of sharing. This is how deep relationships are established.

A Lesson We've Learned

35

A recipe for loving can be found in the joy of cooking together.

UNCONDITIONAL COOKING

Our generation all grew up with caramel and candy apples at the fairs, a fond but sticky memory for all of us. I was on a business trip one day and passing through one of the international airports when I saw, at a very expensive candy store, a new version of caramel apples. I stood and studied them for several minutes, made a mental list in my head with an intention of doing caramel apples with the grandchildren. I highly recommend this activity to any of you for an afternoon of kitchen mess, giggles and fun.

I explained the concept to the grandchildren. The first step of our afternoon was to go to the local store with a good bulk foods section. The children picked out the decorations they wanted for their candy apples. Our array included Smarties, Jelly babies, cinnamon hearts, M & M's , and chocolate chips.

We bought wooden meat skewers to use for the apple sticks, then returned home to browse through a traditional cookbook from the '60s. The caramel apple recipe we found there follows on the next page.

By the time we were finished, the kitchen was a disaster, to say the least! But the grandchildren went home with a box full of caramel apples, to share with neighbourhood friends. We cut cellophane into squares and stood the caramel apple on the cellophane, thereby keeping it relatively germfree. Initially I had thought the grandchildren could take the apples to school to shared with classmates at a break, but learned to my dismay that this is no longer permitted due to the caution we all must take about food for our children from sources that are unknown. Our grandchildren, therefore, took them home. Mothers cut the apples in fours so that the children got a minimum of candy and a maximum of apple, and we understand that this was a very proudly served (and popular!) treat among trusted friends and neighbourhood families.

"Love is, above all, the gift of oneself."

Jean Anoulik

CARAMEL APPLES

Melt one 14-ounce package (about 50) vanilla caramels with 2 tablespoons water in top of double boiler, stirring frequently til mixture is smooth. Add dash salt. Stick wooden skewer into blossom end of 6 unpared crisp medium apples. Dip apples in caramel syrup and turn until bottom half of apples are completely coated. (If syrup is too stiff, add few drops water).

At once roll bottoms of coated apples in chopped California walnuts. Set on cookie sheet covered with waxed paper. Chill till the caramel coating is firm. Top sticks with large pieces of corn candy, if desired.

We laid out shallow dishes with each of the different materials in them. We dipped the apples in the caramel (Note of caution here – it is very easy to burn oneself with the caramel dip. I recommend that the adult do the actual dipping.) Once the caramel mixture was on the apples, the grandchildren rolled the apples in the various mixtures.

Worthy of note: If you take too long to roll it in the M & M's or the Smarties, they melt! We quickly learned to alternate between rolling the caramel apple in the decorations, and patting them on with our hands (by which time the caramel had cooled enough to safely handle them by hand).

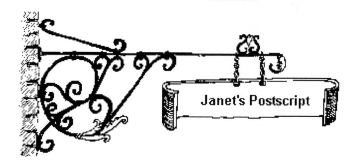

Janet's Postscript

We chose the following recipes because they are part of family traditions and history. I cannot overemphasize the importance of the conversation and interaction. Tell your grandchildren about the other times you've served the dishes you are preparing together; what the celebration was, who was there, what they were like. Tell them about the bloopers, the successes, and other connected family traditions.

When we interviewed the students, cooking with grandparents or the sharing of food were one of the most frequently mentioned favourite activities.

The opportunities to teach such things as measurement, use of kitchen instruments and equipment, nutritional benefits, names of ingredients and safety issues are endless.

The value of the exercise is not the end product, it's the process, the discussion and the togetherness that make the experience so precious.

TRY THIS #140

DOUBLE TROUBLE PEANUT BUTTER COOKIES

(These were the cookies with which I snagged Grandpa
and now they're favorites of his grandkids ... another family tradition)

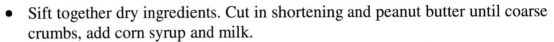

1 1/2 cups flour	1/2 cup shortening
1/2 tsp. soda	1/2 cup creamy peanut butter
1/4 tsp. salt	1/4 cup light corn syrup
1/2 cup sugar	1 tbs. milk

- Sift together dry ingredients. Cut in shortening and peanut butter until coarse crumbs, add corn syrup and milk.
- Shape into a roll 2 inches in diameter and chill thoroughly. Slice into 1/4 inch thick rounds.
- Place half the slices on ungreased cookie sheet and spread with 1/2 tsp peanut butter.
- Place second slice on top and seal the edges with a fork. Bake at 350 degrees for 10 minutes.

These will be family favourites in no time!

TRY THIS #141

GRANDMA'S RICE KRISPIE SQUARES WITH A NEW TWIST

1/4 cup butter or margarine	1 cup dried chopped fruit
5 cups miniature marshmallows	1/2 cup unsweetened coconut
1 cup raisins	4 cups Rice Krispies

- In large pot over low heat melt butter. Add marshmallows and stir until melted and blended. Remove from heat.
- Add raisins fruit and coconut, then cereal, stirring until thoroughly coated.
- Press firmly into buttered 9 inch pan. Chill. Cut into bars and watch them disappear!

My mom makes variations of this recipe for Easter for all the grandkids. When the mix is ready, instead of putting them in the pan, she shapes them into bird's nest. With a bit of colored straw and filled with Easter eggs, they're a big hit!

TRY THIS #142

GREAT GRANDMA'S INCREDIBLE COFFEE RING

(Margaret Swain)

I remember when I was a very small child ogling this incredible coffee ring and listening to the oohs and ahs of Mom's guests at special events. Later Mom taught me how to make it and I've served crowds of twenty, great for impressing staff or new family members and always a must on Christmas morning. Now I've taught my own granddaughter how to make it and she's only seven. This recipe is worth the price of the book! I've rarely shared it but mom gave me permission to include it. Maybe it will become a tradition in your house too.

This is an overnight recipe which is a real advantage as it rises while you sleep. Start at 5:00 at night if you're planning a 9:30 bed time.

1 tsp. yeast	2 cups lukewarm milk
1/2 cup sugar	1/2 cup oil
2 tsp. salt	1 egg
6 cups flour	

butter, brown sugar, raisins and nuts for filling
butter icing sugar, milk and fruit for decorations

- Dissolve yeast in 1/4 cup of milk and add 1 tsp. sugar 1/2 hour before you start, to give it time to start dissolving.
- Beat egg, sugar, oil and remaining milk in large mixing bowl.
- Add yeast mixture.
- Mix in flour and knead until shiny. (Kids love this part.)
- Wipe out and grease the large bowl, put dough back in and set aside to rise for 1 and 1/2 hours or until puffy. (I put it in the oven after warming the oven slightly, then turning it off. If it is too warm it will kill the yeast.)
- Punch dough down, turn it over and put back in oven for another 1 and 1/2 hours.
- Roll it out on a floured surface to the size of a cookie sheet. Spread with butter generously, sprinkle with brown sugar, raisins, nuts of your choice, the more the better.
- Roll it up starting with the long side until you have a long tube. Twist it to form a circle and seal the ends together by squeezing. Place on a large metal pan, the large ones from delis are great. (When risen, this is much larger than a regular pan.)
- With scissors snip into the tube close to the center of the dough. Make snips every 2 inches or so. Twist each piece onto its side, then put back in a cool oven for overnight rising. Remove in the morning while preheating the oven to 350°F.
- Bake for 25 minutes. While still warm, spread with icing, nuts, cherries or other fruit.

TRY THIS #143

GRANDMA JOAN HALL'S EASY, QUICK & DELICIOUS BANANA CAKE

1/2 cup shortening
1/2 cup each white and brown sugar, creamed with shortening
1 egg
2 tsp. baking powder combined with 1 and 1/2 cups of flour
3/4 cup milk added alternately with the flour
2 tsp vanilla
2 bananas, beat with 1 tsp baking soda

Bake at 350 degrees for 1 hour in a 9 inch pan.

THE BEST ICING

- Cream 1 tbs butter
- Add 8 tbs icing sugar and beat
- Add 2 tbs milk and beat
- Add 1 tbs boiling water and beat
- Add 1 tsp vanilla and beat

Voila!

Snapshots

Julia "cooking"
Surprise, Mom!
Age 3

A Lesson We've Learned ③

Our aboriginal cultures have a lot to teach us about unconditional love.
Theirs is passionate, wise and deep.

I have had the privilege and honour to have worked with Bella Bella Community School and its elected School Board. Bella Bella is a First Nations Village on an island off the North West Coast of British Columbia, Canada.

I say a "privilege and honour" because I have had a unique and special opportunity to soak up the Heiltsuk culture and I have come to know a number of the women and men well; their quiet strength and determination, their pride in their culture, their joy in their children.

Unconditional love **is** Bella Bella and its celebration of children.

A number of the women I have met have been new grandparents, my age, and it was not long before we were sharing our "passion for our grandchildren." It was the dancing eyes and sparkling laughter of Grandma Pauline Gladstone which prompted me to ask her if I could interview her.

Pauline is in her forties, proud grandmom of Gary, age 2, and Jordan, age 4 months. Her story of her unconditional love for these two children included many insightful thoughts.

Pauline's words about the difference between parenting and grandparenting:

"I was just a child. I knew I had to feed them and keep them clean, change their diapers regularly, and make sure they're in bed at a sensible time. Now I understand what I should have been."

About the birth of her first grandchild:

"The birth was so beautiful, it was a miracle, there was blood all over him – it was a fabulous feeling, I can't explain, I couldn't stop crying. Life is so wonderful. The whole family was there, the room was full of family, even the mother, Ang's, own grandparents."

About what she loves most about being a grandmother:

"To be able to hold him, to be able to experience every little move, to walk with him, to treasure him. I sing to him; every lunch hour, I phone and sing "itsy bitsy spider" and his mom says he does the actions as I sing."

About what she wants to teach them:

"To value education, to speak openly about their dreams, and to achieve them, to choose a career that is right for them, to know that nothing is out of reach."

About their future:

"To know that at different times of their lives they can choose to be different; they don't have to do it all at once."

Janet's Postscript

- Bella Bella is a celebration of children
- Bella Bella is a place where I saw the richness of the meaning of extended family in the First Nations world
- In Bella Bella I saw the definition of unconditional love
- In Bella Bella I saw the determination of a culture to re-invest in their children as a promise of the future they want and have a right to
- In Bella Bella I saw the commitment of all to one – all adults to any child.

At a settlement feast, or potlatch or community celebration, a chief will carry a newborn in a ritual pattern around the gathering, then raise the child in the air with an introduction to all gathered amidst applause and blessings. Babies are honoured, acknowledged and welcomed everywhere. Adult gatherings are swarming with happy, busy and involved young people in modern games like basketball and traditional dances. Two year-olds exhaust themselves dancing the dance of the Raven, dipping beak to energized drumming. On every street in the village, the conversations and greetings are first for the young one in the stroller, only then to their companion(s).

These people are rebuilding their communities now, taking back their land and their culture. They have their priorities clear – they are investing in their children.

Thank you, Pauline Gladstone and the people of Bella Bella. You've helped to teach me the meaning of unconditional love.

TRY THIS #144

A GRANDBABY SHOWER

- At the birth of a new baby or at the arrival of visiting grandchildren, create an event to proudly present them to your friends and neighbours. Make it a child-centered event.
- Scatter balloons here and there.
- Invite guests to bring a child too; if not their grandchild, a neighbour's child, or their own children.
- Ask each person to bring the name of their favourite children's book or ideas for favourite activities.
- Structure simple games that are child-oriented, and get the adults into play too.

Our culture is accustomed to "showers" before weddings and babies. The time may be right for grandbaby showers!

Snapshots

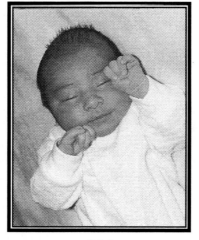

Clea
born 1999
Bella Bella, B.C.

"Of all the joys that lighten suffering earth, what joy is welcomed like a new born child?"

Caroline Norton

TRY THIS #145

HAND AND FOOT RECORDS

Have children press their hands or feet into damp sand, making the impressions one to two inches deep. Mix up plaster of paris as directed and pour it gently into the sand prints.

If you intend to collect these on a wall, put loops of coat hanger into the plaster as it starts to get hard. After 20 minutes or so, carefully take it out to dry.

These make great gifts for far-away grandparents or for mom and dad. Hand or foot prints can be shellacked, painted and decorated as you desire.

TRY THIS #146

GARDEN STEPPING STONES

Embedded in the wall of Bella Bella Community School are the handprints of the young children of the day.

Make garden stepping stones each year with the grandkids' handprints as the centrepiece. Put the name and date nearby, and decorate the stones with "found" materials – coloured glass, marbles, shells, pebbles.

For a mold use a square cardboard box (pizza boxes work well) which can be peeled away when the plaster is firm, or try the bottom of an old pail for a circle.

You will need:
- mortar mix from a hardware or building supply store
- if you use a mold, be sure to coat the inside of it with petroleum jelly

Stir the mortar as little as possible. Once it has been poured, let it dry completely before removing it from the mold. Decorate, then shellac and paint it as desired.

TRY THIS #147

A HANDFUL OF LOVE

Also in Bella Bella, hundreds of brilliantly coloured childrens' handprints adorn a large wall. How about your carport, or basement hallway or just a piece of fabric strung on dowelling at both ends to make a wall hanging?

As the children are growing up, perhaps on birthdays or when their annual visit comes around, they get a chance to add their "new" handprints, date, height, weight and age…an evolving family celebration!

Simply buy water-based paints and mix thickly so colour is intense. Practice once or twice on paper so they get the idea…then do it!

"All, everything that I understand, I understand only because of love."

Leo Tolstoy

A Lesson We've Learned 37

The connection is not dependent on the amount of time spent together, it is the quality of the small and sometimes long-distance connections.

SOMETHING FROM GRANDMA...ALWAYS:

Long-Distance Parents And Unconditional Love

My mom has been doing needlework from patterns for years. When her first grandchild was born, she decided to do a sampler with all the special things about that child. Before the child is four – until you have some idea of really what the personality is like – she decides what is special about this child. She does a sampler with the name and the date of birth. Then she will add all these special things; for instance, she'll put their horoscope sign. For her grandson Sam, for example, he loved dinosaurs so she did a dinosaur and she always does some character from Beatrix Potter. Some things she can't find patterns for, but she went ahead and did a tow truck for him. For Anna she had to do a little raggedy doll called Bebe Rose. For one of my nieces, she had to do "Madeline" because Madeline was a passion for her. It's that child as he or she was at four.

It's beautiful work and it's also something that they will always have of grandma, that grandma did that's their special sampler. It's the connection to the modern world, but such an old-fashioned idea. She's done it for all her grandchildren, all ten of them.

LETTERS: AN OLDIE BUT A GOODY!

My mom also is a good letter writer; always has been. What I notice about her letters to the kids is that she'll respond to what Sam's interests are. We go down every summer to the cottage, which is a wonderful place for kids, and Cam is fascinated by the wildlife. When she wrote him, she used to print it all until he could read writing, so even when he was about five he could pick out words and then he could read the whole letter.

She'd say, "I saw the loon today; I don't know where the babies are," or, "The beaver swam past here again today…"and her letter to him would be about wildlife.

To Anna it would be something like, "I made chocolate cookies. Do you remember when we made them when you were here this summer and I went into town and we went to the store where we got you that little hat." The letter is interesting to them because it is all about their interests. She sends Easter cards, she sends Valentine's cards. They love it, it's mail for them; it's addressed to Mr. Sam Dodd. They really love that kind of thing, and phone calls. She's really good about phone calls. Especially since this $20-a-month deal from the telephone companies, I'll say, "Phone Grandma," so now they will grab the phone and say things like, "You know what, Grandma, I got the goal in my soccer game today."

We didn't used to do that, but now we do all the time. We'll phone her for these brief little calls.

Christine Sanders

MOVING TOWARDS TECHNOLOGY?

One other thing is that we used to send videotapes to them fairly frequently and, although they never sent us back a videotape (neither one of them is very technological), now that our kids are older teenagers they wish that Grampy had e-mail. That's something that we need to resolve: he thinks that he's just too old to learn those kinds of things. Yet, I think that they would have a really ready connection if the e-mail was there. He seems to think that letters serve a different purpose; they are a chronicle, historical as well, and you can tell a lot about a person just by what they write about and the way they write something. He feels that way strongly. We've been trying to talk him into it, but I don't think he's going to be budged. Maybe it shouldn't be us, though, maybe it should be Bria and Ian saying, "Grampy, if you had e-mail we would be able to send you messages a lot more frequently."

Barbara Menzies

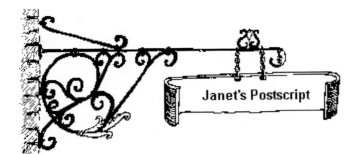

Janet's Postscript

During the interview, Barb and Christine frequently expressed their regret that their parents were so far away and couldn't have the daily or weekly connection some of us are fortunate to have.

Yet, as I reviewed our three-hour taped dialogue, it was clear to me that their kids are certain about their unconditional loving connection to their grandparents. Barb's kids are almost grown, while Christine's are young, but the stories were consistently making that point.

The "Try This" activities offer creative ways to stay in touch, whether near or far.

TRY THIS #148

BE BRAVE: TAKE ON TECHNOLOGY!

In a recent Vancouver *Sun* article, Gillian Shaw headlined "digital imaging" as a snap. There is a wide range of photo software available, geared to amateur use. You can create on-line photo albums, personalized cards and calendars.

Film processors such as London Drugs offer the option of digitized photos if you don't want to purchase a digital camera. Two recommended photo software programs:

- Photo Suite II is approximately $49.99.
- Photo Deluxe 3.0 is approximately $73.99.

Some of Gillian Shaw's ideas:

- put the whole grad album on line
- take pictures of the whole family today at a special event and make a Photo Parade, an animated slide show that comes with Photo Deluxe
- make a collage of one child's week
- make family posters with creative captions
- make personalized cards and goofy cartoons

Grandpa Fishing

You just may start something!

TRY THIS #149

SENDING DO-IT STUFF

- Pack up a large gift box with gorgeous ribbons and lots of tissue inside and send them a play dress-up box – for a princess – old jewellery, glittery high heels, a high-fashion funky dress . . . whatever their interests. Ask for photos to be sent back.

- Add materials to support drawing, painting, textiles, modelling, carving and construction activities as follows:

  Drawing: Drawing with pencil, crayon, felt-tipped marker, chalk, pastels, and improvised tools such as sticks, Q-tips, etc. use a variety of surfaces (damp, wet, dry), and paper types (dark marks on light, light marks on dark). make line drawings, shape drawings, contour and continuous line drawings.

  Painting: Painting with a variety of brush shapes and sizes, sponges, fingers, and improvised brushes. Use a variety of surfaces (damp, wet, dry), paper and card types, coloured surfaces. use a variety of paint methods (stain, wash, resists, tempera, dye).

  Textiles: Paper collage, fabric collage, yarn pictures, stitching on a plain background. Use a variety of fibres and fabrics, sorting and matching yarns and fabric. Fabric construction, paper weaving, fibre weaving, knotting, and tying.

  Modelling, carving and construction: A variety of materials for modelling such as clay, plasticine, baker's clay. Carving, using materials such as soap, clay, styrofoam. Construction using materials such as balsa, cardboard, styrofoam, paper, paper mache, paper folding to make puppets, masks, dioramas, built enviroments, containers, stuffed paper forms, mobiles.

Most of these materials can be purchased in art supply stores and/or office supply stores. Materials are usually exhausted, so why not send a package of different things every six months?

TRY THIS #150

FOCUS YOUR LETTERS

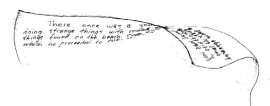

Review the "Try This" ideas offered in this book. Adapt any one of them so you can use the activity over long distance. For example:

- Choose a book for both of you to read, then illustrate the book and send the images back and forth to promote discussion.

- Write a story starter. Exchange it a number of times, adding a new twist in a new paragraph, new character or new direction. This can be fun as it grows.

- Identify a topic of mutual interest. Research it privately, then send it to each other for sharing and discussion.

TRY THIS #151

PHOTO DIARY

Send a disposable camera. Each of you can do a daily diary showing what you did, who your friends are, the high points and low points. The next letter can focus on new things you learned about yourself.

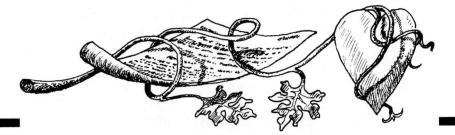

*"We form a circle of hope.
We pass the flame to one another.
If my candle goes out, yours will light it.
Together they make a brighter light...
And each candle promises something of its own:
That darkness is not the last word."*

David McCauley, American Friends Service Committee

A Lesson We've Learned 38

With the unconditional love of an extended family, we can discover and create multiple connections and lifelong relationships.

CELEBRATING FAMILY ROOTS WITH FAMILY FUN

When I was really little, my grandparents had moved to Toronto, as did a number of my aunts and uncles, so they rented a cottage on Lake Huron, where my grandparents, their four children, their spouses and all the grandchildren came to holiday together. We played in Lake Huron and were probably there for a week. We had a fabulous time with the kids. Everybody was everywhere. We were swimming together. There were wonderful swings on the porch, we all ate together. It was just a really, really good time.

We've talked about this over the years as my generation now has their own little kids. So two summers ago at a wedding, then last summer again at a wedding, everyone agreed this is a great idea, so we've gone and done it. We've rented seven campsites. My mom's generation will be in hotels close by.

There are four kids in my family, all with spouses and six grandchildren. My aunt has a daughter with her husband and two kids, both kids bringing two girlfriends as well. My uncle has three boys, two of which are married and have three grandchildren. My other uncle is bringing his family of five kids and four out of the five will be there with their spouses and five grandchildren. (Author's note: I count 39.) The youngest kid is probably just over a year old and the oldest kid is fifteen or sixteen.

Everyone has committed to come. We've chosen a campsite which is halfway between the families, between Toronto and Montreal. We have all the campsites on an inner circle with a gorgeous family beach. It goes out very gradually and slowly in the sand. The kids will bring their water toys. We'll probably end up sharing our foods and telling stories around campfires. We're just going to hang out, tell stories, Go for walks, play on the beach and have campfires . . . just like we did when we were kids.

Elsa Swain vanVliet

Janet's Postscript

This is a new and interesting idea to me. It has been customary for our family members to gather at Christmas, but we have never all gathered somewhere for a holiday outing or family fun.

Half of my family lives in Port Alberni and the other half in Victoria – 200 miles apart. Why couldn't we meet at Rathtrevor Beach, or one of the islands for a picnic and family games?

Barbara told us a great story about meeting the grandparents and holidaying on a houseboat at Shuswap Lake, and they came from all over Canada to do it.

Brad and Yvonne live an hour away, and getting together for dinner means a long drive. Why not meet them at Witty's Lagoon for a beach afternoon ending with a barbecue?
- or at a park
- or an antique car show
- or a folk fest
. . . or . . . or . . . or . .

TRY THIS #152

MULTIPLE POSSIBILITIES

Think "action!" Take garbage bags full of old tried and true toys:

- tennis balls and rackets
- pails and shovels
- badminton equipment
- boxes for collections
- storybooks
- bubble blowers
- craft knives
- water play toys
- frisbees
- a glue gun
- acrylic paints and paper
- nails and hammer and string
- lots of balls
- books to identify birds, insects, flowers, etc.

Your chosen destination will determine your list.

TRY THIS #153

TRIED AND TRUE OUTDOOR GAMES

Brainstorm the games you enjoyed as a child. You may also need to brainstorm the rules!

- Horseshoes
- Kick the can
- Treasure hunt (hide the clues)
- Croquet
- Hide and seek
- Dodge the ball
- all kinds of tag

- Scavenger hunts finding natural items such as a spider, a web, a seed, a nut

- Badminton played with a balloon with a bit of water – in it works!

- Goofy Golf with obstacles made from tubes, shoe boxes, pails with the bottom cut out, drainage pipe

Author's note: The best book I've come across is "The Kid's Cottage Game Book" for detailed and creative family fun.

TRY THIS #154

MORE FAMILY FUN

Family Beach Activities:

- painting pictures on sea shells
- sand castle or sculpture contests
- water experiments
- building rafts
- water basketball (tire is basket)
- kite flying
- braiding bullrushes or seaweed
- feeding the birds
- water polo
- a tree swing (tire and rope)
- netting crabs or other water creepies (always put them back)

Playing with Plentiful Nature: Craft Ideas

- pinecone animals
- leaf printing
- daisy chains
- flower pressing
- rock people, painted
- leaf rubbings
- flower drying

Decide before you go so you can bring the materials you need.

*"God made the beauties of nature
like a child playing in the sand."*

Ascribed to Apollonius of Tyana

TRY THIS #155

T-SHIRT MEMORIES

Ask everyone in the family to bring a new or clean light-coloured T-shirt. Take fabric paint with you (available a craft stores). You'll also need water, and sheets of cardboard for the inside of the shirt while you're working on it.

- divide the family into pairs, an older person with a younger
- decide on the theme: beach, bugs, sky, flowers, fancy line designs, etc.
- help each other create the shirt design on paper first, practise on scraps of old cloth, then go to it. Perhaps as a family you could decide to add the name of your event and the date to commemorate your family party.

For this activity take:
- T-shirts
- paint brushes
- water
- glitter and sequins for those who want to be fancy
- chalk fabric marker to draw designs

If you just want to be carefree, hang the shirts on a makeshift clothesline and splatter paint all over them – with panache!

You can also colour on shirts with wax crayon, then once you're back to civilization and electricity, you can iron the shirt (wrong side out) to make it permanent.

Insert cardboard to stop paint or dye from staining the back of the shirt.

"...because they are children
and for no other reason
they have dignity and worth
simply because they are..."

Barbara Coloroso

A Lesson We've Learned
39

There's a grandparent nearby for each of us... blood is not always thicker than water.

...JUST THAT KIND OF MAN, GRANDPA

Both of my grandfathers died when I was fairly young, my Mom's dad when I was two and a half, and my Dad's dad when I was seven. So while other kids had a grandpa, I didn't. And there was this old fellow whose wife had died – everybody referred to him as Emil – and Dad said to me that Emil is really lonely, and I got it in my head that he could be my grandpa and I could be his grandchild.

And so from the time that I was seven until I was thirty-five, Grandpère was part of my life. And he gave me my first sewing machine and it had been his wife's. And when I decided that I wanted a real sewing machine, an electric sewing machine, he paid for half. And when I was seventeen and decided that I wanted an apartment of my own and my parents said, no absolutely not, Grandpère interceded on my behalf and talked to my Dad and he said let her go, she'll come back. Don't worry about it, let her go. Young people need to do this.

When I was married, it was he who did the toast to the bride. When I was sad in that marriage, it was he that I called upon, even before I talked to my folks. When I needed to have a car, it was Grandpère who came up with the Volkswagen Beetle that had 100,000 miles on it already, and talked my Dad into fixing it up.

It was Grandpère who needed my help to get apricots off his tree so that he could make jam. It was Grandpère who told me stories about the kind of relationship that I wanted to have – he called his wife "my lady."

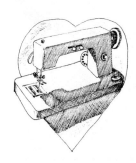

And it was Grandpère who got to be 102 years old and I helped him put his nightshirts on.

Before he died I said to him, "Thank you, thank you, thank you for everything." I was crying and he told me not to be sad, that he was getting ready for the great adventure. He was somebody who I discovered later had been adopted as grandpa of sorts or uncle or father or whatever by all kinds of people. He was just that kind of man.

Daphne

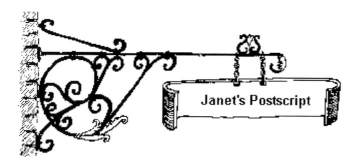

Janet's Postscript

For years, schools have launched "Adopt a Grandparent" programs so that all kids would have someone older and wiser to talk to, in recognition that some children's real grandparents have passed on or live far away. The idea has its limitations, since only a small part of the school day can be devoted to this kind of "reach out" activity.

Yet Daphne's story holds promise for the kids who need this kind of connection outside of their own family resources. Care needs to be taken to ensure the child's safety.

The suggestions in the following "Try This" ideas are intended for any interested adult.

TRY THIS #156

A GRANDPARENTS WANTED SOCIETY

Remember, for every grandchild who has a grandparent far away, the converse is true. There are grandparents far away who have no grandchildren nearby.

Why not start a proper society, similar to Big Brothers (who have long waiting lists) to offer the kids connections. Create a community commitment to kids by gathering a nucleus of people to start the organization. Research the mandates, policies and procedures of other community organizations. Include police, social workers and educators on your initial Board to properly establish the safety net for kids. Find corporate sponsors.

It won't take long, and you will have created a new community network to connect and protect our youth.

TRY THIS #157

POWERFUL BONDS BETWEEN YOUNG AND OLD

Gather a group of young kids together through their parents. Make regular visits to seniors residences in your area.

Most residences have recreational choices for their clients. I took my mom on a tour of a number of them recently, and among the offerings were:

- jazz combos
- harpsichord and singer
- nutritional presentations
- candlelight and pianist
- financial advisor presentations
- field trips all over the city

And new features about children:

- Christmas crafts with kids
- public speaking events by children
- school choirs singing
- individual musical performances by children

I applaud this type of connection but in most cases it was a one-time-only event.

One of our schools, Greenglade Elementary, sent their writing club on a regular basis to buddy-up and write stories and poems together. North Saanich School had the same seniors to their school regularly for Home Ec. Class lunch, and the seniors had them back for tea as a thank-you. More recently, a teacher, as part of her Master's degree, has volunteer students interviewing a senior over time. The electricity and excitement of senior and student together brings tears to the eyes.

What I saw happen, in these cases, were the powerful interpersonal understanding and bonds created between young and old, and many extended beyond the walls of school to weekend personal and family get-togethers.

. . . and everyone benefited.

Check out the seniors residences in your area. I know you'll be welcomed and your kids' lives will be enriched.

TRY THIS #158

NEIGHBOURHOOD KIDS HELPING SENIORS

Organize the neighbourhood kids into work parties. Develop a list of services or activities they could provide to seniors as gestures of kindness and support. Have an adult go with them from door to door of seniors who still live at home. Help them rehearse their speech beforehand.

They might:

- mow the lawn
- weed the garden
- trim hedges
- wash windows
- shovel snow
- clean the shed
- carry heavy items

Be sure when you've finished that you spend time in discussion about how their contribution was received by the senior, how they felt approaching the door, how they felt as they left.

Help them to see the bigger picture. What would life be like if we all were to lend a helping hand, even when it's not requested?

The results may be long-term relationships with the seniors as permanent connections. It may also be the beginning of the development of social conscience among our young people.

"Friendship is a sheltering tree."
Samuel Taylor Coleridge

TRY THIS #159

A SENIOR SERVICES STUDY GROUP

Gather your young people together and with the help of a phone book identify the agencies in your area that make significant contributions to the lives of seniors, e.g.:

- Meals on Wheels
- home care services
- Silver Threads, etc.

Support your group by helping them arrange to accompany people who provide services to seniors, and arrange for them to go along as observers and/or assistants. Structure their visit by creating a series of questions they will need to respond to when next your group meets, e.g.:

- Why is this service important?
- How could you help to provide this service?
- What qualities did you see in the people there that you admired?
- If you could do something that would support seniors, what would it be?
- What values did you see?
- How would you describe them?
- Who are elders in our country's indigenous people? Do they differ from our elders?
- How would we encourage other youth to support our elders?

Maybe "blood won't be thicker than water!"

A Lesson We've Learned 40

Unconditional love is like being best friends. It's the difference between "flat and flying, between the mundane and the magical."

GRANDFATHER TO GRANDSON: ON LOVE AND MARRIAGE

June 2, 1998

Dear Matthew:

You have no doubt heard the saying, "There is always the right time for everything." And with your wedding day just around the corner, this qualifies "in spades" as the time for a chat with you, about you, and about you and Stephanie and some stuff about life before, during and after the ceremony.

Nothing very heavy, mind you. Just light. A few quick thoughts and impressions that make your future as man and wife look so good and hopefully even more so. Just what we all want for you.

Here is something that I find neat. Just as neat as can be. Over the years, many, many years, whenever I think of you, and let me tell you it is not at all an infrequent thing, I seldom if ever can see you alone. Trying to see you without Stephanie is like trying to see Romeo without Juliet.

And when I see that and think about it, I think Wow! You and Stephanie have a powerhouse thing going for you as you go for married life.

You are time-proven and -tried and -tested "best friends." How tremendously important and tremendously promising for your life together. Not just "in love", but two ***best friends*** in love with each other. That is not always the case! And from what I have seen, I can say that without both, it just doesn't work as well.

"Who, being loved, is poor?"

Oscar Wilde

The "best friends" dimension makes the difference between ordinary and the extraordinary. Between the flat and the flying. Between the mundane and the magical. Take it from me.
I speak from happy experience.

Why is that so? Well, let's just think about it and jot down some points that prove the point.

- "Best friends" add to and nourish each other's self esteem and personal growth.
- "Best friends" are close, very close, without smothering, or over-leaning on each other, or encroaching too much on each other's "space".
- "Best friends" know that if there is anything better than to be loved . . . it is to be loving.
- "Best friends" keep the romance part of their relationship alive and active. They do romantic things that surprise and please. They keep stoking the fire. I think romance is the "decoration" on the "icing on the cake."
- "Best friends" are and remain a "winning team." In it for the long haul. They have a super staying power.

In short . . . "best friends" practice the Golden Rule . . . Day after day – year after year – they do and give unto their partner what they would like and want their partner to give and do unto them.

And now that I am in a Bible-quoting mode, let me end with these loving words to you and Stephanie – two of the very "best friends" I know:

Quote . . ."*May your cup runneth over*" . . . with mutual respect and understanding. With the right combination of togetherness and space. With confidence and trust. Lots of caring and lots of support. With talking and listening and laughing. And with some silence too. With lots of calm and lots of excitement. With lots of hugs and lots of romance. May you go through life together doing little things and big things that surprise and please. Always in love, and with lots of love.

You have it all going for you to go that way. And you go with love and best wishes from Pat and myself. So sorry that we are not able to be there with you on your wedding day.

Love, loads of it to both of you

Don

Janet's Postscript

Grandpa Don's letter to Matthew, his grandson, in my opinion is so full of lessons, written on the occasion of Matthew's marriage:

- best friends
- being in love *and* being best   friends
- romance
- The Golden Rule. . . and more…

It made me think of the many passages our children encounter in their very short childhood. Wouldn't it be wonderful if we made a commitment to participate in each passage with wisdom, experience and our blessings? We have learned so much from our mistakes and from our successes.

What if we took our cue from Don and wrote a special message to our grandkids on each occasion of passage. What might they be? They'll be different in each culture and spiritual connection, but to name a few:

- birth
- christening and other spiritual events
- starting kindergarten
- graduation from kindergarten, or elementary or secondary school
- starting middle school or junior high
- starting senior high
- university or post-secondary certification
- the wedding
- the first child

At each stage of our children's evolution there is wisdom and insight that could help them on their way. These letters could become a legacy, a treasure that can be passed on for generations.

Once more, give them the gift of time . . . and wisdom.

Snapshots

TRY THIS #160

DEVELOP A FAMILY MISSION STATEMENT

Businesses, for many years, have established Mission Statements as a way of stating the common purpose of their organization. This can be done by families, too. If you can't get together as a family due to distance, parents or grandparents can begin the development of such a statement, then send it to the others for suggestions or input.

The steps are simple.

Brainstorm and list on a large piece of paper taped to the wall the words which focus on:

- what you want your family to be (characteristics)
- what you want your family to do (contributions and achievements)
- the values and principles upon which the being and doing are based

A friend of mine started the sentences with:

We will seek to . . .
Our home(s) will be a place where . . .
We will value . . .
We will try to keep ourselves free from . .
Our promises to each other will . . .

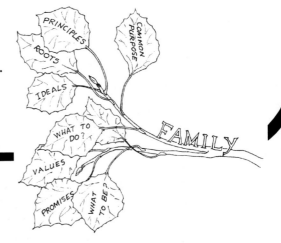

"To forget one's ancestors is to be a brook without a source, a tree without a root."
Chinese Proverb

TRY THIS #161

NARROWING THE FOCUS

You could start by brainstorming the ends to each of the above sentences.

Then use what is called a "weighted vote." Ask family members (near and far) to choose the words which are most important to them by putting a (1) beside the most important word, a (2) beside the next most important word, a (3) beside the next most important word (for each of the sentence completions).

Once you have the results collected give
(1) a value of 5 points
(2) a value of 3 points
(3) a value of 1 point

Total the value for each word and you will have narrowed the focus.
Try then to finish the sentence stems using the words with the highest number of points.

TRY THIS #162

MISSION CHECKPOINT

Before you complete your Mission Statement, use the following checkpoints to scan for important values and principles:

- sense of worth
- strength
- direction
- principles
- perspective on life

- self-esteem
- identity
- standards
- decision-making

Many organizations try to define their key notions in one sentence, but this is difficult to do. A paragraph is fine.

TRY THIS #163

A FAMILY FOCUS ON ITS MISSION

Create a poster for your Mission statement using a collage of photos or a group photo taken at some celebration with the Mission Statement at the bottom. Have it framed and send it to each part of the family.

Remember:

- all family members should be invited to participate
- each sub-family may want to have their own version of the bigger family statement
- individuals may want to create their own, based on the overall statement
- the statement should be reviewed and revised regularly

Properly developed, your mission statement can be used to proactively pursue the basic direction for both short-term and long-term planning. As well, decisions can be measured against your intentions.

Unconditional Love

Conclusion: NEAR OR FAR, IT'S UNCONDITIONAL

I asked two very dear friends, Christine Saunders and Barbara Menzies, to permit me to interview them about long-distance grandparenting, because I know their children had developed an unconditional love relationship with grandparents who were thousands of miles away.

Some of their quotes are lessons in themselves and a fitting conclusion for our chapter on Unconditional Love – whether near or far, it's do-able. Thanks, Barb and Christine, for your insights.

- . . . she makes them accountable for their behaviour in her own way, but it is in a much more gentle way. She appeals to their better self and they rise to it. She'll say, "Oh, Sam, I'm so disappointed that you did that; that's not like you. You're usually so kind to your sister. I'm sure she's feeling badly and you will want to make it better . . ." Before you know it, Sam is apologizing.

  Christine

- The other thing she does, and I don't even know if I agree . . . distraction . . . The child's having a temper tantrum – instead of saying this is not okay, go to your room (which is what I'd do) she'll say, "I think there's a hummingbird at the feeder, quick!"

  Christine

- Bria has always looked upon her grandparents as a treat, as being something to really look forward to, that it was special to see them at all.

  Barbara

- I see the grandparents as kind of being troubleshooters – smoothing the waters.

  Christine

- I think it is really important to have another adult in your life – especially a significant adult – who is able to see you in a different way than your parents do.

  Barbara

- They told her to always know that they'd be there for her if she needed them . . . that was really special to her.

  Barbara

- Our kids got letters from them once every two or three weeks from the time they were small – short but regular

  Barbara

- When she wrote to him – and she used to print it all until he could read writing – she'd say, "Do you remember when we . . . or "I saw the loon again today" and sometimes she puts money in with a note, "Please phone grandma."

  Christine

- My dad is the book grandpa – he buys them at Christmas and birthdays.

  Barbara

- My mother hates travelling more than anything in the world, but she drags herself out here four times a year to see her grandchildren.

  Christine

- I've organized several family vacations to make lemonade out of lemons, to make up for the times they haven't been able to come by for Sunday dinners. Once we rented a houseboat, and I'll never forget looking at the backs of their heads on a beautiful gold pond with grandkids between them. Kids could do kid things, grandparents could just be there to watch and enjoy.

  Barbara

Snapshots

Chapter 5

Grandparents:
Teaching With the Winning Touch

Chapter 5

Grandparents:
Teaching With the Winning Touch

Education is a Critical Key to Their Future

I am particularly proud to have played a role in the development of British Columbia education system as Superintendent of Educational Innovation for the Ministry of Education.

Along with hundreds of leading educators, our team was responsible for re-designing the education system, based on the results of the report of the Sullivan Royal Commission.

The results of this work set the stage for major change in the system, and positioned B.C. as one of the world leaders in educational reform. We were inundated with worldwide visitors and requests for presentations at international conferences. I was asked to speak at the World Congress in Education in Australia in 1994 as a representative of B.C.

Much of the work presented in this chapter was a part of my keynote address there. I dedicate this chapter to the countless educators in B.C. who made the Sullivan Royal Commission's vision a reality. As well, I would like to acknowledge the researchers who provided a solid base of the latest world research on the development of children as our guiding light.

The root of our work was the vision of the "Education citizen." Schools in our province are dedicated to assisting in the development of citizens who are:

- thoughtful, able to learn and to think critically, and who can communicate information from a broad knowledge base;
- creative, flexible and self-motivated and who have a positive self-image;
- capable of making independent decisions;
- skilled and who can contribute to society generally, including the world of work;
- productive, who gain satisfaction through achievement and who strive for physical well-being;
- cooperative, principles and respectful of others, regardless of differences;
- aware of the rights and prepared to exercise the responsibilities of an individual within the family, the community, Canada and the world.

Greater detail about concepts, skills and suggested activities can be found in the following three documents:

- *Supporting Learning*
- *The Primary Program Foundation Document*, and
- *The Intermediate Program Document.*

All three resources are available from the B.C. Ministry of Education.

We grandparents could be the second most influential teacher in our children's lives. The following information will help you track the development of your grandchildren so you can support, coach and teach them…with the Winning Touch.

Cheers,

Janet Mort
1999

Beautiful Babies

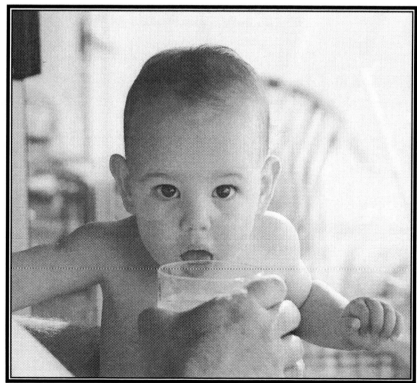

Trevor
Age 1

A Lesson We've Learned

41

"The key to unlocking the door to an unlimited future is reading and getting the best education."
Jean Chretien, Prime Minister, Canada

Learning to read is important as a skill throughout our lives. It is especially associated with success in school, and is therefore a major area of concern for the home and extended family.

How do children learn to read? It is a developmental process that begins in infancy, as children are getting ready to read from birth.

TRY THIS #164

MAKE READING A NECESSITY

Families can support their young learners by:
- reading to them daily
- including traditional reading such as nursery rhymes and fairy tales
- demonstrating many aspects of reading in daily lives (recipes, signs, newspapers, etc.)
- providing opportunities to visit libraries and bookstores
- planning activities to build the child's knowledge of language in general

TRY THIS #165

READ TO THEM DAILY

The single most important thing we can do is read to them often:
- pre-school children like predicable books with rhyme and repetition, as well as folk tales
- ages 5 to 7 prefer a continuation of earlier books, plus nature and picture books
- ages 7 to 9 like longer texts, essay novels and true stories
- ages 9 to 11 like novels, adventure stories, mysteries and nonfiction
- ages 11 to 13 enjoy demanding novels and magazines

TRY THIS #166

ENCOURAGE INDEPENDENT READING

To encourage independent reading we can:

- continue to read aloud, even after they are able to
- be a role model
- provide appropriate material (magazine subscriptions, library cards)
- capitalize on their interests and provide a regular time for reading with both of you reading your own books silently

Learning to read happens over a long period of time. The following chart indicates a developmental pattern in a global way. It is important to remember, however, that each child learns at his/her own speed and style. At times they will surge ahead, and at times they will reach a plateau.

Beautiful Babies

Natasha
Age 1

Reading: A Standards Guide for Grandparents, Parents, Teachers and Students, Kindergarten to Grade 3

These skills develop in young children over a period of several years. This chart is intended only as a broad guideline, since learning readiness and demonstrated success will vary. Choose one area to focus on for each visit. If you live far away, you can achieve the same results using tapes you make yourself, and accompanying books. Have them send the tape back with a description of why they liked the story, or better yet, a recording of them reading it to you.

Reading	Kindergarten to Grade 1 (ages 5 and 6)	Grades 2 and 3 (ages 7, 8, 9)
	Children…	**Children…**
	Teachers encourage reading by placing picture books, signs, posters and other things that are easy to read around the classroom.	Children learn to recognize many words by how they look and where they are in a sentence. Reading becomes easier as students read for longer periods of time. Children are encouraged to read alone.
Word Recognition	• learn how sounds and letters make words (phonics) • substitute a word that makes sense when they don't recognize a word and can't figure it out using phonics • recognize by sight the basic words and phrases that appear frequently in their reading materials	• apply rules of phonics as well as other ways to identify unfamiliar words (e.g., word structure, context, dictionary) • focus on reading fluently and make an effort to correct their own mistakes • recognize a large number of words by sight, and read faster silently than orally (see Lesson 42)
Reading for Information and Enjoyment	• read and re-read storybooks and informational books they have chosen • read orally from their own writing and familiar materials • listen to and talk about stories that have been read to them	• concentrate for longer periods of time (twenty to thirty minutes at a time) on material they have chosen • adjust their approach to fit the purpose and material (e.g., read familiar stories faster than new stories) • rely increasingly on reading to find information
Increasing Recall and Understanding	• look over a book to get ready to read • think about how certain words or pictures help them know what will happen in a story • remember and retell familiar stories	• predict storyline by previewing story or book before reading • ask questions • retell main ideas • read "between the lines" to make inferences about characters and their behaviour

Reading: A Standards Guide for Parents, Teachers and Students, Kindergarten to Grade 3 *(continued)*

Reading	Kindergarten to Grade 1 (ages 5 and 6)	Grades 2 and 3 (ages 7, 8, 9)
	Children…	Children…
Thinking About What Has Been Read	• begin to recognize patterns (repeated words and phrases) in words, stories and poems	• recognize an increasing variety of story types and understand the elements that make up a story • speculate about the author's purpose
Using What Has Been Read	• write and draw about stories and use story characters, events and language in play • express likes or dislikes for particular books or topics • make connections between personal experiences and what they are reading about (e.g., may tell a story about something similar that happened to them)	• express personal views about characters' motivation and behaviour • explain reasons why they like or dislike a book or type of reading material • explain characters' actions and story situations in drawing and writing
Research (Using Reading to Find More Information)	• recognize books as a source of information • use pictures to get information	• use text features such as a table of contents, headings or illustrations to help find information • begin to recognize the purpose of specific reference material such as pictures and glossaries • begin to locate and record information
Reading for Lifelong Development	• show curiosity and interest in books of all kinds • talk about their reading • enjoy looking at books and listening to stories	• will talk about reading with other children • enjoy reading, and may choose to read if given a choice of activities • concentrate for longer periods of time on reading books they have chosen

Reading: A Standards Guide for Parents, Teachers and Students, Grades 4 to 7

The grade cluster four to seven is used in the reading and writing charts because learning these skills is an ongoing process that takes years to develop.

Reading	Grades 4-7
	Children...
	Students begin to read many types of stories (e.g., science fiction, mystery, adventure, romance). They start to use books such as an atlas, dictionary or encyclopedia to find specific information.
Word Recognition	• figure out unfamiliar words by using context clues and phonics, and by analyzing parts of the word • use a dictionary to locate word meanings
Reading for Information and Enjoyment	• recognize different purposes for reading • use different reading strategies for different purposes
Increasing Recall and Understanding	• review what they already know about a topic and make inferences by "reading between the lines", make predictions and ask questions • summarize, retell and interpret information
Thinking About What Has Been Read	• analyze particular elements such as style or theme in novels, articles, short stories and poetry • identify, discuss and write about common themes in literature from different countries and cultures
Using What Has Been Read	• make and support judgements about what they read • write and talk about their responses to what they read • make connections between previous knowledge, personal experiences and the reading of new material
Research (Using Reading to Find More Information)	• locate information from several different sources to complete research projects • use reference materials such as maps, charts, graphs and library materials
Reading for Life-long Development	• select reading material from a wide range of fiction and nonfiction • begin to value the role of literature in our culture and our society

10 Reasons to Read to Your Child

1. Because when you hold them and give them this attention, they know you love them.

2. Because reading to them will encourage them to become readers.

3. Because children's books today are so good that they are fun even for adults.

4. Children's book illustrations often rank with the best, giving them a lifelong feeling for good art.

5. Books are one way of passing on your moral values to them. Readers know how to put themselves in another's shoes.

6. Because, until they learn to read themselves, they will think you are magic.

7. Because every teacher and librarian they ever encounter will thank you.

8. Because it's nostalgic.

9. Because, for that short space and time, they will stay clean and quiet.

10. Because, if you do, they may then let you read in peace!

A Lesson We've Learned 42

If our children can read these words "by sight", they'll be 245 steps ahead in the reading "game".

Research studies have identified the most frequently used words in the English Language. As well, these words have been grouped according to readability level, but you can start them anytime.

Practising these words with children until they can read them by sight (not by "sounding out") is an important exercise.

Use these checklists to keep track of their progress. The most effective system is the use of flashcards (the words written on recipe cards) or use Post-it notes and stick the ones they can read on the wall, for everyone to admire.

Make up games to make the exercise fun and give them lots of encouragement. This is a great investment in reading success.

Snapshots

Great-grandma Margaret and Natasha Margaret
1997

BASIC SIGHT WORDS

Pre Primer	*Primer*	*First Grade*
☐ 1. a	☐ 1. all	☐ 1. after
☐ 2. help	☐ 2. am	☐ 2. again
☐ 3. I	☐ 3. are	☐ 3. an
☐ 4. jump	☐ 4. ate	☐ 4. any
☐ 5. little	☐ 5. be	☐ 5. as
☐ 6. and	☐ 6. black	☐ 6. ask
☐ 7. big	☐ 7. brown	☐ 7. by
☐ 8. can	☐ 8. but	☐ 8. could
☐ 9. down	☐ 9. came	☐ 9. every
☐ 10. find	☐ 10. did	☐ 10. fly
☐ 11. make	☐ 11. good	☐ 11. from
☐ 12. not	☐ 12. have	☐ 12. give
☐ 13. one	☐ 13. he	☐ 13. going
☐ 14. play	☐ 14. into	☐ 14. had
☐ 15. red	☐ 15. like	☐ 15. has
☐ 16. away	☐ 16. must	☐ 16. him
☐ 17. blue	☐ 17. new	☐ 17. his
☐ 18. come	☐ 18. no	☐ 18. her
☐ 19. for	☐ 19. now	☐ 19. how
☐ 20. here	☐ 20. on	☐ 20. just
☐ 21. in	☐ 21. our	☐ 21. know
☐ 22. look	☐ 22. out	☐ 22. let
☐ 23. me	☐ 23. please	☐ 23. live
☐ 24. run	☐ 24. pretty	☐ 24. may
☐ 25. at	☐ 25. ran	☐ 25. of
☐ 26. funny	☐ 26. ride	☐ 26. old
☐ 27. is		☐ 27. once
☐ 28. my		☐ 28. open
☐ 29. it		☐ 29. over
		☐ 30. put

BASIC SIGHT WORDS(continued)

Second Grade	*Third Grade*
☐ 1. always	☐ 1. about
☐ 2. around	☐ 2. better
☐ 3. because	☐ 3. bring
☐ 4. been	☐ 4. carry
☐ 5. best	☐ 5. clean
☐ 6. before	☐ 6. cut
☐ 7. both	☐ 7. eight
☐ 8. buy	☐ 8. drink
☐ 9. call	☐ 9. done
☐ 10. cold	☐ 10. draw
☐ 11. does	☐ 11. fall
☐ 12. don't	☐ 12. far
☐ 13. fast	☐ 13. full
☐ 14. first	☐ 14. got
☐ 15. five	☐ 15. grows
☐ 16. found	☐ 16. held
☐ 17. gave	☐ 17. hot
☐ 18. goes	☐ 18. hurt
☐ 19. green	☐ 19. if
☐ 20. its	☐ 20. keep
☐ 21. made	☐ 21. kind
☐ 22. many	☐ 22. laugh
☐ 23. off	☐ 23. light
☐ 24. or	☐ 24. long
☐ 25. pull	☐ 25. much
☐ 26. read	☐ 26. myself
☐ 27. right	☐ 27. never
☐ 28. sing	☐ 28. only
☐ 29. sleep	☐ 29. own
☐ 30. sit	☐ 30. pick

BASIC SIGHT PHRASES

☐ 1.	will go	☐ 26.	so long
☐ 2.	will walk	☐ 27.	you were
☐ 3.	will look	☐ 28.	your sister
☐ 4.	we were	☐ 29.	from home
☐ 5.	we are	☐ 30.	will read
☐ 6.	my brother	☐ 31.	all night
☐ 7.	his sister	☐ 32.	about him
☐ 8.	my father	☐ 33.	will think
☐ 9.	with mother	☐ 34.	for him
☐ 10.	your mother	☐ 35.	will buy
☐ 11.	his brother	☐ 36.	has made
☐ 12.	about it	☐ 37.	went down
☐ 13.	I am	☐ 38.	at home
☐ 14.	for them	☐ 39.	her mother
☐ 15.	can live	☐ 40.	could eat
☐ 16.	all day	☐ 41.	can play
☐ 17.	could make	☐ 42.	her father
☐ 18.	is coming	☐ 43.	can fly
☐ 19.	must go	☐ 44.	too soon
☐ 20.	would like	☐ 45.	down there
☐ 21.	with us	☐ 46.	it is
☐ 22.	some bread	☐ 47.	I was
☐ 23.	you are	☐ 48.	is going
☐ 24.	too little	☐ 49.	would want
☐ 25.	was made	☐ 50.	to stop

BASIC SIGHT WORDS PHRASES *(continued)*

☐ 51. they are	☐ 76. are going
☐ 52. some cake	☐ 77. we have
☐ 53. to go	☐ 78. they will
☐ 54. they were	☐ 79. ran away
☐ 55. up here	☐ 80. look at it
☐ 56. was found	☐ 81. she said
☐ 57. can run	☐ 82. will be
☐ 58. so much	☐ 83. won't have
☐ 59. down there	☐ 84. where are
☐ 60. up there	☐ 85. want some
☐ 61. went away	☐ 86. know how
☐ 62. at three	☐ 87. too much
☐ 63. it was	☐ 88. found that
☐ 64. he was	☐ 89. by myself
☐ 65. he is	☐ 90. look around
☐ 66. must be	☐ 91. in a while
☐ 67. has found	☐ 92. very soon
☐ 68. at once	☐ 93. give back
☐ 69. at school	☐ 94. when will
☐ 70. the white sheep	☐ 95. there are
☐ 71. a new book	☐ 96. better than
☐ 72. to the nest	☐ 97. right now
☐ 73. I saw	☐ 98. try again
☐ 74. here is	☐ 99. just before
☐ 75. they went	☐ 100. their own

A Lesson We've Learned 43

When we insist on accuracy in a young child's writing, we run the risk of inhibiting their inspiration to write.

Young children usually write the way they talk. A child's first experiences with the written word should bring a sense of pleasure and achievement. We need to encourage a child's interest in the printed or written letter or word.

In the early years, children scribble and make letter-like shapes. They begin to discover the connection between the letters of the alphabet and speech sounds. Initially, children use what we call "invented spelling" – the way it sounds to them. For example "lik" for "like". They have not yet learned the rule of the silent "e". There's no rush. As the child matures with more and more experience with reading and writing, conventional spellings start to emerge. The more reading experiences the child has, the sooner proper spelling will appear.

At one time we thought children couldn't write until they had been taught to form letters and spell. In the past, the adult wrote their stories for them and they copied.

Today we know that writing is a developmental process that begins with toddlers who "scribble". Then "letter-like" shapes appear as "play writing". The development of their writing skills is enhanced by experimentation and risk-taking with a focus on meaning.

. . . and don't worry…as they have more and more practise they will ask for your help with spelling. If you can't read their story, ask them to read it to you. As long as it's done soon after they wrote it, you'll be surprised how well they read their own script.

Spelling is difficult for young children, and they need the opportunity to make meaning of their own ever-growing knowledge of letter-sound relationships.

The chart on the next page will help you support them as developing writers.

Writing: A Standards Guide for Grandparents, Parents, Teachers and Students, K-3

Writing	Kindergarten to Grade 1 (ages 5 and 6)	Grades 2 and 3 (ages 7, 8, 9)
	Children learn basic writing skills. They are encouraged to use drawing, scribbling and combinations of letters to try writing.	Children can now do more writing on their own. They will write so others can read what they have written, and they often choose what they want to write.
Why We Write	Children: • explore ways of representing thoughts on paper (most attempts at writing are intended for the students themselves, rather than others) • share words and experiences that are important to them	Children: • share personal experiences and interests through writing • show awareness and interest in having others read their work • use a variety of ways to record and represent ideas
What We Write About	• recognize that print has meaning, and explore ways of representing the letters, names and words they see in books or other places • read parts of what they have written if asked immediately after they finish writing • show interest in letters, sounds and words	• write about immediate personal experiences and interests • include ideas and events they imagine or remember • read their own writing
Style	• explore the form of writing by attempting to represent sounds, words and ideas	• rely on concrete words that represent people, places and things that are important to them • use some descriptive words (frequently repeat a favourite word or phrase) • write in short, simple sentences
How Letters Make Words (Form)	• write from left to right • represent sounds, words and ideas on paper using scribbles, drawing and some recognizable letters • write familiar words that are important to them, such as names	• learn to connect words to form basic sentences • understand and use story structure such as a beginning, middle and an end • write in a variety of simple forms (lists, journals, stories)
Spelling, Grammar and Punctuation	• begin to spell phonetically • recognize letters, names of letters and sounds • print letters, but often use capital letters at first, and reverse some of them • focus on beginning sounds, then ending sounds (e.g., md for mud), then middle consonants (e.g., wgn for wagon) and finally vowels	• use spaces to separate words and spell an increasing number of words correctly, particularly those that are phonetic • use their knowledge of phonics to help them spell many words (e.g., speshaly instead of especially) • show increasing concern for correct spelling and basic punctuation

Writing: A Standards Guide for Parents, Teachers and Students, Grades 4 to 7

Writing	*Grades 4-7*
	In this grade range student learn to write a first copy of their work, and then review it for errors before writing a final copy. Students think about the relationship between what they are writing and who they are writing for, and the best way of presenting the information.
	Children...
Why We Write	• show an increasing awareness and consideration of audiences for their writing, both within the classroom (teacher and other students), and outside the classroom (parents and friends)
	• write for a variety of purposes, such as sharing ideas, to help themselves understand and remember information, to get what they want or to persuade someone to agree with them
What We Write About	• present ideas in a clear, simple and direct way
	• use a variety of sources for ideas, such as books, friends, experiences, imagination
	• show evidence of abstract thought and generalizations
	• learn to revise writing to organize and elaborate on ideas, and to clarify meaning
Style	• show increasing ability to use words with precision, including descriptive language such as similes, metaphors and synonyms
	• attempt to make sentences, paragraphs or sections work together
	• use some specialized language when writing about research or technical topics
	• begin to write more complex sentences
How Letters Make Words (Form)	• show clear form and follow the rules for forms of writing that have been taught (e.g., specific types of poetry such as haiku or research reports)
	• make smooth transitions from one idea to another
	• use paragraphs appropriately in longer pieces of writing
Spelling, Grammar and Punctuation	• follow basic rules for sentence structure, although sentences may still contain errors in the use of pronouns or modifiers
	• proofread drafts of work to identify and correct errors in spelling, punctuation and sentence structure
	• know an increasing number of rules for standard spelling
	• begin to edit work independently

A Lesson We've Learned

44

Awareness of how to deal with and express emotions in a socially acceptable manner leads children to function independently and in cooperation with others.

TRY THIS #167

EMOTIONAL AND SOCIAL DEVELOPMENT

The way people view themselves determines the way they feel, think and learn. Children need to develop positive feelings of self-worth to enhance living and learning. We need to provide experiences that help our grandchildren to:

- develop a positive realistic self-concept
- accept and express emotions in socially acceptable ways
- accept and demonstrate empathy
- accept challenges

- feel pride in accomplishments
- develop independence
- enjoy living and learning

Children who are confident and secure are ready for new learning. Successful learning, in turn, enhances self-esteem...and the cycle continues.

TRY THIS #168

ACCEPTING AND EXPRESSING EMOTIONS IN SOCIALLY ACCEPTABLE WAYS

Children need to observe modelled behaviour that fosters the development of interpersonal skills. Our time with them offers opportunity to deal with and gain competence in living with others. Talking about problems, fears and concerns leads children to the understanding that these emotions are common to all people. Then we have the opportunity to help them understand that all emotions are acceptable but some reactions to emotions are unacceptable.

We need to use patience and perceptiveness to understand the personal point of view of our grandchildren as well as help them understand the point of view of others.

The following checklist will provide you with an opportunity to support, understand and guide the emotional and social development of our grandkids:

Considering the Social and Emotional Development of Our Grandchildren, Birth –7

Birth – 3 years	3 – 5 years	5 – 7 years
Children...	Children...	Children...
• may demonstrate visible expressions of emotion (temper tantrums)	• may display their emotions easily and appear very sensitive and impulsive (crying fits, "No!")	• may continue to show intense emotions (one moment will say, "I love you" and the next, "You are mean.")
• actively show affection for familiar people • may show anxiety when separated from familiar people and places	• begin to feel more comfortable when separated from familiar people, places and things (visiting the neighbour, nursery school, babysitters)	• may appear anxious once again when separated from familiar people and places (beginning school, sleepovers)
• are naturally very curious about other children and may watch and imitate others • generally play alone, and may or may not attempt to interact with others	• may play alone or beside others, but are becoming more aware of the feelings of others. May be frustrated at attempts to socialize but hold no grudges	• are learning to cooperate with others for longer periods of time, and friendships may change frequently
• strive toward independence with support and affection (sitting up, crawling, walking, dressing, feeding, toileting)	• begin to assert independence by saying "No" or "I can do it myself!" May dump a cupful of water onto the floor while looking directly at you • see selves as family members and as boy or girl in the family	• continue to develop feelings of independence by becoming able to do certain things (making a simple breakfast or riding a bicycle) • may begin to talk about self and to define self in terms of what they have or own • may feel they are being treated unfairly if others get something they do not

245

Considering the Social and Emotional Development of Our Grandchildren, Birth –7
(continued)

Birth – 3 years	3 – 5 years	5 – 7 years
Children…	Children…	Children…
• begin to see themselves as people and appear self-centred • begin to see themselves as strong through directing others: "Sit down."	• See themselves as powerful and creative doers. If the child can't reach something, he or she will get a stool	• begin to see themselves as bad, good, clever, and may seem very hard on themselves
• May become possessive of belongings (special people, toys, special times)	• May continue to appear possessive • May feel if something is shared for a brief period it is gone forever	• begin to develop the ability to share possessions and take turns

Beautiful Babies

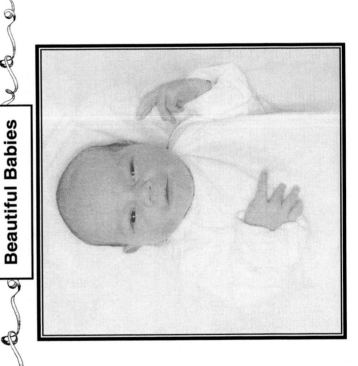

246

Considering the Social and Emotional Development of Our Grandchildren, 7-13 years

7 – 9 years	9 – 11 years	11 – 13 years
Children…	Children…	Children…
• may continue to show bursts of emotions and impatience less frequently • may show emotions that are both judgmental and critical of themselves and others	• may appear relatively calm and at peace with themselves, and occasionally become angry, sad or depressed, but these moments are usually short-lived	• may begin to show intense emotions, bouts of anxiety, moodiness. Emotions may come close to the surface (cry and anger easily)
• continue to feel some anxiety within the larger community when separated from familiar people, places, things (going to camp, sleepovers, shopping malls)	• often hide feelings of anxiety when introduced to new experiences by appearing overconfident • continue to be very sociable and spend time with parents, friends of the same sex, and often have a "special" friend	• continue to hide feelings of anxiety with friends and family, often appearing overconfident, with a know-it-all attitude • generally get along well with their friends and continue to show an interest in having a "best" friend, but fights and arguments may occur from time to time
• are becoming more outgoing • are developing closer friendships with others and may begin to play mainly with children of the same sex	• are generally positive about themselves and begin to understand what they are good at doing; may comment easily, "I can do that" or "I can't do that."	• start to question adult authority • sometimes engage in self put-downs – in conversations with others, may say, "I can't do anything right!"
• show a generally increased sense of self-confidence	• often define self by physical characteristics and possessions, as well as likes and dislikes	• may begin to define self in terms of opinions, beliefs, values, and expand sense of self by attempting to copy the culture of current fads (clothes, music, sports)

Considering the Social and Emotional Development of Our Grandchildren, 7-13 years *(continued)*

7 – 9 years	9 – 11 years	11 – 13 years
Children...	Children...	Children...
• will eagerly take on tasks and activities likely to be successful, but usually will not take risks • may define self as a particular name, age, size, hair colour or other characteristics ("I'm Elizabeth Anne and I'm seven years old!")	• often vary between the sexes in their view of what is important in dress and physical appearance • are sensitive to criticism and display feelings of success or failure, depending on how adults and peers respond to them	• gradually are gaining independence from parental influence • are sensitive to criticism and display feelings of success or failure, depending on reactions of others
• are sensitive to criticism and display feelings of success or failure, depending on how adults respond to them	• continue to develop the ability to work and play with others • may not want to be disturbed when involved in an activity or a game	• may become self-critical • may appear to become possessive with own belongings, especially with younger brothers and sisters • may view younger brothers and sisters as a bother or a nuisance when involved with peers, and feel discriminated against in family situations
• continue to develop the ability to share possessions and to take turns if they understand something is not always "lost" by doing so	• are continuing to develop an appreciation of their own and other cultural heritages. Can talk about similarities and differences • continue to develop the ability to respond sympathetically to others and may try to help them	• may begin to appreciate the rich multicultural heritage of their own country, while cherishing family culture in relation to the whole • may begin developing the ability to empathize with another's feelings in understandable situations
	• begin to "weigh" consequences of own actions	• begin to "test" consequences of own and others' actions

A Lesson We've Learned 45

"Living in harmony with other human beings may be one of the outstanding challenges for the whole human race."

Social Responsibility

The way people view the world is directly related to the early development of attitudes and values. Children need to develop the awareness and behaviour of a socially responsible person. They need experiences which will help them to:

- become responsible citizens
- cope with change
- appreciate cultural identity and heritage
- value and respect individual and cultural similarities and differences
- respect and care for the environment

Social responsibility is learned at a very early age. Children must be helped to not only live comfortably with self and others, but to move beyond the personal level toward the ability to appreciate social problems and to contribute cooperatively to their solutions.

After all, development of the values inherent in these statements begins at a young age, and in our families first.

Beautiful Babies

Taylor and Austin
1999

Considering the Social Responsibility of Our Grandchildren, Birth - 7

The following checklist will help you watch over, understand and guide your grandchildren through this complex and critical skill set:

Birth – 3 years	*3 – 5 years*	*5 – 7 years*
Children...	**Children...**	**Children...**
• appear insensitive to the views of others, yet show interest in them • are generally self-centred in their views • look at the world mostly from their own viewpoint (may think the sun sets because they go to bed) • may cry when they see or hear another child crying • physically explore the environment to the best of their abilities using their senses (seeing, hearing, tasting, smelling and feeling)	• are becoming aware of others, and beginning to take part in social play groups • may play "beside" rather than "with" others • are beginning to see that their views differ from those of others, but remain self-centred • may show aggressive feelings toward others when something does not go their way • are beginning to sense when another person is sad, angry, happy	• are developing the ability to take part in social play groups and for longer periods of time • may prefer to play alone at times or with others • are developing the ability to see that others have feelings and different views than their own • may begin to respond to others in times of distress if they are supported and encouraged to do so
• are natural explorers, eager for new experiences	• become interested in exploring the environment outside the immediate home. May be interested in growing seed, weather, seasons, the moon and sun	• are developing an interest in the community and the world outside their own
• are beginning to distinguish between familiar and unfamiliar faces	• continue to eagerly explore the world around them	• may begin to show an awareness of basic necessities (food, clothing, shelter)

Considering the Social Responsibility of Our Grandchildren, Birth – 7
(continued)

Birth – 3 years	*3 – 5 years*	*5 – 7 years*
Children...	Children...	Children...
• are becoming aware of their own feelings and respond to others' expressions (become upset if caregiver is also upset)	• are becoming more aware of family and social relationships	• may begin to notice how people are similar and different from one another
• begin to recognize that consequences follow actions	• may sense another person's unhappiness (such as another child crying) and not know how to help	• are developing the ability to respond sympathetically to others if they are hurt, upset or crying
	• become aware of consequences of own behaviour	• begin to understand the consequences of own and others' behaviour

Beautiful Babies

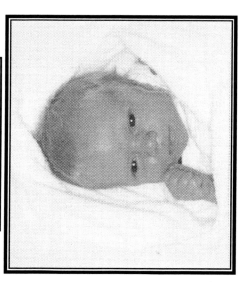

Glendon
hours old!

Considering the Social Responsibility of Our Grandchildren, 7-13 years

The following checklist will help you watch over, understand and guide your grandchildren through this complex and critical skill set:

7 – 9 years	9 – 11 years	11 – 13 years
Children...	Children...	Children...
• are learning to work in groups and are developing the ability to get along with others	• continue to learn to work in groups if this activity is supported	• may show that their relations with friends are increasingly important
• can lead sometimes, and can follow at others	• may become upset or distressed if they have problems with friends	• continue to develop the ability to work cooperatively and collaboratively with others
• are developing the ability to see how others act and what they expect in certain situations	• begin to understand the idea of the differing contributions of groups members to a common goal	• are developing the ability to understand that there are several sides to an issue, but are just beginning to show evidence of being able to take other views into account. Still consider own point of view the right one
• may be developing close friendships that are helping them learn to understand how others think and feel	• are developing the ability to take a third-person view, in which they see situations, themselves and others as if they were spectators, but still do not coordinate these views	• continue to develop the ability to see the worth of others' viewpoints if this is supported
• continue to develop the ability to respond sympathetically to others if they are supported and encouraged to do so	• may be developing the ability to see that others have different viewpoints but still do not coordinate these views with their own	

252

Considering the Social Responsibility of Our Grandchildren, 7-13 years
(continued)

7 – 9 years	*9 – 11 years*	*11 – 13 years*
Children...	Children...	Children...
• continue to be curious about the world around them and may show interest in learning about other people (food, clothing, shelter)	• continue to try to develop the ability to respond sympathetically to others, but still have difficulty in taking any point of view but their own	• continue to develop the ability to respond sympathetically to others, and may begin to consider other points of view
• are developing an interest in and enthusiasm for specific issues pertaining to their world, and can define simple actions to help (returning aluminum cans for recycling)	• continue to develop an awareness of how own family meets basic needs	• continue to develop an awareness of how family needs affect others
• are developing an appreciation of their own and other cultural heritages through special events, festivals, foods, folk songs and other concrete experiences	• are developing personal views of important issues and values pertaining to their world, and act upon their beliefs (making posters)	• are becoming more committed to their beliefs and personal views of the world around them (writing letters to newspapers)
• continue to develop the ability to respond sympathetically to others if this is supported	• are continuing to develop an appreciation of their own and other cultural heritages. Can talk about similarities and differences	• may begin developing the ability to empathize with another's feelings in understandable situations
• begin to understand the consequences of own and others' behaviour	• continue to develop the ability to respond sympathetically to others, and may try to help them	• begin to "test" consequences of own and others' actions
	• begin to "weigh" consequences of own actions	

A Lesson We've Learned 46

By giving our kids a solid foundation of family values, we will provide them with the capacity to withstand the inevitable growing pains and stress of life.

Raising Moral Children

Dr. Marianne Neifert, in an article called "Raising A Moral Child" *(Parenting Magazine, June/July, 1999)* identifies a number of ways we can help children develop desirable emotional skills. She is also author of *Dr. Mom's Parenting Guide.*

She concludes the article by saying:

> "Just knowing that you've raised a
> kind, generous, decent child
> can be the most gratifying reward of all."

1. **Show your love.** When a child feels valued, he's more likely to be the best he can be.

2. **Practise what you preach.** Children watch the way we handle our emotions and how we interact and solve problems.

3. **Help him sort out his emotions.** Don't negate his feelings, help him define and articulate them.

4. **Praise good behaviour.** Compliment them when they do something admirable…in front of other family members. Show you are proud of appropriate actions. Eventually their own satisfaction will be their motivation.

5. **Tell tales.** Use movies, books, family stories and your personal experiences to teach and discuss lessons.

TRY THIS #169

ENCOURAGING FAMILY VALUES

Dr. Neifert recommends the following strategies:

Show empathy
- respond promptly to their emotional needs

Demonstrate generosity
- teach how good it feels to share

Demonstrate problem-solving
- help him find a variety of possible solutions to a problem, then evaluate them by discussing the pros and cons of each one before choosing

Demonstrate optimism
- teach them to search for answers instead of dwelling on problems

Demonstrate perseverance
- the ability to keep on trying when faced with difficulties is connected to increased confidence, responsibility and healthy risk-taking

Show respect for self and others
- a child who is treated with respect will be more likely to give it to others

Encourage honesty
- avoid putting them in situations where they can choose to lie. When he's truthful, praise the behaviour

A Lesson We've Learned

"Enjoy the one you have,
not the one you think you should make him into."
Dr. Pruett

Nurturing Strengths: 4 Golden Rules

In his article called "Nurture Your Child's Strengths", Dr. Pruett describes four golden rules to bring out the best in your child. In short, they are:

TRY THIS #170

GOLDEN RULE 1: Always Love the One You're With

Enjoy the one you have, not the one you think you should make him into. Dr. Pruett points out:

- his temperament is his, not yours
- children this age with difficult temperaments are not being willfully irritating; it is beyond their control in early life
- remember their unique behavioural styles are part of their "nature", so be sympathetic
- don't make the baby kiss grandma when she leaves...be sympathetic rather than reprimanding

TRY THIS #171

GOLDEN RULE 2: Nurture Her Strengths
and Lessen Her Weaknesses

While temperament is not a parent's doing, neither is it entirely fixed. How you nurture your child's nature is what building character is all about, one of the biggest responsibilities of parenthood (and grandparenting!).

Dr.Pruett suggests:

- strengths can be nurtured and shaped
- weaknesses can be lessened and channeled into constructive traits
- Dr. Gottman of Seattle, Wa., is quoted as saying that aggression can be managed by encouraging them to express their emotions:
  - acknowledging the emotion
  - waiting for a response
  - labelling it
  - encouraging the child to put it into words
  - finally coming up with a solution to the problem
  -

Beautiful Babies

Natasha and her hat

This creates an emotional connection between adult and child, a long-term connection.

TRY THIS #172

GOLDEN RULE 3: Accept and Appreciate Your Toddler for Who She Is

Dr. Pruett says that children can condition us, and we them, by rewarding and punishing in subtle ways and we need to take care in this area. He proposes:

- that we take care to **not** assign a temperamental tendency to kids or pigeonhole children (whiner or aggressive, etc.)
- our unconscious handling of situations can reinforce a temperamental tendency
- that if children can get their needs met by whining, for example, that will become her "trigger point"

TRY THIS #173

GOLDEN RULE 4: Cherish Your Child's Individuality

"A toddler with a different temperament than your own can take you on an enriching excursion." Remember, Dr. Pruett says:

"Some temperamental fits between adult and child may be easy, some complex, but not good or bad. Adults who accept values and react appropriately to a child's individuality have the happiest outcomes."

- respond to your child consistently
- have realistic expectations
- be a parent (or grandparent!), not a friend

Finally, he says, "The toddler years are the final run-up to a fully wired brain, a process that slows at age 3 . . . This time is rich with potential – greater than you will ever encounter again – to encourage positive traits and to modify those that could pose a challenge to healthy growth and a happy childhood."

Beautiful Babies

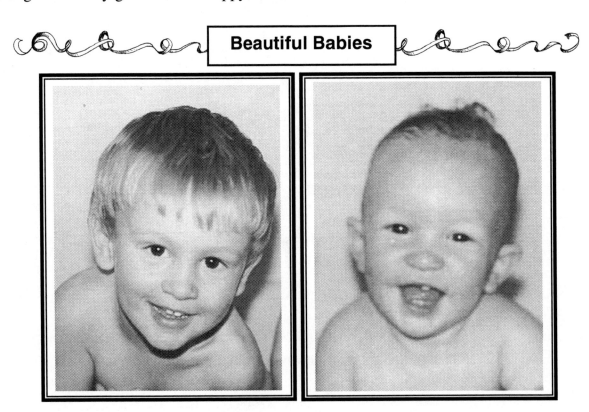

Hayden and Cody

A Lesson We've Learned 48

"If I could tell you what I mean, there would be no point in dancing."
Isodora Duncan – *Coming To Our Senses*

Raising the Whole Child

The Goals of the Primary Program for the Province of B.C. encompass:

- emotional development
- social development
- social responsibility
- intellectual development
- physical development
- aesthetic and artistic development

As indicated in the introduction to this chapter , elaborate skill lists are available for each area in the Supporting Learning document available from the Ministry of Education through the Queen's Printer.

We have chosen to elaborate on the first four of these, as they will be the ones most easily influenced by grandparents near or far, as already outlined in the preceding chapters.

It would be improper, however, to minimize the importance of any of the goals, as each contributes to the development of the whole child; therefore, we present a summary of those remaining.

TRY THIS #174

AESTHETIC AND ARTISTIC DEVELOPMENT

Experiences should be provided which will help the child to:

- foster enthusiasm for the arts
- explore, express, visualize, interpret and create
- represent through a variety of forms
- appreciate the interrelationships between the arts, society and the environment
- respond to the arts

TRY THIS #175

PHYSICAL DEVELOPMENT

Experiences should be provided that will help the child to:

- develop a wide variety of motor skills and maintain physical fitness
- take care of and respect his/her body
- develop an awareness of and practise good nutrition
- develop appreciation and enjoyment of human movement
- learn and practise safety procedures
- work cooperatively in group activities and team games

They will be blessed if we can support them in all goal areas.

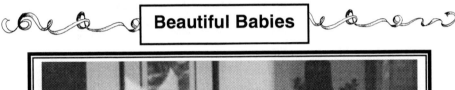

Beautiful Babies

A Lesson We've Learned 49

Play is important...and it keeps us young at heart!

Teach your grandchild through play

Play is a natural and universal learning activity of both kids and adults. It is a lifelong need and pursuit, vital to all human beings. Play is motivated by an inner drive to imagine, explore, experiment, discover and learn. It comes from our inborn desire to make sense of our world.

Children learn through play. Play engages their thought, language and interaction with others. Play gives children the chance to experiment safely, develop social relationships, and imagine and act out roles and relationships in a variety of settings.

Through play children can:

- explore
- imitate
- discuss
- manipulate
- dramatize
- experiment
- imagine
- construct
- plan
- problem solve
- create

Beautiful Babies

Encourage your grandchildren to create ideas and activities while you provide the time, space and materials for play. Play should be a deeply satisfying, creative endeavour as well as an adventure in self-expression and exploration.

P.S. Besides, it's tried and true – play keeps grandparents young at heart!

Brent
6 months old

A Lesson We've Learned 50

50 Ways to Show You Care

TRY THESE #176 to #225

50 Ways To Show You Care

176. Make a difference in their lives
177. Hold a fair for grandkids in your area with clowns, balloons, facepainting
178. Make grandparenting a community focus
179. Start a grandparent's (celebration) support group
180. Keep a place deep in your heart for your grandkids
181. If they're allergic to favourite foods find exciting substitute treats
182. Publicly demonstrate their importance
183. Buy books and let them eat the covers
184. Soothe the tears and give the comfort
185. Look into their eyes when you talk to them
186. Set boundaries that keep them safe
187. Never raise your voice
188. Deliver meals for parents of the newborn, but don't get in the way
189. Be respectful of their parents' feelings
190. Provide or pay for daycare to give their parents a break
191. Create a grandparent's co-op, pool your talents and energies
192. Plan family outings, picnics and parties that are unique and child focussed. Include families by marriage
193. Plan one-on-one time and let them pick the activity
194. Eat as a family as often as you can
195. Subscribe to family and kid magazines to keep current

176. Remember when your child is hurt or frightened, every minute counts. Stay with them.
177. Keep a journal of every contact, near or far
178. Pray for them
179. Create a backyard carnival with a tattoo parlour, corn dogs, jelly bean counting contest and colourful crafts. Invite all the kids on the street.
180. Make big kabobs of fruit pieces and stick them in a watermelon for snacks
181. Buy plain cotton beach/book bags, decorate with fabric paint and fabric markers
182. Take them back to nature
183. Be as silly as they are
184. Teach them to jive
185. Order "child" magazine that can be targeted to your grandkid's exact age
186. Provide swimming lessons for safety's sake
187. Make a gift of topnotch sun screens
188. With parents' permission (be sensitive), take them for a nutritional analysis, then supply the necessary supplements
189. Hide surprises for them to find
190. Talk about hitting, and brainstorm alternatives – "no bullying in this family"
191. Let them see your tears and explain
192. Give them Beatrix Potter's work
193. Take them to visit the elderly
194. Make cards for sick friends with them
195. Help them bake brownies for a homeless shelter
196. Take them to a local walkathon that supports a good cause
197. Don't let distance be your excuse, get creative
198. Find "no sugar added" recipes
199. Count their multiple blessings with them
200. Reconnect with a hug
201. Teach them how to apologize
202. Help them have great memories
203. Find recipe books on "smoothies"* and keep the ingredients for these fabulous blender drinks on hand. Kids love making and drinking them, and they're nutritious too
204. Teach 9-1-1
205. Love them, love them, and love them some more!

Chapter 5

Grandparents:
Teaching With the Winning Touch

Conclusion: WHEN THEY ARE GROWN

If we can articulate a vision of the kind of contributing person we want our grandkids to be in the future, we will have a better chance of helping them make that journey.

One of the most articulate and inspiring statements of intended learning outcomes (the results of learning) I have seen is the work done in the Greater Victoria School District (SD# 61) in British Columbia, Canada.

Over the course of two years, committees of highly skilled professionals developed this vision of the kind of graduates they would be proud of. These Significant Learning Outcomes have been incorporated into individual school goals throughout the district and shared with other districts. Thanks to the Greater Victoria School District for being willing to share them through this book.

Significant Learning Outcomes

Children need to be working to become:

- **Quality producers and performers who:**
    - evaluate products and performances for quality
    - creates quality standards for his/her own products and performances
    - create intellectual, artistic and practical products demonstrating high quality standards
    - revise and rework products and performances until they demonstrate high quality standards
    - use resources and technologies as appropriate

Beautiful Babies

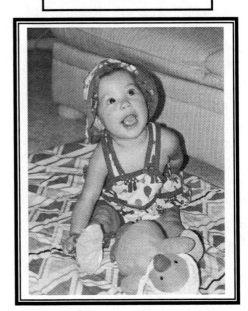

Children need to be working to become:

- **self-directed learners who**

    - set challenging but achievable goals
    - plan effectively to achieve those goals
    - stays focused on and carries through with his/her plans
    - assesses his/her progress, inviting assessment from others, and replanning as necessary

- **perceptive thinkers who:**

    - relate his/her experience to new situations
    - gather, assess and use information
    - explain, form opinions, and create new ideas or products

- **flexible problem solvers who:**

    - discover and define problems
    - relates his/her experience to problems
    - gathers, assesses and uses information to supplement his/her experience
    - structure experience, information, intuition and chance in ways that may lead to solutions

- **community contributors who:**

    - respect the rights of others
    - participate actively in the community
    - cooperate in solving interpersonal problems
    - understand and work within diverse cultures and organizational settings
    - consider the need for change and its effects on the global environment

- **effective communicators who:**

    - conveys his/her thoughts, feelings and competencies to others through a variety of media
    - react appropriately to the expressed thoughts, feelings and competencies of others

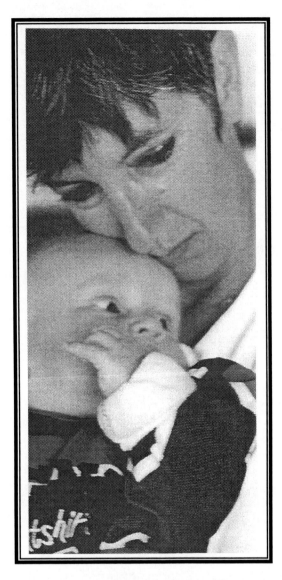

A Passion for Our Grandchildren

Conclusion

Granny Consultant, Wendy Graham

A very special thanks to Wendy Graham, my "Granny Consultant," who sponsored an invitation to grandparents to contribute to this book, through an ad in Sidney's (BC) *New Senior* magazine. (Wendy and I and two of our grandchildren were their cover models.) Some of the stories already appear in the Lessons in this book. Here are some that were too special to be set aside.

Wendy is one of my best granny friends, owner of two retail stores, "Sunday's Snowflakes" (1 and 2) and "Something More" – all in the Victoria, B.C., area. She is on the Board of the local YMCA and one of the wisest and most dedicated grannies about.

We present her collection of stories which were submitted in response to the following ad. They provide a fitting conclusion to *A Passion for Our Grandchildren*.

GRANDCHILD

Who asks me questions
takes time to listen
aware she already has the answers.

Who holds my hand, whispers secrets
that I must not share,
honoring me with trust.

Who sheds tears
at my leaving that
heals all hurts and sustains my soul.

Whose spirit has
at the beginning the knowledge
that at my end I am still searching for.

Who loves me, yet judges not,
but smiles
warming all that surrounds her.

Who sits still for photographs
angelic, loving
before the snap, calls "fuzzy pickles!"

Kirstan!

Shirley-Ann Badminton

TO MY GRANDDAUGHTER

You will be special to me, little girl.
I see you posing as you twist and twirl
In your pretty pink frilled party dresses,
With matching ribbons to hold your tresses
Tied in a bow, and with white socks and shoes.
Is that the kind of granddaughter to choose?

Or one who's romping in jeans and a tee,
Seated aloft at the top of a tree,
Playing kick ball with the boys on the block,
Listening to music (undoubtedly rock),
Off camping and fishing and if you please
Proud of the patches which cover your knees?

Whichever you'll be, rambunctious, demure,
You're my granddaughter, I'll love you for sure.
I'll watch you grow up and know at each stage
Of your childhood I'll enjoy that age.
If we have problems, who's going to worry,
I'll just send you back home in a hurry!

Elizabeth Symon

TO MY GRANDSON

He comes as a bonus to me, this boy,
He is indeed a real bundle of joy.
It was like having a pleasure rerun
Holding this baby, the son of my son,
His first smile, a tooth, a step on his own,
Watching my grandson to see how he's grown.
Baby to toddler, he is quite a lad,
With that winning way his own Daddy had,
Same spirit of mischief, same sense of fun,
Like Father, like child, and just like my son!

Elizabeth Symon

Re: The Art of Grandparenting

Attached please find my submission for your consideration in a collection of stories about grandparenting.

It is a eulogy I wrote for my grandma and delivered at her memorial service in April of last year. Needless to say, it was a very difficult but necessary thing to do.

Having just had my first baby (Olivia – born May 11), I now have first-hand experience of the overwhelming love one feels for their offspring. It's absolutely fantastic to watch my parents with my baby, and I think it has given me some appreciation of what that relationship must have meant for my grandma.

Anyway, good luck with your collection. It's a great idea!

Alison Giles

FOR GRANDMA – FROM AL

When I was a little girl, my Grandma was a giant. She was a tall, dignified, elegant woman – she was the tallest grandparent I had. One of my memories from a visit to England when I was 10, was of her calling Grandpa and me in for lunch. We had been puttering around in the vegetable patch at the bottom of the garden, and when she came outside to call us in, her head was well above the hydrangeas that grew along the south side of their bungalow in Devon. I think she always found it slightly amusing that her daughter and eldest granddaughter were vertically challenged – much like Grandpa. She was taller than those giant hydrangeas, and she could almost always reach the top shelf in just about any kitchen – and, of course, it's taken me some time to realize that she was a giant in other ways too.

I was fortunate to have had four grandparents until well into my teens. I realize now that I was exceedingly lucky to have had a grandparent until age 33. Not everyone gets that chance. And that grandparent/grandchild relationship is one of the best. Grandparents love to tell anyone, especially those who can't wait to be grandparents, about how great it is having grandkids because they get to do all the fun stuff – and almost none of the difficult stuff. Well, think how great that is from a child's perspective! You have someone with almost unlimited time and patience, someone prepared to play copious card games, someone who believes in the importance of dessert following a meal, someone who knows where the chocolate chips are and can get them for you, someone who's prepared to clean up your mess instead of making you do it, someone who indulges you with Battenburg cake and cupcakes with thick chocolate icing, and someone who gives you a ten-dollar bill "just because."

One of Grandma's qualities was loyalty. She was loyal to England, to the Queen, and to the game of golf. But it was her loyalty to family that eventually prompted Grandma and Grandpa to emigrate to Canada in their late 60s. They did this to be with their only daughter, son-in-law and their growing family. Our grandmother was an integral part of all three of our lives. When I was three months old, I was shipped off to Grandma and Grandpa Forrester's for three weeks while Mum and Dad wrote final exams at university. When Rosalind was about eighteen months old, Mum became very ill with appendicitis, and Grandma flew out from England to Terrace, B.C. to take care of Mum and Ros, while Dad worked. And, when Mum returned to university to complete her teaching certificate, Grandma and Grandpa took care of Elizabeth, who was not yet in school. They took us the majority of our doctor and dentist and orthodontist appointments while we were growing up, and helped Mum and Dad out whenever they could.

Grandma also had a history of community service, having volunteered with the Ladies' Auxiliary at Saanich Peninsula Hospital, the CRD Health Clinic in Sidney (mostly weighing babies), and the St. Andrew's Morning Group and Altar Guild. She considered it important to have a sense of the spirit of a community.

Grandma had a huge capacity to love. If she could have had half a dozen children, she probably would have. Mum and Grandma didn't always see eye to eye on a number of issues, but in spite of this, Grandma would have done anything for Mum. She absolutely adored babies, flowers, social occasions, and Elvis. I'm not talking about the rock star who lived in Memphis, but the Siamese cat who lives on Beaufort Road. Grandma was the first to admit she wasn't really taken with pets, but when it came to Elvis, she was smitten. When Dad used to threaten to pitch Elvis outside because he'd been up to one of his howling and yowling episodes (and he really is a yowler), Grandma was quite convinced Elvis was simply communicating, and she, in turn, would threaten Dad right back.

It goes, without saying, that we are growing up in a generation vastly different from Grandma's. Ours is an instant generation. We want everything, and we want it now. Hers was a generation where you saved until you had enough money to buy things, where you never took food for granted, where you never put off 'til tomorrow what you could do today, and where homemade items were treasured because they represented time spent on something worthwhile that spoke from the heart.

In spite of this generation gap, Grandma strove to be contemporary. She found computers baffling, but would nevertheless get on a keyboard and have a go at computer golf anyway. She knew how to handle Automatic Teller machines, self-serve gas stations, and long-distance dialing. She was a champion of the balanced cheque book. She had a strong work ethic and always inquired about our work. She was among the pioneers of women who worked outside the home, having worked as an office manager for a general contracting firm in Stoke-on-Trent in England.

She was adept at knitting, sewing, and baking. She rarely said no to a Fair Isle sweater, a difficult dress pattern, or a complicated recipe. Grandma was a master of the lost arts. She was an excellent typist, an enthusiastic correspondent, and excelled at crosswords.

When Grandma moved in with Mum and Dad almost three years ago, she down-sized significantly, and either sold many items or gave many things away. Among the treasures she kept, we've discovered sentimental cards from Grandpa, icing roses from their 50th wedding anniversary cake, and photographs of the two of them – he in black tie and she in a long gown she'd made herself, attending formal occasions. These items speak volumes about Grandma. She had always missed Grandpa and made no bones about it. Grandma loved a social occasion and birthdays. She celebrated her 88th birthday on Christmas Day, and three days later attended Elizabeth's wedding. It was important to her that we were all settled down and married. These were events that added to her satisfaction. These last few months weren't easy for Grandma. She recognized that Saanich Peninsula Hospital was likely the best option, given the circumstances. For Grandma, appearances meant a great deal. She was a smart old bird and managed to be self possessed, composed, and retain her dignity in a situation which afforded very little.

There is nothing quite like the pain of loss. Although these words aren't mine, I think this is what it all boils down to: A hundred years from now, it will not matter what my bank account was, the sort of house I lived in, or the kind of car I drove – what will matter is that the world may be different because I was important in the life of a child.

Grandma was fond of gin and tonic, a good cribbage game, golf, *Coronation Street*, the smell of cigar smoke and sweet peas. I'm hopeful that even if you don't imbibe, play cards, golf, watch British soap operas or smoke, should you have the good fortune to catch the scent of a sweet pea, you'll think of my Grandma and smile. And she would be pleased. We'll all miss her.

My name is Zola Beatrice Auld and through my Mom's writing hand, I'd like to share with you why my Nonna and Grandma mean so much to me. When I was born almost 22 months ago, I nearly didn't make it due to a severe abdominal blockage. A wonderful surgeon helped me, along with a great team of caregivers to ensure that I received the essential nutrients and then my mother's milk until I could nurse well following the surgery.

Both grandmothers have been my supporters and never once have given me less than their complete love and devotion. They look after me early in the morning until mid-afternoon while my parents work. I am a delight and a challenge. Having Down Syndrome means that I have to be shown new or different skills at times when it seems ripe for me to learn. Nonna and Grandma sing to me, show me so many ways to tell them, "I love you," help me know when to go to use the potty, bring me to parks, playgroups, and special learning classes. They mirror my attempts at feeding myself and encourage me to try all sorts of activities. I am a social girl who likes to be in the thick of things, and sometimes I need direction as to the better way to go.

I feel so lucky, if not completely fortunate, to have grandmothers who have taken such an active role in my early, formative months. I'll continue to thrive while they watch me walk, run, jump, climb, dance, play and sing. Thank you, "Noma" and "Gama".

Zola B.
XOXOXO

P.S. I love the "Brring, Brring" of the phone

OUR GRANDPARENTS

Great listeners
Really thoughtful
Appreciative audience
Never angry
Doing fun things with us
Patient and kind
Always loving
Remembering our roots
Encouraging our efforts
Noticing our growth
There when we need them
Super friends

by Max Way
(age 8)

I HAVE A GRANDDAUGHTER

I have a granddaughter just one year,
she is heavenly sent and does not know fear!
She is adorable and so clever
is she crying often? No, never….!!!

I am with her every second week
as much as four times then I am beat!
She wakes up and patiently wait,
till I get there not too late

We walk together and she talks
baby noises to the folks
She is dainty and light as a feather
we come home and play together

Then her Daddy arrives and I must go
How difficult to part from my little
beau!

Wilma Roberts

THANKS NOAH

He skips around the corner.
Blond hair bobbing playfully matches
his magnetic blue eyes.
He's two…
"Hi Gwamma", rings through the hall.
Smiles flood our faces.
An angel bringing light to the day.
Thank you for the opportunities
you have given me,
to be amazed over a bug, a "slub" or a "big tuck".
You're forever my gift.

Marlene Johnson

MY LITTLE GRANDSON

"Grandma, help me!
I fell down and skinned my knee."
As I bandage the wound
I kiss the "boo-boo," so it will heal soon.
My grandson embraces me in my arms,
Secure and safe from harm,
Pulling, tugging my hand
Playing follow the leader.
I follow my Little man.

"Grandma, come and see
A secret to share with me."
He whispers, "I love you," in my ear
Such joy makes me shed a tear.
Just one of the many joys
A grandma's memory holds.

Mrs. Teri Sirvio

MY GARDEN

I've been working in my garden, picking raspberries and peas
If you would like to have some, bring a little carton, please.
The strawberries are over now – blackcurrants, too
Languish in my freezer, for pies, when weather's blue.
The birds and bees all love them, and when Curtis comes to call,
"Let's pick blackcurrants, Grannie," he shouts to one and all.
"Just pick the black ones," I tell him every time,
"I will," he answers cheerfully, giving me a line.
He's only three, and next year I guess won't want to bother,
So I enjoy him while I can, just as I did his Mother.

The years go by so quickly, and other interests call,
But now I'm still in favour for he has me playing ball.
We kick it and we throw it, and it keeps us trim and fit,
No rules or regulations, and we don't mind that one bit.
When he's old enough for tennis, or hockey, and such
I'll bow out very gracefully, and not really miss it much.
I never was much good at sports, but this he doesn't know
I'll enjoy each day that comes along and watch him grow.
My peas and berries help, and my nature study lessons
He stuffs bugs in bottles, and asks so many questions.
We put suet out for Jays, and wheat seed for the Quail,
Watch the birds at the feeders, water flowers with a pail.
Busy, busy, busy, no stopping for a minute
"Til Mother says, "It's time for bed."
Goodnight, my little poppit.

Doris E. Carr

AS WE GO STROLLING THROUGH THE PARK

Today is special. Our daughter-in-law is bringing our grandson over for a while. She needs some free time to be able to do some shopping. We are pleased, and look forward to taking him for a walk in his stroller.

He is a happy little fellow and, of course, because we are his grandparents and love him dearly, he is a wonder to us in every way.

Walking along Dallas Road, and then through the park, we feel almost young again, taking turns at pushing the stroller. Lawson smiles at the people passing by, who in turn give us an approving glance and nod. Of course they know we look old enough to be the grandparents; but, even so, we can make believe and reminisce a little, remembering . . . a generation ago, it was our own, and we felt so proud then, as we do now. And after all, as anyone can see, he does have his grandfather's smile!

Hélène and Alan Smith

THOUGHTS OF NANNA AND GRAMPA

A person who provides routine in someone's life is seen by them as someone who can be counted on. My grandparents did this . . .it is the thing that I remember most about them.

When I was five I spent a year living with Nanna and Grampa because I was old enough to go to kindergarten, but there wasn't one in Nipigon. I'd be at school most of the day. The other half of the day Nanna looked after me. Mom didn't have to hire a babysitter that year because my other sister and brother were both in school. There was a big difference from the little house I knew in Nipigon to the brick two-storey in Port Arthur.

It was very quiet in Nanna's house, and I can remember things like being able to hear the clock tick. On Mondays Nanna did the wash in the basement, and she gave me a pail so I could wash my doll clothes beside her. On the other days of the week, Nanna had certain chores that she always did and I helped her. When she dust mopped the floors, I helped with my own dust mop that was just the right height for me to use. When she watered the garden, I helped and used a little watering can that was just for me. I learned the names of her flowers and the stories that sometimes went with them. Saturdays after supper and after all the dishes were done and when Nanna was having a cup of tea, she read the funnies in the newspaper. I remember sitting on her soft lap.

Grampa had his routines, too. He tapped the barometer every day and predicted the weather. Every Sunday, he went to the garage and started the car and warmed it up for a while. He never went anywhere in it, he just took care of it. Some Sundays, he would take me for a walk while Nanna was at church. He took me to places I didn't know existed. We walked along the docks, through the train yard and stopped at the station, and I'd ask all kinds of questions. After the walk, we rode the bus home, and Grampa would signal me when it was time to pull the cord to make the bell ring. Grampa always had the same kind of mints in his pocket, and I always knew that somewhere along the way I'd get a mint.

My world was small and life was routine but wonderful. The little things were special.

I guess I'm saying that that year could have been very hard on me. I was away from home, but the simple routine of the days with Nanna and Grampa made me feel secure, and I know it was easier on them to let me help them in their routines, rather than them trying to find things for me to do by myself.

Christine Nuttall

WENDY'S SUMMATION

There is something magic in being a grandparent.

From the time they are born, you can wrap your arms around those children, encompass them with understanding, joy, and a love that knows no bounds.

You can enrich their lives and yours, as well as being a safe haven for them throughout their lives; provide them with fun and excitement and enchantment; provide them with overwhelming joy and love; and enjoy the magic of being a grandparent.

Wendy Graham

Janet and granddaughter Natasha, and
"Granny Consultant" Wendy and grandson Cody

An Invitation To You:
"A Day in Our Lives"

We have already begun *A Passion for Our Grandchildren – Volume II*, a collection of journal entries written either by children and/or their grandparents. We invite you to submit entries about you, your grandchildren and/or your family.

Journal entries might be about:

- a weekend visit
- a special event
- the story of a birth or death, beginnings and endings
- celebrations
- excursions
- ways you've bonded and connected with your grandchildren, near or far
- ideas you used from *A Passion for Our Grandchildren – Volume I*, and the impact it had on your relationships

Consider:

- feelings
- activities
- recipes
- special moments
- lessons learned
- "kids say the darnest things!"
- places to go
- crafts
- gifts or keepsakes

Journal entries should follow a timeline – refer to Lesson 11 – and could be accompanied by photos, children's art or sketches, preferably in black and white.

Send your story to the following address:

A Passion for Our Grandchildren: Volume II
Janet Mort
818-6880 Wallace Drive
Brentwood Bay, B.C.
Canada
V8M 1N8
e-mail: jmort@direct.ca
Fax: (250) 652-7889

We will be sure that you are credited for your submission.

ISBN 155212281-6

9 781552 122815